Taking the Local Train

A QUEST FOR STABLE ADULTHOOD IN THE "ME" DECADE

P. J. Lamb

ISBN: 978-1-54399-304-2 (soft cover)
ISBN: 978-1-54399-305-9 (eBook)

Acknowledgements

Thanks to the people who supported, encouraged, or gave advice to this work. This includes, in alphabetical order, Dan Barbush, Tara Bess, Marty Bolton, Marc Cooke, Lisa Kindrick, Pam Lamb, Chris Malaney, Jack O'Brien, Paul O'Neil, Jeanna Orphanidys, Katie Orphanidys, Randy Proctor, Karen Schober, Nathan Van Coops, Pete VanderVoort and all the staff at BookBaby.

Taking the Local Train

Introduction

This is a story of two men who became friends while serving in the military, their journey through life from their early 20s to mid-30s, and the directions their lives took after getting out of the service. One was a Mexican-American from the Southwest, the other, an Irish-Italian from the East coast. The time frame is the 11-year period from 1971 to 1981. Names of many people and places are either disguised or vague.

Not only does this story reflect the opinions, values and personalities of these men, but also the American society, as well as the world in general. Much of the story includes topics that guys their age were interested in - sex, drugs/alcohol, pop/rock music, sports, military, politics, friends, family, travel, education, jobs/careers, cars, intimate relationships, living situations, and the gradual challenge of becoming an independent adult. American values regarding these things are quite a bit different in the 21st century when compared to the '70s, which, like the late '60s, were relatively hedonistic times for many emerging adults. Tom Wolfe appropriately named it "The Me Decade."

The saga begins with two Vietnam veteran GIs adjusting to life in the Army in Germany. One had been there for over a year, the other just arrived. Most GIs who came to Germany dealt with dollars, not Deutschmarks (DM), which was the currency used outside any American military installation in Germany. In early 1971, the rate was about 3.50 DM to $1.00; 16 months later, it was 3.15 DM to $1.00. The military work environment, which shaped their choice of jobs for years to come, was a general hospital. Coping with the Army life thousands of miles away from home enabled them to focus on these themes: do a good job while on duty; travel and party otherwise, instead of merely biding time until discharge, as many others in the service did. One wound up staying in the military for a total of nine years and then working in jobs mostly in the medical field; the other decided to pursue higher education after discharge while subsequently working in hospitals. For each of them there were periods, at times for months at stretch, when life was generally pretty easy. At other times, life seemed to be an absolute struggle to get out of a situational rut.

As with most people, they had a lot of fun times, as well as major disappointments. The adventure begins in Europe and ends with a separation of over 2000 miles away from each other, for the last half of this time period. During those times when they were miles apart, they maintained their close friendship through phone calls, cassette tapes, and letters. At that time, there were no modern means of electronic communication as compared to the 21st century. There was no such thing as the internet, and it was rare that anyone even had any kind of a computer. Cell phones didn't even exist until years later, and long-distance landline phone call rates were pricey. In the years 1971 through 1981, we all trudged through the Vietnam war and its end, Nixon and Watergate, Ford and Whip Inflation Now, Carter and Iran, and the beginnings of Reagan conservatism. The all-volunteer Army at the end of the draft may have contributed to the racial tension and rising substance abuse in the military. Gun violence was spreading. Even though the Women's Liberation movement was taking off, scoring with sex partners (for both sexes), or partying with alcohol or drugs, reflected an era of pleasurable experimentation for many Baby Boomers in those days. Getting high or drinking on days off, weekends, or vacation was fun, or at least stress-relieving for many people, as were opportunities to travel. With advances in birth control techniques, most people felt good and safe about sex. Nobody ever heard of AIDS until 1981; herpes was rare. LGBTQ people were outcasts who got little or no respect, especially in the military. The wave of disco music came and went, but then rednecks and country music were coming "in" during the early '80s'. "Rapping" meant informal discussions moving back and forth, not the sing-song rhyming music that began at the end of the '70s. "Ghosting" meant temporarily disappearing from work for personal reasons, usually without telling a supervisor, for 10 to 30 minutes - not cutting people off cold. Only some people had cable TV until the late '70s and even then, only 15 to 20 channels at most were available (many people still used "rabbit ears" antennae).

Baby Boomers in their 20s and 30s during that era adjusted and either "rolled with the punches" or prospered. The changes were exciting, even though the two guys who are the protagonists here eventually traveled in somewhat different directions, personally and occupationally, especially when they were in their thirties. For them, this time period was not zooming along on an express to success; it was more like taking a local train with stops and detours along the way. But their long-term quest was still the same - to develop stable, enjoyable lives as gradually maturing human beings.

This book is dedicated to anyone who served in the military in Europe in the 1970s.

Chapter 1

El Guru and the New Guy

Anyone who first met him could tell by his walk and speech that Specialist 5th Class Raimondo Domenico Guererro, a US Army medical corpsman stationed at a hospital in Bad Kreuznach, Germany, came off as a Chicano "macho man." He just turned 23, and stood about 5'6", had a fairly dark complexion, thick black moustache, wore glasses, and spoke with a slight Hispanic accent. In the military, most guys addressed each other by their last names, but by first names among friends. He preferred his initials - R. D. - which led many of his friends and close acquaintances to call him "Artie." Periodically, he enjoyed smoking a bowl of hashish with the heads who called him "El Guru," a nickname he liked even better. But he never called himself "Raimondo" unless it was imperative to use his given first name. El Guru served in Vietnam from close to mid-1968 to mid-1969 - one of the more volatile time frames to be there. He saw intermittent action in Vietnam with an infantry unit, and for helping repel an attack one night and saving the lives of a few others, he was awarded a Bronze Star. El Guru liked the work of the medical corpsman, but not as a combat medic; so, he extended his active duty service time for three more years to go to Germany, work in a hospital, and explore Europe. Because of his experience in Vietnam, and from talking with various Europeans while traveling in Europe, his attitudes toward war, military, drugs, sex, and politics in the US took a 180 degree turn from what it used to be when he enlisted in 1966. He became a flaming liberal - even with some radical ideas - who could be outspoken regarding his beliefs, whether others liked them or not. Just as many people admired him for this (mostly the younger, educated, willing to converse types) as those who disliked him (mostly the rednecks, conservatives, or "lifer" types). El Guru didn't have many close friends, but he did interact frequently with people who had similar interests, which also included travel, sports, and music. Everyone agreed, however, that El Guru was good at his job - he was the leader of the evening shift medics on the OB-GYN ward. Even though he was pretty much a chauvinist (women's liberation emerged in 1969 and it was definitely an adjustment for most military men), he always treated the civilian and military nurses as well as patients with respect, in and out of work. He was determined to learn from his time in Germany - both personally and occupationally - possibly to compensate for having a high school level education.

Greg James was the new guy in the hospital, and initially came off as being the aloof, cool guy in the corner, taking in what was going on around him before interacting. He was not thrilled about the prospect of spending 1971 and most of 1972 in Germany. Greg was 23, white, middle-class, from the East Coast, college educated, of average height and build and just came from a year in Vietnam. In 1969, after he got drafted, he decided to go into the Army on delayed enlistment to become a social worker and add an extra year to his tour of duty instead of two years via the draft. His persuasive Army recruiter told him that after basic training, he would have to be cross trained as a medic first at Ft. Sam Houston, Texas, because social work was in that group. Then, after that 10-week training, he would be assigned to the special school for social work training in Denver, and with Nixon's plan to end the war, his duty station for the remaining service time would be stateside. He fell for this, like many geriatrics might be duped by a scam. After Ft. Sam Houston, he received orders to go to Vietnam, and he could not avoid it because of the fine print in the contract that implied he had to accept a duty assignment of anything in the medical field (or words to that effect). When he got to Vietnam, the only slots open for social workers OJT(on-the-job-training) were with the Green Berets in Nha Trang (which he wanted no part of), but he was fortunately stationed at a clinic and made the rank of Specialist 4th Class (Spec/4) quickly. He experienced hardly any action in his eleven months there, luckily. When his time was up in Vietnam, Greg was about to return to the US unassigned, which meant he could select almost any duty station stateside. However, 30 minutes before his flight back to the Oakland Army Terminal, he was notified his orders were changed and he was going to Germany, but with a month of leave time. Greg was the only unhappy GI on the plane. He thought, "I just came from a war and they want me to go play freakin' war games in Germany!"

After a couple of weeks at home, Greg spoke with a new recruiter in his hometown for almost an hour, who reassured him he would try to help him but had to discuss the matter with his Commanding Officer. He told Greg to come back to his office in 24 hours. Late the next day, Greg went back to see the recruiter, who told him, "When you get to Germany, give the CO (Commanding Officer) or his NCO in charge this letter (which came from the recruiter, signed by his Commanding Officer) as soon as you can. It's a request to be assigned to a general hospital and become a social worker by OJT." Greg did this and sure enough, his orders were changed the day after he landed in Germany. He was assigned to a general hospital in Bad Kreuznach and would train as a social worker at a psychiatric clinic in the building.

The guys in the barracks were divided into four groups and each tried to pull any new man stationed at the hospital into their "camp." There were the "heads" - "How's the dope over in (Viet) Nam, man? You can't get grass here, but we got hash, and that's even better than pot." Or, "A bunch of us may be over at Mark's room doing a bowl or two most midnights if you want to drop in." There were the "juicers" - "C'mon down to the EM club. It opens up at 5 and they always have a good band. Sometimes nice chicks are there." Or, "Once you start drinking German beers (half liter bottles; mostly higher alcohol content), you'll never go back to Budweiser or Pabst." There were the "Jesus freaks" – "Prayer will get you through your time here." Believe in Christ. Don't get tempted by all the sin that occurs here." Or, "There are six of us that have a Bible study two nights a week in Bob's room, and we always have room for another if you want to join." The "straights" were the others; they were an amorphous lot - "It's just like a regular job, so are you gonna re-up (stay in for more time in the service)?" Or, "I got some good new stuff (books, sports magazines, music cassette tapes) if you want to use any." Most of the "straights" were concerned about the Army, the hospital, their jobs, women and sex (wives, military and civilian nurses, girlfriends back home, experiences, and fantasies), families, plans after military service was over, what was happening in their home towns, and politics. Many just wanted to hang around the barracks after work and on weekends.

El Guru and Greg did not gravitate to any of these groups exclusively, although El Guru sometimes smoked dope with the "heads" and Greg started spending some time with the "juicers". But they both eventually liked or disliked some people in all of these groups and most of the guys in the hospital would discuss at least some of the issues pertinent to any of these four groups at any given time.

Chapter 2

Coping with Army Life in Germany

Near the end of March, there was a late afternoon monthly training session which was mandatory for all personnel in any medical positions who were not on duty. That month, the session was about how to disassemble, clean, and reconstruct an M 16 A1—the current US Army rifle of choice. Sgt. Browne, the training instructor, delegated this task to people in pairs at various tables in the room. "Guererro, James, here you go. You got 45 minutes. Should be easy for you war vets." Grudgingly, they took the weapon apart.

James said, "Damn it! This is what I meant about coming from a war and doing this Mickey Mouse shit. You know this is made by Mattel, the toy company. When the hell will we ever use these things here?"

Guererro replied, "James, quit your bitchin' and let's get this damn thing done and get out of here. I used an M-14 in Nam and at the end of my time, an M-16. You used the A-1 model over there didn't you?"

"I was issued one, but I never used it."

"What the hell, man? Are you a Conscientious Objector?"

"No, I got lucky and I was stationed at a clinic on the coast in III Corps (mid-to-southeast Vietnam). I did see a few bad things, though; everybody does there at one time or another. One night I was on CQ (Charge of Quarters) and there was a guy 30 yards away who got booby trapped and blown into a million pieces."

"Don't tell me about it. I was mostly with the 9th Infantry, out humping in the boonies for some of my time there. I re-upped to see the saner part of the world - not like in America with Nixon and his bullshit political system."

"Guererro, see if you can handle the details of this thing and I'll get the big pieces in place. If it works, it works. If it doesn't and the Russians invade the hospital, whoever uses it is fucked, unless maybe we can make a deal with them." Both of them laughed.

Guererro then said, "We just might have a better system if the Russians took us over. Hey, James, I know you work with the shrink, Dr. Goodman, and I heard you enlisted instead of getting drafted. You're conservative, aren't you?"

James said, "Don't stereotype me like that. I'm not the damn CID (undercover Criminal Investigation Detective). I didn't ask to come over to Europe. You remember that night of the Ali-Frazier fight? There were about 25 guys watching it and you, me, and the two blacks were only ones rooting for Ali. So. What does that tell you?"

"I remember that now. So, what did you learn from your time in Vietnam?"

"I learned that the Vietnamese only want to prolong the war because their economy never had it so good with us there, and they don't give a shit about who wins the war."

"Right on, man. I also learned that I never want to fire a weapon against anyone ever again, and I don't want to see anyone get killed again. I know you play softball here and some of the guys on the team don't like me because they are so damn conservative, but you seem like you're OK. You wanna do a bowl someplace later?"

"No, I don't touch that crap. Let's go to the EM Club and have a couple of beers."

"You better watch it. I was there last week when I saw you getting blitzed to the max and I heard you were still a little drunk the next morning. Word around the hospital is you damn near lost your job and they were gonna send you back working on a ward because of that. You also damn near picked a fight with that big dude who works in X-ray - he's the heavyweight champion of the hospital."

"I really learned a lesson from that and it won't happen again. Tell you what, let's stay straight and come on down to my room after chow. I got some good cassette tapes we can listen to music and rap a while."

"If you got a decent radio, we can listen to Radio Luxembourg. Some songs they play will be hits in America several months from now, guaranteed. I seldom hang around the barracks or the EM Club. I usually go downtown or get out of town whenever I have enough cash. Luxembourg is my favorite place. I got to meet a DJ from Radio Luxembourg at a party last year and I want to meet a chick they're promoting, who is gonna have an album coming out probably later this year. Maybe Friday night, we can go downtown to one of the bars here. I know some German chicks who hang out at the Scotch Club and I'll meet you there after my shift is over. You call me El Guru or Artie, and I'll call you Greg. I like that name," Guererro said.

"OK," Greg said smiling. They shook hands, finished assembling the M-16A1, and left the training session. A long friendship had its origin.

That Friday night, Greg flagged a taxi outside the barracks and went downtown to the Scotch Club at about 10:45. The place was like a typical long American bar, but with about 15 tables, a DJ and no dance floor. It was fairly full - half were GIs and half were German, nobody was older than about 35. El Guru got there at about 11:30; both were in civilian clothes. Greg bought him a beer and at one point related how Lt. Col. Goring (the Executive Officer at the hospital) asked Greg to consider coaching a Little League Team of all German kids. (Goring was the Little League Commissioner.) Greg asked El Guru to help him but El Guru wanted no connection with the hospital brass unless he had to. That's why he worked permanent evenings.

Greg wondered who could speak any German in the barracks who liked baseball. He asked about Dave Wilson, but El Guru thought he would be too argumentative and the kids might be afraid of him. Instead, he suggested Buck Williams from Personnel, who was one of the straighter people.

"Far out. I'll talk to him tomorrow."

Just then, El Guru noticed two very drunken American GIs sitting at a table across the room trying to move in on a couple of German ladies in their mid-20s. One guy in particular was getting loud and had a slurred speech. El Guru said, "Hey, I know one of those chicks. I almost picked her up a couple of times. We gotta rescue them from these assholes."

He walked over to the table with Greg following, quickly sat down and said, "Anna! Guten Abend! Wie Ghet's?" She smiled, and he hugged her and kissed her. She whispered loudly to him in half English, "Artie, get us aus-schnell!" El Guru said to them, smiling, "Ist Mein Freund, Greg!" Anna introduced them to her friend Gitta, and El Guru motioned them to an empty table not far away, gesturing to a waitress and he quickly ordered drinks. One of the drunk GIs said, "Those bastards work at the hospital." The other GI loud said, "Well I'll be goddamned!" Then he fell out of his chair and passed out, as some people left in the bar laughed.

Soon it was midnight, and El Guru and Anna (who was feeling no pain, apparently) were getting very cozy. Greg wasn't having much luck communicating with Gitta, and she wanted to leave. El Guru whispered to him, "You're losing her. You got to be aggressive with these German chicks. Tell her she's sexy. A lot of these chicks understand basic English, so what have you got to lose?"

El Guru and Anna got up to leave, holding hands. Greg told Gitta that she was beautiful and he was horny, and went to kiss her. She slapped his face and stormed out of there. El Guru noticed this, and called to Greg, "Go to the bahnhof and get a cab."

"What's a bahnhof?"

"The train station. Two blocks away to the left. There's always a cab outside the station."

Later in April, Greg and Buck hit it off well and they began coaching the German kids' Little League team. One German kid, Jürgen, was the best player on the team and he spoke perfect English. In return, he taught Greg and Buck conversational German. An MP named Dan, who spoke some German, joined Greg and Buck as a third coach. The team lost by 10 or more runs for the first 6 games, although the boys seemed to enjoy learning the game. The night before Greg's birthday in mid-May, El Guru said to him that he was staying here this weekend because he ended things with Anna peacefully - she was getting emotionally involved; he felt she was too shallow, and he couldn't handle that with her. He asked Greg if he was ready to go back downtown to the Scotch Club again.

Greg said, "Can't we go to another place? It's Friday night and there has to be other bars in this town."

"There are good places, but some are off limits, thanks to Kevin Monday, that guy on your softball team. He got into some fights and now Americans are banned from them. I can speak Spanish and get into a couple of them, but you probably can't."

They decided to go back to the Scotch Club at 11:30. The place was packed. After Greg and El Guru had a few beers at the long brass railed bar, at a table up against the wall, an older, 35ish, black GI was with two German women. He saw Greg, pointed to him and yelled, "Hey, home ... come here!" Greg and El Guru came over, and the GI smiled and said, "I know you, man - you're the dude who hit that triple off me last week. But we beat you hospital boys." El Guru said that it was Greg's birthday, and the GI bought them a round of drinks while introductions were made around the table. One lady said to El Guru, "Mexicans bring me good luck."

They had a long, pleasant conversation about the military and where they all were from originally. El Guru decided to stay, while Greg left because he was getting drunk. Later that morning at 6:30 am, El Guru knocked on Greg's door. Greg let him in and El Guru said, laughing, "You were fucked up last night, weren't you?"

"I'm hung over now. Did you pick up that woman? Did you bring her good luck?"

"She was too drunk to function."

"Glad I didn't miss anything."

"Happy birthday, Greg."

Over the next couple of weeks, El Guru and Greg had mostly conflicting work schedules. Greg learned quite a bit from Dr. Goodman at the psychiatric clinic sitting in on interviews and making ward rounds, but Dr. Goodman disclosed that he was leaving the Army during the 4th week of May. Greg had just gone up before the E-5 board and was promoted to Specialist 5th Class (Spec/5). El Guru was spending his time off traveling to Luxembourg or smoking hash and giving his opinions about politics and sports with some GIs late at night.

As soon as Dr. Goodman left, the rumor was that Colonel Lindberg, the hospital commanding officer, would close the Psychiatric Clinic. Two psychology techs (ironically named Moen and Groen) were brought in for TDY (temporary duty) from Mainz. They lasted only one week, however, due to a dwindling clinic patient load. One day the following week, Col. Lindberg and the Nursing Director paid a surprise visit to the clinic. Greg was yelling out the window to El Guru, who was going on duty for the evening, about how excited he was to be taking a four day leave to go to Paris with some people on the softball team. The other social work tech, Donnie, had propped his legs up on his desk drinking coffee, and was reading a comic book (he didn't care - he was getting discharged in two weeks).

The next day, Greg and Donnie were notified that the clinic would close after the first week of June, and Greg would be reassigned to the Medical/Surgical ward. At least, Greg got 90 days of OJT so he could apply for a secondary MOS (Military Occupational Specialty) as a Psychiatric Social

Worker, which is what he had enlisted for in the first place. El Guru told him to try to work permanent evenings, because it had the advantage of not being around the hospital brass as much. Then they would have more time together to go out evenings or explore some towns in the region during some days. Greg talked to SFC (Sergeant First Class) Jim Owens, supervisor of the medics who made up the schedule for the unit, and he agreed to let Greg work permanent evenings. Owens was a good guy, not a rigid "lifer."

During the second and third weeks of June, El Guru was busy in his ward, which had a full census almost every day and night. A couple of premature babies were hanging on for their lives and he worked some overtime hours for several nights. One night at the mess hall, El Guru met Greg at dinner and said, "I've had to clean and disinfect the DR (delivery room) a lot. It's just as important to do this to prevent infections as providing services to any pregnant lady who walks in the place. How are you doing up there?"

"I like the shift. Not a lot of mindless 'do this, do that' errand boy stuff. One guy who was a former psych patient told people I got demoted, and I had to set him straight."

El Guru asked how the Little League team was doing, and Greg told him that they lost all the 11 games so far. However, their star player Jürgen (who was left-handed) was brought with some other kids over to the field Saturday. They suggested that he try hitting left-handed and suddenly, line drives off the wall were coming off his bat. Buck discovered that Jürgen was a natural switch hitter, but Jürgen could get angry and start cursing in German on the field. Greg told El Guru that he and Buck had to take him aside and calm him down several times.

El Guru said, "You know, maybe I should have helped out with the team. I really like kids and German kids are cool. They say what they feel but they respect grownups, too, unlike these young American Army brats. I hope that's not the way the world is going now."

Greg replied, "The German boys are good kids, and I enjoy teaching them. They're having fun but the more they lose, they get frustrated - even more than me. I hate to lose at anything. A lot of nights I dream of Jürgen, Andre, Wolfgang, Dieter, Tomas, Karl, and the others. I'm so glad Buck is with me. I couldn't do this alone. They really like him."

"I'm gonna stay here this weekend. Let me bring you downtown to the Capri Bar. It's an off-limits place but dress up and wear shades, act European – cool - and we'll be OK."

"Sounds exciting. I'll try to borrow a sport coat from someone. I was practicing my French a little when I went to Paris a couple of weeks ago."

"I meant to ask you, how did that Paris trip go with Manny, Romo, and Purina?"

Greg related that Paris is a big international city with people trying to con you out of money, like running up and taking your picture near the Arc de Triomphe with a Polaroid camera and screaming at you to pay for it. It took them three tries to get a hotel because of anti-Americanism. If you try to jaywalk, drivers will either try to hit you or scream at you if they miss. He said that Romo didn't like the food and one time he ordered a Steak Tartare at a restaurant; it came back with what looked like raw ground hamburger with a fried egg on top and he was pissed. Purina just wanted to see the sights and hang out at the hotel and go to bed early - he's a super straight dude. Manny had asked where the Bastille was and they laughed - it was destroyed in the late 18th century. They climbed the stairs halfway up the Eiffel Tower, saw the Notre Dame Cathedral, walked along the Left Bank of the Seine, and spent four hours in the Louvre, but saw about an eighth of it. But they had a good time. Greg concluded, "It takes at least five days to see Paris, though."

"I didn't really like Paris when I went there a couple of years ago - it's like the New York of Europe - too big of a city for me," El Guru said.

After El Guru got off work that Friday at 11:30, he saw Greg down the hall, angrily unlocking the door to his room and he sensed that something was wrong. After he approached Greg, he asked him if he had just come back from the EM Club. They went into El Guru's room to talk. Greg told him that a melee broke out between some of the new guys who were transferred here from Frankfurt last week and the club regulars. El Guru's friend Dave Wilson didn't help any. "He was at a table with Greg and a few other guys - Rabbit, Lefty, and Kevin - and after a couple of beers, in that loud, obnoxious voice of his, he started bitching about one of the nurses who worked nights on the Med-Surg ward - Karen Gallen."

El Guru told him that they hated each other. "But I like her because she does things the correct way; she and Wilson clash over this, and Wilson is stubborn."

Greg said, "He threw one of those red bags of infection control waste out the window into the dumpster three floors below and she saw him. She yelled that she would write him up for that. They screamed at each other, and it was the end of the shift, but he didn't stay for the report and he walked off the unit. So, tonight at the club, he starts hollering how she's a 'cringing, Catholic, conservative, shriveling, sniveling, spineless bitch!' And some drunk at the next table - one of the guys sent from Frankfurt - yells at Wilson to sit down and shut up, and they started fighting. Kevin loves to fight, and he got in the middle of it. Then, some bastard throws a lit firecracker at me that went off about 6 inches from my head. I didn't get hurt, but all hell broke loose in a big fight. Fortunately, I didn't get thrown out of the club. Nobody knows who threw the firecracker at me, but I was really pissed and got out of there. I'm calming down. I'm realizing that you're better off going downtown or out of town, anyway."

They decided to go to the Capri Bar the following night. Although it was presently off limits, El Guru again said if they dressed up and looked cool, they might be OK. He added that the only time anyone should go to the EM Club is if there were no cooks eating at the mess hall, because the food would be bad that night.

The next night, Greg borrowed a sport coat from Stevens, one of the friendlier guys who got transferred from Frankfurt. El Guru wasn't in his room. He saw Dave Wilson in the hall, who said that he wanted to go downtown with them. Greg, who was afraid that Wilson would do something embarrassing, told him that they would be at the Scotch Club.

Greg ran downstairs to a cab that was outside the barracks. "Capri Bar, bitte," he said.

As he opened the door to the Capri Bar, Greg put on his shades. The place was upscale, but crowded, with subdued lighting. People of both sexes were fairly well dressed, and of a wide range of ages. A quartet was softly playing instrumental jazz in the background. When Greg said coolly to the bartender, "Un cognac, sil vous plait," and handed him a 10 DM bill, some heads at the bar suspiciously turned toward him. He took his cognac and left the change on the bar. He sauntered slowly around the bar near the tables, to check out the place. He then turned to take a sip of his drink, and bam! An elbow bumped into his and spilled half of his drink on his shirt. The other elbow belonged to El Guru (also wearing shades), who immediately cursed in Spanish. Then he grabbed Greg's arm and whispered, "What the hell - it's you!" Some people were laughing. They went over to a corner.

El Guru said, "I'm drinking cognac. You got it all over my sport coat!"

"You got cognac all over my shirt! These goddamn people must think we're a couple of blind men, with our shades on. It cost me 10 DM for this."

"Why the hell did you pay 10 DM for a cognac? I only paid 5 DM."

"I spoke French to the dude and left a big tip. I planned to drag it out and be cool; be European, like you said."

"But now half the place thinks we're a couple of American assholes."

"We put on a good show." And they both started laughing.

El Guru said, "The best way to cope with your time here in Germany is to do the best job you possibly can at work, but as soon as you're off duty, you got to relax or party somewhere away from the hospital. You got to get out of town some weekend."

"At least we didn't get thrown out of this place. Maybe they thought we were tourists. I want to go somewhere where there are no American GIs around. In another two weeks, I will get the German kids, or one of the German people at the hospital, to teach me how to get a train ticket, order a meal, get a hotel room, ask a girl to dance, and wing it as best I can from there."

"That's all you need," El Guru replied.

Chapter 3

In and Out of Work and a Trip to Cologne

On the last day of June, Greg was scheduled for CQ, which meant that after 5:00 pm, a designated military person at a rank of Spec/5 to Sgt 1st Class was in charge of operations of the barracks until 8:00 am the next morning. This was done on a rotating basis; and even though it resulted in having the next day off, a lot of guys tried to get out of it if they could. El Guru told him that CQ at this place is a pain in the ass unless you have an easy night.

Greg said that at the end of the day he had to report to "Deputy Dog" (the First Sergeant; many guys called him this because he appeared to be incompetent and stories from higher ranking men bore this out), or Chuck (his Company Clerk).

Greg asked El Guru about what duties were expected for the CQ at the hospital.

El Guru replied, "Deputy Dog left early today, so see Chuck. You walk around and make rounds every hour, tell guys to keep the noise down, log in a report of any real suspicious activity, break up loud arguments and fights, and tell anyone to get chicks out of their rooms, if they have them. It's your first time, so you can play dumb. You have to give a report to Deputy Dog in the morning. This is great. I can smoke a bowl with the heads tonight."

"Don't make it obvious. I don't want to get busted."

"You won't. I'll keep it cool. Depending on how the night goes for me on the ward, I might get stoned alone. Or I might go totally straight. No beer, booze, or dope."

Chuck gave Greg brief instructions. It was an easy evening. El Guru stopped just before midnight and he asked El Guru about how his evening went.

"It was busy. One lady had a wicked childbirth, and it looks like the kid is going to make it OK, but she was hemorrhaging, lost a lot of blood, and they may have to send her to Landstuhl. Another lady gave birth to a kid two days ago and all she's doing is crying. Too bad you can't see her."

"They call it post-partum depression. I didn't see anyone like that with Dr. Goodman."

An older black GI, "Lefty Luke," staggered into the main door of the barracks drunk. Lefty was a tall, slender Private E-2 who was in his mid-40s but looked older. He was in the Korean War and was staying in the Army to make it 30 years if he could. He worked at the OPC (Out-Patient Clinic) in the hospital and he was busted from a high rank of Staff Sergeant in the mid '60s all the way down to Private, for incidents related to his alcoholism. He was like a "mascot," had a great sense of humor, and people felt sorry for him. He did not like being in Germany, so he sat at the corner of the bar at the EM Club on the hospital grounds most nights and drank. This was about the 10th night straight he was drunk. If he still felt any effect of alcohol the next morning, he would take a long cold shower to sober up. Guys would cover for him at the OPC by giving him menial clerical work, cleaning, etc.

"El Guru, help me," Greg pleaded.

They grabbed him as he was about to fall, and dragged him upstairs. Lefty insisted on trying to open his door alone but he had a lock that always stuck. He brushed Greg and El Guru away, jammed his key into the door and kept yelling, "C'mon you tired ass dude!" When he finally got it open, he wanted no help getting into bed. As they walked away, they heard a loud crash. Lefty fell and cut the right side of his head open. El Guru told Greg to call the ER, and said that he would stay with Lefty. Lefty wound up getting admitted to the Med-Surg ward after two medics helped haul him up there. El Guru went to bed.

Several more drunks came in, and there was one argument between the two of them that Greg broke up. The phone rang on and off about what had happened to Lefty and other things, for the rest of the night. Greg got no sleep (he was told by El Guru that he should get at least three hours on and off). At 7:45, he went to see Deputy Dog.

Deputy Dog looked at his name tag. "James? Do you know how to count money?"

"Yes, I am James (smiling). Sure, I can count money," Greg thought. "You and Chuck can't even do that?"

"Can you count money fast?"

"Yeah. Why?"

"C'mon. We got to get the tables set up for the pay line. I want you to sit next to Captain Bolling, count out the money and help Sgt. Browne check the ID cards. Hey, why did you come here anyway?"

"I'm reporting in from CQ last night."

"Then give me that report, get out of here and come back to me at 16:00 hours (4:00 pm). Go to the Mess Hall to see if they need help with the headcount. Get your money later at the Registrar's office."

Greg walked away saying, "This is stupid." He went to the Mess Hall; they said they didn't need any help, and so he went back to his room and crashed.

The following Wednesday, El Guru convinced Greg to take the train and go to Bad Muenster with him in the morning and spend a few hours there. He said Bad Muenster was a nice little town, people were friendly, and that they had been working their asses off lately. They arrived in Bad Muenster at 10:00, walked around the town, played miniature golf, ate lunch at a café, and rented a two-person paddle boat to cruise on the river. The weather could not have been more perfect for a day in Germany; sunny and warm instead of the cool, cloudy days they had there lately. Their minds were a million miles away from work.

They slowly paddled and drifted, as if time stood still. Suddenly, as they docked the boat, El Guru said, "Holy shit! It's almost 2:00. We got to get out of here and go to work!"

They ran to catch an arriving train. Greg exclaimed, "We gotta get tickets fast!"

"Screw the tickets. We don't have time. The trains only stop here for one minute!"

El Guru hopped on the train, yelling to Greg, "C'mon, dammit!"

They both got on the train, just as it was pulling away and Greg yelled, "What the hell are we gonna do now? We didn't pay for this?"

"If we get caught, we'll try to give the guy a few DM. Just keep moving back to the next car. If you see the conductor wanting to check tickets, just keep moving back."

They did this for what seemed like an eternity and jumped off the train from the last car when it was their stop. They ran to the front of the bahnhof, yelling "Taxi!" They jumped into the taxi and wound up making it to work on time.

"We shouldn't pull this crap again," Greg said.

"Let's just call that the Bad Muenster Special, "El Guru replied.

The Little League season ended the next night. The kids only won one game but they had fun. After the last game, Buck Williams talked with El Guru and Greg about his future plans. Buck was slowly transferring out of Personnel to start working 3-11 with Greg on the same ward. He wanted to finish his college degree and get a dual major. He already had enough credits for Political Science but was over a year short for Pre-Med. Goring approved this deal provided Buck was on call to babysit his kids at any time.

El Guru said that he wanted to go to college someday and major in Political Science but he had heard about brand new Physician's Assistant programs at some schools. Greg disagreed with Buck's plan because he thought that since Buck was 23, he wouldn't get out of the Army until January, and wouldn't be going back to school until that September. By the time he finished his Pre-Med degree, got through Medical school, Residency and Internship, he'd be over 30 with a load of bills to pay - even with the GI bill.

"I don't care. Over the last few months, I realized that this is what I really want to do and I want to learn all I can here," Buck said.

El Guru worked a stretch of nights (11-7). Two weeks later, Greg went to see him at the OB ward just as he was getting out of report to start his shift. Greg told him he had a three-day weekend. He was going up to Cologne to check it out just to be adventurous, like El Guru suggested. He didn't think there were any American GIs up there.

El Guru said that he had to work Friday night but he could meet him in front of the Hauptbahnhof (main train station) on Saturday. Greg responded that the trip was only a few hours by train, according to Herr Walther (the hospital's community ambassador) and that there was also some good sightseeing.

"I can get there at 6. We can go to your hotel, have dinner, and go to some bars."

"Great. I'll meet you at 6, and I should know what to see and do there by then."

Greg bought a ticket to Cologne "einfach" (one way). He didn't know he could've bought a round trip ticket, even though he had to change trains in Bingen. He enjoyed the scenic ride along the Rhine, seeing all the quaint wine towns, the majestic castles on the banks from a distance, and the pillars that were left from the Remagen bridge after WWII. Right after he got to Cologne, an American civilian with a Nebraska sweatshirt asked if Greg could give him a couple of DM so he could get a locker. Greg did this, got a locker of his own, and wound up buying the guy a bratwurst and pommes frites (French fries) near the station. His name was Ron, and he was traveling around Europe, working when he could, and he had just spent a couple of days in Cologne. He was going to catch an all-night train to Munich in a few hours to meet someone who promised him a temporary job.

They ambled over to the Information booth a block away and Greg got a map. Ron told Greg a couple of areas to avoid, but suggested Greg to go into the Dom (a Cathedral near the train station), because of the fantastic architecture. He also told him to take a walk over the bridge to get a nice view of the Rhine and the city. Alt Koln, a restaurant up the street, had a glockenspiel that came out on top of the entrance every hour, and Ron told him they had good meals that were not expensive. Ron said he stayed at the Hotel Berlin behind the train station the night before, which was not a long walk from where all the "action" was at night. Greg thanked Ron, got his bag out of his locker, checked in at the Hotel Berlin, got washed up, changed, and ventured out for a night on the town. He found his way to Hohenzollern Strasse, went into a bar to have a beer, and talked to some people. Hardly anyone spoke English there, however (Greg knew how to order a drink in German, at least). After the beer, he walked down the street to the Scotsman's Club, a discotheque. It was about 10:15, and he overheard people speaking English at a nearby table. He went over there, and talked briefly to two guys from England who were just getting up to leave. After Greg introduced himself, one of them said, "This is a good city, and you'll have a good time, but Dusseldorf is better. Everybody is friendly in this whole region."

Greg thanked them and sat down at their table as they left. There were about 50 people out on the floor dancing to "Coco," by the Sweet. Fifteen feet away, there was a gorgeous looking blonde in about her mid-20s with a fantastic body, who was laughing and joking with an old man. Once the old man walked away, she looked over at Greg and smiled. Immediately, Greg was smitten. He smiled back and thought, "Man, I've got to make a play for this chick somehow." At that very moment "Brown Sugar" by the Rolling Stones was being played by the DJ. Greg went up to the woman and asked her to dance, but she couldn't understand him until someone explained what Greg wanted. She didn't speak any foreign languages at all. The DJ played a slow song next, and as they danced, Greg thought, "She is built, nice to hold, but there has to be a better way to communicate with this lady."

After this song, they went over to his table and Greg tried writing things down and drawing pictures. He was able to discern that her name was Diana, and she was staying in Cologne for the summer. Then she shocked Greg by leading him by the hand out of the bar and apparently wanting to go to her hotel. They got a cab outside and Greg said, "Hotel Berlin, bitte." She said, "Nein," and insisted on her hotel. The cab driver was laughing as he spoke back and forth with her - they seemed to know each other. The ride was only about 4 or 5 blocks away. The cab driver smiled and said in broken English as he took Greg's cash upon exiting the cab, "Have gut time, Herr."

The hotel was seedy. There was an old couple and a big guy playing cards in what was apparently the lobby. As they went upstairs to her room, the older man barked out, "mach schnell (be quick)". Greg thought, "Uh Oh! Is she a hooker?" She started taking off her clothes and took off Greg's. Greg thought, "What a body!" He tried to kiss her, but she put out the palm of her hand and gestured to his wallet. Against his better judgment, he couldn't totally resist her as they negotiated eine strude (one hour) vs. ganze nacht (all night). They were done in a half an hour. Neither one of them enjoyed it that much. She got dressed fast and left. Greg was pissed at himself for being suckered into this, but something caught his eye - she had forgotten her keys. He got dressed, snatched the keys, went downstairs to get another cab that was nearby, went to his hotel, and went to sleep.

Greg didn't venture out of his room until about noon the next day. After grabbing something to eat (he learned Schinken meant ham), he hung around the train station for a while before visiting the Dom. "What a fantastic church. I wouldn't mind getting married in here someday," he thought. After leaving the Cathedral, he meandered over to an area where there were houses from the 1400s that somehow had remained unscathed by the bombings from World War II. Then he sauntered through the Neu-market, a modern mall. After leaving the mall, he took a walk across the bridge over the Rhine to take a picture of the city.

El Guru showed up at the train station at 6:00. When he asked Greg if he was having a good time, Greg told him the story of what happened the night before, and El Guru said, "You should've known better. You never, ever, pay for any chick."

"I've had a long dry spell. But you're right. I won't let that happen again."

They went to the hotel. El Guru noticed that Greg signed in as "Greg-ory James" for their room (the desk clerk got them a room with two beds; Greg paid for 2 nights).

"No, don't use your real name checking into these cheap places. From now on, I'm Paul Hornung and you're Jim Taylor, but we spell their last names differently - Horning and Tailer. They don't know who those guys are over here; they don't know American football."

They went out to eat at Alt Koln, and they thought it was a cool place. There were three Americans and an Italian guy at the next table, and Greg and El Guru struck up a conversation with them. The Italian guy, who was about 40, spoke fluent English and said his name was John, but for some reason the people called him "Rollo." Two of the people were a couple from Boston, and the other was an attractive older redhead (Kay) in her early 30s from California, who was a recent divorcee. As El Guru and Greg were finishing up their dinner, Rollo called them over to join them and he ordered a liter of wine to pass around. They were all interesting people. Kay was flirting with Greg, but he seemed gun-shy after what happened the night before.

Rollo kept cracking jokes and then he pulled several watches out of his pocket and tried to sell them to everyone at the table, to no avail. Rollo then invited everybody to come down to the Rheinwalk. The Boston couple said they were going back to the hotel, and Kay said she was going with them, but told them that she might show up at the Santa Cruz club later if she got bored. Then she winked at El Guru and Greg.

El Guru and Greg argued briefly over whether or not to follow them. They went to the St. Marlena on Hohenzollern Strasse where they talked with some chicks who were with a big group of people, but once El Guru came on with his heavy rap lines, they were turned off. They went to another bar for a beer, and later strolled into the Scotsman's Club. While they were having a beer at a table, Diana came in, dressed very fashionably (black dress, high heels). She sat down at the table next to them. She gave a seductive smile to Greg.

"That's the chick from last night," Greg said.

"This bitch picked you up here?"

"Yeah. She's a fox, but she's a cheap whore. I still have her keys in my pocket."

"What? Let's get out of here, now! She's probably got some thug thinking you're a dumb American and he's gonna beat the shit out of you for taking her keys!"

They got up to leave. Greg threw her keys at her. As they were going out the door, she got up from her table and left.

El Guru said, we have to go to the Santa Cruz now - I noticed it's not far away. At least they may speak Spanish there."

The Santa Cruz was a lively bar with good music, but Greg and El Guru slowly got drunk and Kay never showed up. They took the train home the next morning.

In early August, a bunch of guys at the hospital were ETSing (getting out of the Army), including most of the softball team. One guy on the softball team in particular, Benny, who worked in Hospital Administration, was leaving and he threw a going away party at the EM Club from 8:30 to 11:30 at his expense (free beer) on July 31st. Benny had an equal number of people who liked him and didn't like him throughout the hospital but a crowd came to the party, regardless. Very few people would want to pass up free beer at the EM Club on a Saturday night, and after their evening shifts were over, El Guru and Greg were shocked to see the throng of people who showed up at Benny's expense. El Guru asked a guy at the bar incredulously, "Didn't Benny make enemies?"

"Some people came for revenge, I guess," he smiled.

The band played contemporary rock, and people were dancing in the aisles because there was no room on the dance floor. Guys came with their wives, and some German chicks from downtown (including two barmaids from off-limits clubs) made the scene. Dave Wilson was dancing down the aisle and spilled a beer, knocking a slice of pizza onto some woman's lap, but she was so drunk she didn't seem to mind much. El Guru and Greg each had a beer, but El Guru stunningly said, "I've never seen so many drunken people at this place since I first came here. This is gonna cost Benny a shitload of money! He's leaving in a couple of days."

Benny, who rarely drank, was getting drunk himself, and the club manager seized the opportunity to close the place early to prevent any fights or illegal activity on the premises. Greg saw Lefty Luke in the corner of the bar downing another drink, and he was obviously smashed.

Greg asked him, "Lefty! You just spent 10 days on the ward with DTs!"

"Doc says there ain't nothin' wrong with my liver yet. I ain't got cirrhosis."

Benny got up from his table and was wobbling. El Guru and Greg tailed two other guys who walked him out of the EM Club and back to the hospital barracks as the club closed down. Benny started crying, begging

God to forgive him for getting drunk for the first time in his life, and how much the party was going to cost him.

"Wait until he gets his first wicked hangover," Greg said.

"Wait until he sees the bill for the party tomorrow," El Guru added.

"Good thing for him payday is Monday," Greg replied.

Chapter 4

An Eventful Late Summer

During the first two weeks of August, work on the ward was busy for El Guru, but fairly slow for Greg. Greg and some other medics and nurses taught Buck Williams a lot of things he needed to know about being a ward medic. This included proper ways of taking temperatures, pulses, respirations, blood pressures, rendering some special treatments (e.g., IPPBs, K-Pads, cleaning wounds), how to chart notes, how to look busier than you actually are, and when to hide on or just off the unit to take a break (termed "ghosting"). Also, evening shift was the best time to talk with patients and Greg used it to improve his mental health interviewing skills. The last hour before the change of shift was usually the quietest time; ward staff discussed their personal lives or any other non-medical issues frequently. El Guru and Greg continued a lengthy discussion about such issues at the Rhiengraffen, a gasthaus (small restaurant), a few blocks away at dinner after work one night.

Greg told El Guru that the trips to Cologne and Paris made him realize that since he had another year left in the Army, he should try to explore other areas of Germany and Europe, be more familiar with European ways of life, and meet more German people and party on weekends whenever he could. Staying in the barracks and going to the EM Club a lot, like other guys did was, for him, essentially "doing time." Like El Guru had suggested to him, he also wanted to do the best job he possibly could, because that was the way he would gain more respect from people. El Guru said he felt exactly the same way, and he wondered how the skills they learned as medics would translate to civilian life someday. He said he was undecided, at this time, about whether to go back to school for a degree or get a steady job. Greg said that he was going to try to get into a Masters program somewhere, hopefully for the fall of '72.

They discussed which women they liked who worked at the hospital, including civilian and military nurses, as well as German civilians. They agreed that although they liked almost all of the non-military nurses, and some of the single military nurses, at this point in their lives they had no interest in getting married (almost all of the civilian nurses were married, anyway). El Guru told him they couldn't date the military nurses unless both parties wanted to get married, and even then, it was a long shot. But they agreed it would be nice to have a steady girlfriend somewhere in Europe who liked some of the same things they did.

They then talked about music. El Guru said, "Hey, are you listening to Radio Luxembourg, yet? It seems like a lot of the songs the DJs play become hits back in the world months later."

"Yeah. Groups I never heard of before - T-Rex? The Sweet? Slade? They played their songs at bars in Cologne and even downtown here."

"It's a different world once you get out of the GI areas. You get treated much better in places where there are no Americans. That's why I take off for Luxembourg when I can. Never go to Heidelberg - a lot of military brass there. But if you have to buy something cheap, go to the PX at Wiesbaden. You can get good deals on clothes there. When you go to a town with no military people lurking, try not to look or act like a typical GI."

Greg remarked what he noticed about working evenings is that people gain weight by eating an extra meal a day, and possibly a beer or two after work. El Guru said, "You don't gain weight by smoking a bowl. Hey, let's go back to your room and listen to the ball game. The Reds are playing somebody tonight. Or we can dig Kid Jensen on Radio Luxembourg."

"The Pirates are gonna go all the way this year, Artie."

"Or maybe the Orioles."

Work, partying, future plans, sports, music, politics and traveling was their "world."

El Guru couldn't wait to get to Luxembourg for a four-day weekend after working ten evenings. When he got there, he didn't go out of his hotel room because he was so tired. (After working ten straight evenings on the ward, medics and nurses were really dragging, especially if the ward was busy every night.) Late the next afternoon, in the big park, he was throwing a football with a couple of American kids. A chick was watching as he chased an errant throw, and he cursed in Spanish. She said, "You no catch, senor?"

She had him at "senor." He threw the ball to one kid, smiled at her and walked over to her. Up close, she was prettier that he had seen from a distance. Her name was Marguerite. She was 23 and had recently moved to Luxembourg with relatives temporarily until the end of the year. She was working as a secretary for a company based in Portugal that was expanding operations. Her parents lived in Marseille, France. She spoke several languages.

El Guru asked if he could take a walk with her to a sidewalk café about a quarter mile away to have dinner with her. She agreed, and as they strolled along, they spoke to each other, half in Spanish and half in English. El Guru felt things were going very well, so after dinner they went to a bar where there was soft, romantic music playing. After one drink of Sangria, he asked her to spend the night with him. She called her relatives and asked for their permission to stay in town. After she hung up, she told El Guru that she couldn't, but she didn't have to be home for a few hours. They made love for over an hour. "This is more than just sex," he thought. "I like this girl." They talked for a while before she left. They agreed to meet at the same café for lunch the next day before he went back to the hospital. She gave him her address and phone number. He didn't look up his DJ friends from Radio Luxembourg this trip. El Guru definitely had a good time and wanted to see Marguerite again, hoping that she would be a good girlfriend to see there.

That Monday, while El Guru was fooling around in Luxembourg, MSG Jack Greene from Administration pulled Greg aside on the ward at the beginning of the 3-11 shift and said that the hospital got a new psych tech in - Spec/5 Barry Thompson - to work in Preventive Medicine and do the administrative work for the new drug rehab program.

Greg was disappointed and asked, "Why not me?"

Greene told him that they needed someone experienced to get the program off the ground, and that Thompson had only 4 months left. "You don't have a secondary MOS of 91G (Psychology/Social Work Technician). He has it for his primary MOS. You did a good job at the Psych Clinic. We'll look out for you when the time comes."

"Thanks, but I want to talk to Lt. Col. Goring, anyway," Greg responded.

Buck Williams was working with Greg that night on the ward. Since Buck had worked in Personnel for a year, Greg asked his opinion about what Greene had related to him earlier. Buck told him that they wouldn't make any changes to his primary MOS but that he should see Goring anyway because Goring liked Greg. Greg got permission to see Goring right away. "I hope he doesn't throw me out of his office," Greg thought. Goring could be assertive to the point of being combative, but Greg caught him in a good mood.

Goring told Greg that there wouldn't be a psychiatrist coming here for a long time, and they were freezing all MOSs anyway, in Heidelberg (USAEUR Command headquarters). He said that he heard Greg was doing a good job being the leader of the medics on the evening shift for his ward. He said, "There's a slot open in Baumholder for the same thing Thompson is doing but would you really want to go to a town of 800 people where there are 21,000 GIs, with only one train in and out all day? The other option would be for you to re-enlist and go back to Vietnam, but you don't want to do that, do you?"

"No way to both, Sir. Rumor has it that Col. Lindberg thinks that psychiatry is about the same thing as witchcraft."

"He thought you were interested only in the clinical end of things there, not the administrative. By the way, you and Williams did a great job with those German kids, teaching them baseball."

"Buck was actually the one who ended up doing most of it, but thanks, Sir." Greg had hoped that he would be able to get some more clinical experience in order to help him get accepted to a graduate school for a possible mental health career.

On August 14th, El Guru had the night off and he convinced one of the Jesus freaks to borrow their Bethlehem Baptist Church bus "to take some teenagers to a music festival." At 5:00, he and all the heads boarded the bus, loading up hash joints and laughing as they took off to see the Grand Funk Railroad concert in Frankfurt. At the same time, there was a Rhine cruise for any hospital staff who didn't have to work, arranged by Sgt. Major Dennis. Greg and a dude named Ralph were the only medics on duty at the Med Surg ward that evening; Goring had ordered Buck to babysit his kids because he and his wife were going on the cruise. The heads at the concert all came back stoned. El Guru was only a little high because he had to drive. He stopped at Greg's room briefly, after midnight. He said the band was "out of sight," but he could only smoke one hash joint because he drove. A couple of guys disappeared with chicks and didn't come back.

Dave Wilson, who was on the cruise, came into Greg's room about 20 minutes later and told him, "The people on the cruise were like a bunch of wild animals after we hit Koblenz. Lanier passed out and missed the whole trip back. Rabbit was barfing until he passed out, too. Allie was on the upper deck, going at it hot and heavy with some officer's wife. Bill McAfee was so blitzed he wanted to jump off the boat and Goring punched him in the mouth to stop him. Somebody balled one of the nurses in the men's room. Two doctors got on a train heading north instead of south after they got off the boat - one was yelling, 'Where's my wife?' One German asked the Sgt. Major if this was his group and he said, 'Only some of them are. I don't know the other Americans.' It was hilarious!"

After that, El Guru and Greg talked about their plans for the next weekend. El Guru said that he was going to see Marguerite on Saturday. Greg said that he had a four-day weekend coming after working 10 straight evenings. He said that he was going to Dusseldorf and check it out, but that he might go down to Luxembourg from there, Friday or Saturday. El Guru told him that if he got to Luxembourg, he could meet him at the Black Bess bar on Saturday around 5:00.

Greg got into Dusseldorf Thursday night. There was a big technology convention and the only cheap room he could find was for 35 DM a night. This was slightly more expensive than he usually paid for a bed, a closet, a sink, and a common bathroom with four other people on the third floor. Such cheap hotels had no elevators. Greg knew that Peter Herkt, who was the former German bartender at the EM Club on the hospital grounds, had moved to Dusseldorf and was working at a bar on the Konigsallee. When he got there, he saw that everyone was fashionably dressed. "Good thing I wore a sport coat," he thought. But when Greg got to Peter's bar, the New Orleans Club, he was told Peter was off until Monday. The man at the stool next to him was a conventioneer and spoke broken English. He said that Konigsallee was the "little Paris of Dusseldorf," and he was right - 6.50 DM a beer at that place. Greg dragged out the beer and the guy gave him the name of a classy bar a few blocks away if he wanted to meet some beautiful women.

Greg took his advice and the guy was right. "More women than men here and everyone is a fox," he thought, as he scanned the bar and the dance floor. One of these fine chicks about his age was a few stools away and glanced over at him a few times and smiled. Greg moved over to the stool next to her. She spoke only a little bit of English, but once they started seemingly hitting it off great, she wanted him to buy her a 60 DM bottle of champagne and go to her place. She thought he was in Dusseldorf for the convention. Greg kissed her on the check and said, "Goodbye, Baby," and hurried out the door thinking, "Damn, am I a magnet for prostitutes and bar girls?" A guy stopped him just outside, and speaking in a British accent, said, "I watched you. Why don't you go to the Altstadt? That's where all the action is, where you don't have to spend a fortune. You have young people who are real there - lots of restaurants, discotheques. Go back past that plaza over there and keep walking left. You'll find it."

After a 20-minute search, Greg was about to take a taxi to the hotel when all of a sudden, he came upon an area of four or five square blocks of mostly neon signed restaurants and bars with bands and DJs playing popular and rock music. Happy people were walking around in the narrow streets on the humid summer night; some were singing songs and some were probably a little drunk. But it was 12.45 am, and too late to check out most bars. He walked about Altstadt, thinking, "I got to come back here during next trip. Wait till I tell El Guru. And it looks like there are no Americans around, which is even better."

He made it back to his hotel, checked out the next morning, put his bag in a locker at the Hauptbahnhof, and walked around part of the city. "This town is really nice - as good as Cologne, if not better. What a beautiful, huge park they have," he thought as he strolled along. He later took a train to Brussels, checked into another cheap hotel not far from the center of town, took a nap, and went out to dinner. He walked around La Grande Place, a huge old, open area right in the center of the city. Then he went to explore the area. There was a Vietnamese restaurant where two girls waved their hands at him (the Vietnamese signal to come in) as he walked by. So, he stopped in and asked, "Have nuc mahm (fish head soup)?"

One said, "You GI!"

The other said, smiling, "Have ga chin (fried chicken). Have nuc mahm."

They were from Da Nang and they had moved to Brussels a year ago. Many of the older, and even some of the younger, Vietnamese spoke French along with their broken English. One of the girls had gone to Maine to live with her American GI boyfriend for eight months. She excitedly exclaimed, "Maine number 10! (Bad). He tell me he live at beach (Old Orchard Beach, where many French Canadians spend part of their summers) but buku cold! Next time, GI lie, GI die!" She picked up a steak knife and smiled.

"Cam Anh (Thank you)," Greg said, as he walked away laughing.

Greg didn't find many other people in Brussels friendly. He did pop into a discotheque at La Grande Place that was fairly dead, and later he tried to get into another place where he heard lots of people talking and music, but two guys grabbed him by his arms and pointed to a sign inside the door. "Club Privat, monsieur," one bouncer gruffly said. Greg walked away, humming a line from the song, "Signs," reflecting the situation.

The next day, he left around noon and went to Luxembourg. He put his bag in a locker at the station and decided to walk around this nice, very clean, friendly city. Everyone was helpful to him; he even bought a pair of shoes at a department store. At 3:30, he noticed El Guru sitting alone at a sidewalk café, and he said, "Artie! You look a little down. What happened?"

He said that he would not see Marguerite tonight - probably not ever. He met her an hour ago and she told her relatives all about him, and how he suggested they smoke hash, and how they had sex, and now she couldn't see him anymore. "Her uncle said to her to never trust Americans. He thinks they're all liars and pricks, I guess."

"You have to find somebody with their own place and no relatives to call."

"I don't believe she told her relatives about everything we said and did. Christ, she isn't a virgin and she's old enough to know better."

They talked for an hour at the café and Greg told him all about Dusseldorf. El Guru laughed at the story about the bar girl, but said that Altstadt sounded like a good area. When Greg related his adventure in Brussels, El Guru remarked that he didn't like Brussels; to him, people seemed cold and unfriendly there. He said that Luxembourg was a different world and that even Trier was better than Brussels. Greg asked El Guru if he wanted to go to Trier but he said he was bummed out and wanted to go back to the hospital and lay low. Greg then asked him about Koblenz and El Guru said, "See what you think. There is a good little wine town on the Mosel – Cochem - if you want to check that out."

They both took the train to Koblenz, but El Guru changed trains and went back to Bad Kreuznach. He kept wondering how Marguerite could have told their relatives about their encounter because he liked this girl better than anyone he'd met in quite a while.

"I know there are some good cheap hotels near the bahnhof," El Guru said. "There's a good pizza shop near there, too. Go to the Big Ben. You'll like that bar. I'm going home."

That night, after checking into a hotel and eating a small pizza, Greg went to the Big Ben but like in America, Saturday night was probably date night because the place had only couples or older, unattractive women. So, Greg went down the street to the Toff Toff and ordered a beer. Right away, the bartender, a flaming redhead with a big wide smile, started flirting with him. She spoke in broken English. "When you come, I think (pointing to her head), 'Ah. Amerikaner."

"How can Ich be more European?"

"Why? Amerikaner sind good."

They talked back and forth as Greg had a few beers. He was drawing pictures and writing and explaining in English what German he knew. Her name was Marlies, she was in her late 20s, slightly chunky, and seemed very interested in knowing all about him and telling him all about herself. "Good thing it's kinda dead—there's not even 20 people here," Greg thought. At 11:00 he had to leave because he didn't want to get drunk in a totally strange town. She wanted to know where he was staying. He told her, but he thought nothing would come of this.

The next morning, just as he was about to get his ticket at the train station, he heard a voice yell, "Greg! No!" It was Marlies running up to him. She wanted him to stay with her and spend the day and night showing him all around Koblenz. He took her up on her offer. They went all over the area in her car—they explored a magnificent castle on the Rhine that had Napoleon's arches and later, went back to her apartment. She wanted him to meet her friend, Rosi, who was her next-door neighbor, and Rosi's 7-year-old boy, Franchi. Franchi was shy and didn't want to come in, but Rosi did.

Rosi was "drop dead gorgeous" - a fairly tall blonde about 30, with a big wide smile. She spoke better English than Marlies. Marlies had to pick up some things for dinner at a nearby store. While she was gone, Rosi started flirting with Greg. He tried to draw a picture to explain something and she took the pen and notepad away from him, and drew a near-perfect sketch of Greg, writing underneath, "$100,000 reward!" Laughing, she said, "Wanted Man!"

Greg grinned and seductively asked, "Am I your man?"

She smiled and started to hug and kiss him, but then Marlies walked in with groceries. Rosi said she had to leave and make dinner for her and Franchi. Marlies said something about how he should not flirt with her because "Rosi Ist mein Freund," and Rosi had a boyfriend who was living in Toronto, who was returning in a month. Greg apologized, but he couldn't get Rosi out of his mind.

Marlies cooked a huge Jaeger schnitzel dinner; after dinner, they ate some Black Forest cake and enjoyed some white wine. They sat down on the couch for some "get to know you better" conversation. Her father was killed by the Nazis just before she was born. In the past seven years, she moved from Koblenz to Bad Kreuznach, to Munich, to Heidelberg, to Aachen, and back to Koblenz. She told Greg all about her experiences in those cities. Later, there was some flirting: "Du bist teacher. Ist bin Schulerin." Greg said, "Du bist student. Ich bin Der Furher! Sieg Heil!" They both laughed loudly and Greg spent the night with her.

The next morning Greg saw her in bed without her makeup and thought, "What have I done?" She looked borderline ugly. Then she got up and they both got washed and dressed - with her makeup on, she looked good again. Greg had to get back to the hospital to work that evening, so she drove him to the bahnhof, and kissed him goodbye just before he boarded the train. She knew exactly where he worked and said she would write to him "very soon."

El Guru got eight hours of comp time for pulling a double shift, so he decided to take it on September 1st. Greg had dinner with him the night before at the mess hall, and told him that he also had the next day off because he had to work all weekend. He suggested they go to Saarbrucken for the night, because it was a university town, and just far enough away from any American military facilities. However, the trip was uneventful. They tried to look up a former German hospital employee who reportedly co-owned a restaurant and bar, The Starlite. However, when they got there, they learned that he sold his interest in the place and went to a city in northern Germany. They wound up taking a train home, thinking they would return there at a later date because Saarbrucken seemed like a clean, non-military town.

Greg's weekend featured a patient on the ward who was in for mono-nucleosis. The guy's wife happened to be on the other side of the unit for some medical problem and they were screaming at each other for a couple of brief periods. The staff on the ward learned that she was divorcing him. Apparently, they met each other at a psychiatric hospital; she was diagnosed as manic-depressive and he was suicidal. Buck said, "We could be in for an exciting night."

Greg told Eileen and Barbie Doll (as Buck nicknamed her), "Remember all you learned in psych nursing."

All hell broke loose on the ward at 7:30. The guy got by the staff, barged in on his wife and they started to have a physical fight. A few staff members broke it up and dragged the guy back to his room. A medic named Mike wanted to stay with him and talk him down with Greg's help. He suddenly knocked Mike down and ran down the hall, yelling that he was going to jump through the big glass window at the end of the unit, three floors up. Buck and Greg tackled him, just as he was about to make his jump. All staff on the ward got him back to his room and put him in restraints. A few minutes later, he broke out of the restraints, bit Mike, broke a glass on the night strand, and tried to slit his wrist. Eileen called for help and the guy wound up going to Landstuhl, which had the biggest psychiatric unit in the region. He broke out of Landstuhl the next day, but MPs got him back and he was put on a locked unit.

Several nights later, El Guru was at the EM Club looking for Greg (who happened to be on CQ), and the guy's wife was there. El Guru tried to pick her up (he didn't know who she was), but some other GI actually did. The next day, her husband got out of Landstuhl, went home, found out that his wife spent the night with the GI she met at the EM club, and he swallowed everything he could from their medicine cabinet. He was brought back to the hospital ER, where they pumped his stomach. 10 minutes later, he bolted down the hall. Barry Thompson, who was standing near the ER, yelled to Greg (who happened to be coming out of the hospital canteen) for help to stop the guy. They found him in a room that had some cleaning supplies, and he was just about to down a bottle of turpentine. The MOD (Medical Officer of the Day) got there, and the guy broke down and cried for a half an hour, exhausted. Reportedly, his wife soon went back to the U.S., and he ended up getting a psychiatric discharge from the Army.

The next night, El Guru said, "It has been exhausting lately. We got to get out of here."

Greg replied, "Let's go to Cologne and Dusseldorf next weekend."

Chapter 5

The Oktoberfest

The next weekend, Greg and El Guru caught an afternoon train, and talked about politics for much of the way to Dusseldorf. The *Pentagon Papers* was a book by Daniel Ellsberg that had come out a couple months earlier - El Guru was discussing it with Greg and a German guy who sat across from them on the ride from Bingen to Bonn. El Guru was complaining about how Robert McNamara, Defense Secretary under Johnson, probably prolonged the war. Then he went into a tirade about how Nixon had his so-called secret plan to end the war just to get elected, and that Nixon was going to fight all "left wing conspirators" who would try to take down his presidency because he continued the war by going into Cambodia, and that Nixon's men bugged Ellsberg's' psychiatrist's office to discredit Ellsberg. The guy remarked that Willy Brandt, the German Chancellor, was "as you say - slick." El Guru declared that Brandt was more competent and less corrupt than Nixon. While El Guru droned on, Greg peered out the window and took in the sights on the Rhine, its gorgeous castles, the Lorelei rock, and its many wine towns advertising their festivals for the month of September. The German guy, who noticed Greg checking out the signs for festivals at each stop, stated that 1971, because of the rainier than usual weather in Germany that spring and summer, was going to be a great year for wine. He gave Greg and El Guru a tip on a good, cheap hotel in Dusseldorf as he disembarked from the train in Bonn.

"How come you never went to Bonn for a day or night, Artie?"

"Too uncomfortable. It's the center of their government, they have some high up American government officials there, and there's got to be some lifers and their families hanging around. I know there are some American schools there."

"It looks like a fairly nice town from the train. I'll have to check it out for the day, sometime right after I get a haircut. You could go there any time because you look foreign and can speak Spanish any time you want."

"Still, I'm not interested in it."

About an hour later, they checked into the Hotel an der Oper in Altstadt. They got washed up, dressed, and ate an Italian restaurant. (Italian, Chinese, or Mexican restaurants, if you could find one, gave you more for your money all over Europe.) At 8:30, in Altstadt the streets were already filled up with people in their 20s and 30s; some were casually dressed, others fashionably dressed. They went into a bar for a beer and ducked into an alley to share a joint of hash. They then made their way to La Bamba - the first of several great bars and discotheques. The bartender had a quick smile and quick service. The Alt beer was refreshing, and the pop music was excellent.

Then they talked for a long time with a guy named Jakob - "call me Jim" - He spent half of his time in New York working for Lufthansa Airlines. Jim told them about other bars they might like. El Guru asked Jim about meeting ladies Dusseldorf.

"They would be mostly looking for a boyfriend, not a one-night stand. Many of them just want to be looked at. They dress to impress people."

"Just like back in the US," Greg said.

Jim added that most people over 25, speak little, if any English, and that few Americans or British come there. "Why, I don't know. It is a very nice city," he said.

"I bet you can get to some chicks if you ask them and their friends if they want to do a bowl of hash," El Guru said.

Jim responded, "I would not suggest trying that. True, it might work for some people but a lot of locals keep foreigners who use drugs at an arm's length. But most people here are somewhat friendly. And there are no American soldiers around here so most Germans will keep an open mind about you because you are young."

Eventually, Jim saw a lady friend at a table conversing with some older people and he left Greg and El Guru to join them. They thanked Jim and decided to go to one of the bars Jim suggested. A long-haired guy in jeans, with a rip in his shirt, named Rudy, overheard them and followed them into the Downtown Club, speaking loudly in half-German and half-English. He introduced them to a waitress – a cute honey blonde in her 20s who spoke English. She told Rudy to get home, from what they could decipher. Then she informed Greg and El Guru, "He is what you call the town drunk. He drinks a liter of vodka every night."

El Guru whispered to Greg, "I like this chick. Maybe she has a friend." He asked her about maybe doing a bowl of hash later. She ordered them out of the bar.

They left and Rudy followed them, getting wild - he was singing songs, grabbing some girls by their asses, and telling merchants on the street that they were selling "shit." Then he urinated right in the middle of a side street. "We really got to get rid of this bastard," Greg said. They took off, running for a couple of blocks and went to the Sing Sing. After a couple of beers and getting shot down by a couple more ladies, they decided to leave. Rudy suddenly appeared right outside the bar, half smiling, half angry. "Amerikaner not want (to be) my friend," he said, as he wandered away.

It was just past midnight and after walking some more and starting to feel no pain, they went into a place called The Disaster. The place was literally a disaster - a broken window, heavy sawdust floor, toilet in the men's room almost overflowing, small alt (dark) beers served in what looked to be old glasses, and barstools that were creaky and bent. And the band - somebody said they were called "Kraftwerk" - consisted of guys who wore shades, staring at El Guru and Greg and playing weird music.

El Guru said, "Is this place real?"

"Let's get out of here, Artie. This is the creepiest bar I've ever been to in my life. Appropriately named, though, I'll say that."

Finally, they topped off the night by going to the ABC Club on the way back to the hotel. El Guru loved it at first—nobody in the place looked very straight. The waitress, Lena, had a resemblance to Cher, and wore a sheer blouse with obviously no bra.

El Guru said, "She's too tall for me, why don't you try for her?"

"I don't trust her."

The DJ constantly made jokes running down Americans, and the bartender tried twice to cheat El Guru and Greg out of their change. No tip for him. They decided to call it a night and they returned to their hotel. The next morning, they checked their bags at the Hauptbahnhof and walked off their hangovers by taking in the sights of Dusseldorf, mostly in the big park between Altstadt and downtown. Before this, El Guru bought a new pair of shoes at a department store. After three hours his feet were hurting so badly, he was hobbling like an old man. "I don't want to go to Cologne," El Guru said.

Greg suggested they see Aachen, which was about an hour away. Historical artefacts of Charlemagne were in the Cathedral there, and there weren't any American GIs around. "You're the one who told me you get treated better in the non-GI towns, and I think you're right."

"OK. Vamos."

They arrived in Aachen and checked into a hotel near the train station, giving their names as "Paul Horning and Jim Tailer." They went to the Cathedral that housed Charlemagne's relics. The man at the desk at the entrance only spoke German and they had a hard time understanding him, but it seemed like he said it cost 20 DM to enter. They didn't want to spend that kind of money so they decided to forego Charlemagne and instead, they split a pizza for dinner. After that, they hung out at the hotel, listening to Radio Luxembourg for several hours, before hitting the town at night for their usual bar hopping. After a couple of hours at one discotheque, El Guru was checking out a girl nearby who smiled at him.

Greg remarked about her nice legs; El Guru commented on all of the rest of her body as he looked at her. Before he could get another word out of his mouth, she turned to him with a disgusted look and announced that she was an American. She said she thought they were European and said, "All American men are pigs."

They exited the bar. Greg stated, "You gotta watch your mouth. You never know who you're gonna meet. Maybe we should go back and apologize."

"I don't apologize to anyone."

At the hotel, the desk clerk smiled and greeted them. "Mr. Horning and Mr. Tailer. You like Aachen?"

"Charlemagne's Cathedral museum is expensive - 20 DM," Greg said.

"Oh no, admission is only 2 DM."

"Ooh! We misinterpreted what he told us. At least you have some good places to eat and go out at night, "El Guru said.

"We will be back in Aachen again," Greg said.

"Don't mind us, we're a couple of gringos," El Guru said.

As they went up to their room, Greg said, "That guy at the Cathedral must've thought we were a couple of cheap bastards."

"I thought for sure he said TWENTY DM!"

They stopped into Koblenz on their way back. Marlies was not at the Toff Toff. They went to the Cape Horn, as Greg hoped Rosi would be there. However, they were told she flew to Canada for a week to be with her boyfriend Luigi. El Guru said that he had been there before and remembered Rosi. They agreed to take the next train home because they probably would have just enough money to go to Munich and the Oktoberfest next weekend, which would be their only chance to see it.

Both Greg and El Guru worked for the next five evenings straight, but they both took an annual leave day so they could get another three-day weekend to go to the Oktoberfest in Munich. Buck Williams never wanted a day off and he covered for Greg. El Guru was busy, too. He complained, "My ward is filling up to the max with all these damn women who got pregnant around New Year's Eve and didn't use any birth control."

At 11:15 on Friday night, El Guru told Greg they had to get out of town by 6:00 am because it would be a long ride to Munich by train. They estimated that it would take at least six or seven hours to get there, and they would probably have to change trains one time. This wouldn't give them much time to pack, leaving that early, Greg declared.

El Guru replied, "Don't bother packing. Take a shower, get dressed, and we'll go European - most Europeans don't take a shower or bath more than once a week. You can wash up at the train station's men's room. Just bring a jacket, a long sleeve shirt, and an undershirt."

"Do you think there might be a room at some flophouse where we could stay?"

"I don't know. We can try."

They got on the train to Munich after changing trains quickly at Kaiserslautern. At 1:30, they arrived in Munich. Greg suggested they get a map at one of the welcome stands and follow the crowd. They did just that, and eventually reached the Oktoberfest. They were amazed at the huge fair grounds, the beer tents and the number of smiling people there walking around the narrow lanes, apparently speaking many foreign languages. It was a beautiful day - not a cloud in the sky - about 65 degrees and sunny with a very light breeze. Two very muscular men were turning a huge spit, roasting an ox.

Greg exclaimed, "Look at those dudes! Want to see if we can get a sandwich there?"

El Guru replied, "Nah. We probably can't afford it. Let's just get a bratwurst."

After they ate, they went to the Hacker-Pschorr Brau tent, sat at a table and ordered beers. The steins were huge—almost as big as a pitcher—and the beer was tasty and filling. They cost only about 3 DM each. El Guru said that he was going to walk around for a while to see if anyone spoke Spanish because people were there from all over the world.

"I'm gonna stay here and listen to the band playing the 'Ein, Zwei, G'suffa' song."

Two minutes later, some Americans and their German wives from Ulm, who overheard Greg and El Guru speaking English, asked Greg if he wanted to join them. Greg drank another stein with them, while everyone in the group laughed and talked about their experiences living and traveling in Germany. Then Greg asked if he and his friend, El Guru, could stay with them, and they said, "No," as they got up and walked away.

Greg thought, "Where's Artie?" He looked all around and started walking toward the Lowenbrau tent. The El Guru suddenly tapped him on the shoulder and said, "See that chick over there in the brown jacket? She's alone and lives near the Olympic Village that they're building. I'm pretty sure that I'm gonna score with her."

"You've been rapping to her all this time? You think she'll let me sleep in her car?"

"She doesn't have a car. She took a local train in. I've gotta get back to her. Try to get a place somewhere if you can. If we both come up empty, sit over near the top of the hill off to your right (he gestured). If I'm not back, I'll meet you at the Hofbrauhaus tomorrow at noon."

Greg agreed with El Guru's plan, and he went into the tent, bought another beer, and soon spotted a cute chick in her 30s with two of her girl-friends. He went over to them and learned her name was Erika. Greg tried his best to stay as sober as he could, dragging out his beer. He learned Erika had been married to an American GI and lived in Tennessee before coming back home to Germany. He didn't even rap to the other ladies at all, thinking, "Here is my place to stay. If I can have her, great; if not, I'll be grateful if I can sleep on her couch. At least she's talking to me." He ate some kind of chicken dinner with her, and she agreed to walk with him around part of the grounds near the rides. Her friends left. After finished his beer, he was intoxicated. His speech was starting to slur, as they walked and he held her hand. Then he stopped and hugged her, smiling. He then tried to make out with her, but after one quick kiss, she told him that she had to know him for at least two weeks before she could sleep with him. Barely able to get coherent thoughts out of his mouth, Greg begged her to at least let him sleep on the floor, but she refused. As a consolation, she said she might be at the Lowenbrau tent the next night at 5:00, if they happened to run into each other. She quickly left.

No longer able to control his drunkenness, he staggered as she walked away. Greg was tired, so he hobbled over to the hill, a little more than halfway up, where some people were grazing in the grass, and he sat down, hoping El Guru would show up. He quickly passed out and woke up at 10:30; with hardly anyone around. Not caring, he got up and peed behind a tree nearby. Just about everything had closed down at the fairgrounds, and he was hung over. "It's a damn good thing I didn't get mugged and robbed," he thought. But he needed to sleep off his hangover somewhere - and not on the hill. He walked for several blocks and spotted a dark construction site. He climbed over a wall there and hid, slumping behind a shed there for about two hours. He couldn't stand the cold any longer, so he decided to break into the office and sleep on the floor. At about 7:00 am, he heard some voices at about 50 yards away, coming closer. He got up and jumped out the office window and ran toward a fence. A construction worker spotted him and yelled in German something to the effect of, "What the hell are you doing here?"

Greg yelled back, "Wo ist das Hofbrauhaus?" ("Where's the Hofbrauhaus?")

"Hofbrauhaus? Aus! Raus! Poleizi! (Police)"

Greg jumped over the fence and ran for several blocks toward the middle of downtown. He ducked into a little restaurant and ordered tea, ice water, and a pastry. He took his time and spent some time in their bathroom, also. He felt miserable. He then made his way to the Hauptbahnhof, washed his face and hands, used the public electric shaver costing one DM, sprinkled some spray cologne on his hand to rub into his underarms, sat down on a bench near one of the train tracks and "spaced out" for a few hours, watching trains and people come and go. He started feeling better at 11:30, ate a slice of pizza, and made his way to the Hofbrauhaus. El Guru was waiting outside, and said, "Greg, are you OK? You don't look good."

"I felt like shit this morning. Did you get to stay with that chick?"

"Yeah - stay. She damn near threw me out when I tried to make a move on her. At least she let me sleep on her sofa."

Greg told him all of what had happened to him, and El Guru laughed, "Jesus, man, after what you went through, you should either be in a German jail or dead."

"Hey, the Hofbrauhaus is a famous place. Let's have a beer here," Greg replied.

"Are you sure - after last night?"

"Yeah. I doubt if I'll ever make it back to Munich again."

One huge stein of beer was all they had, and they dragged out their Hofbraus for well over an hour. They marveled at the sheer size of the place and the number of tables, and the strength of the waitresses carrying several full steins of beer in each hand, serving the thirsty people. There were as many people eating and drinking there as in any of the tents at the Oktoberfest grounds. They ate a couple of giant pretzels. "I bet these are as good as any you'd get in New York," El Guru said.

They were back at the fairgrounds at about 2:00. They were walking around near the rides when a guy who looked like a super freak, with a boy about eight or nine years old started speaking French to them. He asked them how they liked the Oktoberfest and how long they were staying in Munich. After a minute, Greg couldn't keep up with his French, and El Guru then asked the guy if he spoke Spanish, to which he replied that he did not. Greg asked him if he spoke English, and he said, "Yes." The man remarked, "I thought you men were French or Moroccan. I know you're not English. You aren't Americans, are you? You don't seem like typical American tourists."

"That's a compliment," El Guru said.

"We are in the military, not civilians," Greg said.

He seemed astonished. He talked with them for almost an hour and it appeared that, politically, he was a leftist radical. El Guru was fascinated with him. The man said that he was glad to see that America was on the way down because of Vietnam. He encouraged El Guru and Greg to desert because he himself was a military deserter once, and he currently worked for a news outlet affiliated with a Munich TV station where he had some broadcasting influence. During the conversation, he wanted to know all about Vietnam. Greg revealed that what he learned was that the Vietnamese people didn't really care who won the war. El Guru said that it was shameful that so many people were getting killed for essentially nothing, and that he hoped such an immoral war would be over soon, but it would be difficult to get Nixon out of office unless someone assassinated him like Kennedy. The guy told them about an up and coming leftist named Lyndon La Rouche (alias Lyn Marcus), and encouraged them to study his writings. El Guru said that his discharge from the army was a year away, but he had thought about working within the system to advocate leftist causes as long as the US was politically conservative. The guy sincerely thanked them for the discussion and left with his son.

El Guru said, "Wow. That was really food for thought. I should have gotten his name."

"But that guy just might be working for the CIA. Don't go getting court-martialed."

As they walked along the fairgrounds, they were entranced by the myriad of people speaking a multitude of languages; some singing, some drunk, some with children; people of all ages, shapes and sizes—almost everyone smiling and happy, enjoying the beautiful fall day and the festivities. Greg suddenly stopped; a lady was smiling at him. He told El Guru that it was Erika, the lady who wouldn't let him stay with her last night. She appeared to be alone.

El Guru told him to go over to her in case she changed her mind, and that Greg had nothing to lose. "If I don't see you, I'll meet you right here tomorrow, same time. For the next hour or two, I'll be near the back row of one of the beer tents."

Greg went over to Erika, who smiled, gave him a hug and a kiss on the cheek and they walked for about a half hour on the grounds, making small talk and eating strudel. They held hands as they went into one of the beer tents. After sitting down, he related his adventures of the past 24 hours. She laughed, at which point he laid it on the line.

"It may be funny to you, but it wasn't for me. I had no place to stay. I like you and it seems you like me too. I will never do anything you wouldn't want me to do. I just want to stay with you. We don't have to sleep together. Like I said last night, I'll sleep on the floor. I'll even sleep on the stairs at your house."

"I told you I can't have you stay with me. I have to know you a lot better."

"Why did you come back here? You found me, you smiled at me. What kind of message does that send to a man?"

"You can sleep outside again. You must have done that when you were in Vietnam last year. No, you will not be staying with me. See if you can get transferred here and maybe we could know each other. That is the only way we can have any kind of romantic relationship."

"I don't even want that. I just want a roof over my head for one night!"

She ignored him and walked away. At the other end of the tent, several rows up, he noticed El Guru, laughing and talking with a bunch of girls in their early 20s. He went over to them and said, "Artie, introduce me to your friends."

"These are Australian girls and I'm trying to teach them a little Spanish. Get a beer and sit down! We're having a good time here."

They decided to go up near the front of the tent to watch the band and sing along with the songs to get into the spirit of the Oktoberfest. The table was not far from where the band was playing, and right after they sat down there, the band stopped. There was a loud argument at the bandstand. Two guys were cursing each other in German. One was the tuba player and the other was an old man who was dressed in Alpine outfit and lederhosen. A few people tried to hold the old man back from going after the tuba player. The girls were watching and one said, "Someone better get that old man away before the bloke blips him." The band started to play the next number, but the old man climbed up the side of the bandstand and dumped his whole stein of beer down the tuba. Everyone started laughing, but out of nowhere, about 20 cops shot right through the crowd, swinging their clubs and dragging the old man away, showing him no mercy amid his loud cursing.

The girls started asking Greg and El Guru about where they were from and all about their time in the Army. Greg talked about Sydney and the wonderful time he had on his R&R last year there; El Guru asked about the Australian government, what laws there were about marijuana, and telling them Germany right now is a better place to live than the U.S. They all got steins of beer and toasted (Prosit!) to all of us. It turned out that these women were all 22 to 24, apparently from wealthy families in Sydney, and they were near the end of traveling in Europe for a month. One of them (Helga) grew up in Regensberg, but hadn't lived in Germany for seven years - she spoke fluent German. El Guru and Greg couldn't believe their good luck - the other five girls never met Americans before, and they seemed to like them.

They all kept laughing and talking as they were drinking their beers. It was dark out, at this point in time. Helga seemed to be the leader of the group. They were staying in a big tent near the fairgrounds and they had a VW van. Later, Peggy and Mary said they had enough to drink and commented, "Maybe we should call it a night. We don't want to get pissed." El Guru looked shocked at that remark, but before he could say anything, Greg explained to him that "pissed" was Aussie slang for drinking so much that you have to keep urinating. El Guru laughed and then spoke about the possibility of continuing the conversation in their tent. Greg admitted that he and El Guru didn't have a place to stay, and he asked if he and El Guru could stay in the tent or in the van. Helga said, "Let's talk among ourselves for a few minutes."

A few minutes later, they came back and Pat told them, "We took a vote and you can stay with us, but we can't all fit in the tent."

They walked to where the tent was and after about 15 minutes of discussion, it was decided that El Guru would stay in the van with Sue and Pat. Greg would sleep in the tent with the rest of them, being in the center of the circle on the ground.

"That's OK with me," Greg said to El Guru, smiling.

Greg wound up cuddling with Maureen, not being able to get a lot of sleep.

He whispered, "What're we gonna do?"

She whispered, "Try to sleep. Maybe somehow later tomorrow, I can make it up to you, but not with all of the girls around. Let's talk about it alone in the morning."

An hour later, Pat came into the tent and somebody asked, "What happened?"

"They're getting it on with each other," Pat responded, in a voice of disgust.

In the morning, as they all woke up, Sue came back into the tent first. El Guru soon followed. He seemed happy. On the other hand, Greg felt a little groggy. They offered Greg and El Guru some tea and pastries to eat, and Maureen wanted to talk to Greg alone. She said they were going to Dachau and then to see Helga's relatives in Munich, but she would meet him under the Ferris Wheel at 8:00 that night.

El Guru was thanking everybody and saying goodbye as Sue walked him out to the gate. Greg did the same about a minute later.

El Guru asked with a smile, as they walked away, "Which one did you get?"

"Maureen, but we couldn't do anything heavy, especially with the other girls right there. I had better luck in Sydney last year."

"Sue was good, but we both understood that we'll never see each other again. She never had a Mexican before and she was curious."

They went downtown and hung out at the Hauptbahnhof for a while, getting cleaned up in the men's room and walking around the area. Then, instead of going back to the fairgrounds, they decided to take a long jaunt out to the Olympic stadium the Germans were building for the 1972 Olympics. They imagined about the Olympics and the Oktoberfest back to back - what a great time it would be!

It took them hours to make their way back to the fairgrounds. They laid out on the grass on the nearby hill for a long time, alternately taking naps before walking around the fairgrounds again. They looked at kids in bumper cars. The German children were very orderly driving them around while the American kids were actually having fun bumping into each other. A drunken Turk was trying to climb over the wall and fell into one of the unoccupied cars. The American kids laughed at this and started knocking him around with their cars as he was yelling at them. Suddenly, two kids converged on his car and hit him at the same time. He was knocked right out of the car onto the railing and started puking his guts out. El Guru, Greg, and even the ride operator couldn't stop laughing as the guy staggered away. The police came after him and his two drunk friends who were staggering nearby who tried to help him. El Guru and Greg decided to "go straight" - no beer for them after all the beer they drank the last two days. They went back downtown, eating dinner at a Chinese restaurant.

"I have to meet Maureen at 8:00 pm under the Ferris Wheel. What are you gonna do?"

"I'm just gonna lay low at the station and we should take a train home later. Out best bet would be to get a local train that leaves for Kaiserslautern around 11:00 tonight. A connecting train from there would get us home at 8:00 am. We both have to work tomorrow at 3:00."

"OK. I'll see what I can do with Maureen and I'll get to the station to catch that train."

Greg went back to meet Maureen but it started to rain. By 8:00, there was a wicked thunderstorm—he got soaked thinking, "Where the hell are you Maureen?" It stopped raining about an hour later and he headed back to the train station but something caught his eye - two empty big glass Paulaner steins next to one of the tents. He snatched them up and slipped them under his jacket, bolting toward the Hauptbahnhof. "One great souvenir for me, and one for Artie," he thought. One block away from the station, he rounded a corner running when suddenly five German guys, walking arm in arm and singing, slammed into him and CRASH! Greg was knocked down and both mugs were broken, lying in the street. They helped him up but he started crying, yelling, "goddamnit!" He ran into El Guru as soon as he got to the station and told him what happened. After he vented for about a half hour, they didn't say much to each other and tried to sleep during the long ride back to Bad Kreuznach.

Chapter 6

Greg Goes Home and El Guru Surprises Him

After they got back to the hospital barracks, both of them slept for about five hours. Greg took a shower, got dressed for work and picked up his mail. As he went back upstairs to his room, he stood in his doorway and opened a letter for Marlies and stopped. She wanted him to come up and see her this week. He decided to write her a quick letter to tell her he had just enough money to go up to Koblenz and back, but she would have to subsidize him, or else he couldn't see her until November.

The census was 27 on the ward when he got there - he was working with Barbie Doll, Buck, and an SFC medic named Warren. They had 11 admissions that evening which was probably an all-time record for a non-disaster, and the four of them were extremely busy. All of them did about an hour overtime before they could sit down to give the report to the next shift. Shortly after 11:00 pm, a couple came up to the unit with a child, apparently referred by someone on call at the OPC, wanting to get some kind of a shot for their son. Greg told them that they would have to wait for a while until the next shift came on. About 30 minutes later they were complaining and Greg told Barbie Doll, who yelled outside the nurses' station to no one in particular, "Don't they realize the four of us are running half this freaking hospital all by ourselves!" She went over to the parents and said sternly, "I'm very sorry, but we have some other people we have to take of immediately that are more important than one shot." Greg explained to the parents about all the admissions, and the MOD (Medical Officer of the Day) should have gone to the OPC to give the shot himself. Barb gave a fast report to the 11-7 nurse. Warren got off the phone saying, "Do you believe this crap? We're getting five more admissions coming up in the next half hour!" Buck volunteered to help out for the next shift. Barb replied, "OK. Thanks, Buck, but the rest of us are leaving. We have enough people covering on 11-7 to take care of the rest of this." Greg had never seen her so upset. But this was the ninth evening of a 10-day stretch for her and tensions were high for the evening shift staff on the ward.

El Guru stopped in to see Greg later, who told him what happened. He wondered why nobody called him because they had five staff on his ward and it was an easy night. Down the hall, Lefty Luke was yelling, struggling to open the door to get into his room. They went to help him but he did get and he dropped a couple of cans of beer outside. El Guru said, "We need these. He won't even remember them. Let's go to your room."

As they were drinking and talking, there were two loud voices coming toward Greg's door. El Guru opened up the door to see Jerry and Allie. They were two friends originally from Wisconsin who worked at other parts of the hospital. El Guru took one look at them and said, "Shit, you guys are stoned. You got any more hash?"

"We got a big joint left," Allie said, grinning.

"Come on in, light it up and pass it around," El Guru eagerly suggested.

Greg inquired, "What the hell were you guys arguing about?"

Allie loudly said, "Fucking Vietnam. We shouldn't be there unless the other people in the fucking UN are there!"

Jerry said, "Well, they're there."

Allie yelled, "Not as many as we have, goddammit. But they're supported by those fuckers!"

El Guru asked, "What fuckers?" (He and Greg both started laughing.)

Allie yelled, "Fucking Russia. They should get kicked out of the UN! The UN is supposed to run the world. They're supposed to keep things under control in the fucking world!"

"They can't keep things under control in the fucking world. The UN can't keep anything under control," Jerry said loudly.

Allie argued, "They're supposed to make all the rules."

Jerry screamed, "No, they don't make rules!"

Allied replied, "Well they're bullshitters. No, they're fucking liars is what they are."

Greg asked, laughing, "What's the difference between a bullshitter and a liar?"

Allie explained, "A bullshitter just talks around things and gives reasons that aren't really the truth. A liar just out and out fucking lies to your face."

Jerry said, "Allie, bend down, put your head between your legs. Take hold of your ears."

Allie gave him a strange look and said, "What are you gonna do, you goddamn pervert?"

Jerry yelled, "Just do what I say!"

Allie did that and Jerry said, "Now pull your head out of your ass, you fucking dummy!"

Everybody laughed. Then Jerry remarked, "I go up before the E-5 Board tomorrow and I'm probably still gonna be higher than a kite. If I get to be Spec/5, I'll be making $299 more a month than a PFC now."

Allie interjected, "No, you got it wrong. They won't pay you that much. If they do, your paycheck will be fucked up because they paid you too much."

"They don't fool me, boy," Jerry responded.

"You'd lose more money to me bowling. You never beat me bowling," Allie declared.

Jerry responded, "That's just because I had one fucked up night tonight."

Allied replied, "OK. Let's all go bowling again—right now—and we'll see."

El Guru pleaded, "C'mon Allie! I don't think you're that fucked up."

"I got to go to work tomorrow, anyway," Allie whined.

"You don't know what work is," Jerry retorted.

Allied declared, "I'll tell you what work is. It's when you show up and feel like shit and you have a lifer on your ass harping on you to get the job done. Your eyes are 'balooted' and red. You're all fucked up. Now that's what work is."

Allie slid out of his chair and onto the floor as he finished his rant. They all laughed.

Greg said, "You guys better get out of her and get some sleep. Artie, open the window and get that smell of hash out of here. Jerry, good luck with the E-5 Board tomorrow. Man, you're gonna need it."

As they got up to leave, Jerry said, "Maybe I'll be like Buck Williams and tell 'em I don't want E-5. That'll piss 'em off. I only got about eight months left anyway."

After they went out the door, El Guru said, "I can see them self-destructing. They're both good guys when they're sober."

"I'm exhausted from this whole night," Greg replied.

Greg got a letter back from Marlies right away. She wanted him to see her Sunday, which happened to be his only day off until he went back home to the US on leave. She said she could meet him at the train station at 4:30 and she would wait for him if he missed that train. She also indicated that he would not need any money. Greg decided to go. She was there waiting for him as he got off the train, and she gave him a big hug and kiss but immediately he sensed that something was not right. When he stepped back to look at her, she looked like she had gained about 25 pounds. She took him by the hand and drove him to a place that looked like a delicatessen; she told him to wait outside because the owner didn't like Americans. She was in there for almost a half hour and suddenly appeared with several big bags loaded with food and she told him (with a big smile) not to look because, "Ist surprise." When they got to her place, she opened up the bags and said, "Zwei hanchen!" There were two big roast chickens. This was followed by a huge bowl of Kartofellnsalat (potato salad), several other vegetables, a chocolate cake, and other pastries. Then she quickly set the table with all the food on it and they started to eat. Greg thought, "What have I done? Should I get out of here?" As she talked, she ate an entire chicken, half of Greg's chicken, half the potato salad, most of the vegetables and half of the chocolate cake. Rosi stopped by to say hello for a few minutes and as soon as Marlies went to the bathroom, Greg asked Rosi what was wrong with Marlies that she was eating so much and had gained so much weight. Rosi told him that Marlies' doctor diagnosed her with some kind of glandular problem and now she had gained 40 pounds in the last three to four months and all she wants to do is eat. "My God, I got to get rid of this sweat hog," Greg thought.

Greg told Marlies that he was tired, and maybe they should go to bed early. She insisted they share a bottle of wine, of which she drank three quarters, and listen to music on the couch. She wanted to go to bed an hour later. In bed, Greg made believe he was making love to Rosi. Marlies then said that she did not want to get married, but just wanted to have a baby.

Greg thought, "That's it for this lady." He left early the next morning. When he got back to the hospital, he wrote a letter to her saying that he was sorry, he couldn't see her anymore, and that he was starting to fall in love with Rosi. She did not respond to him.

The next night, he told El Guru what transpired regarding the quick trip to Koblenz.

"Jesus, Greg, you just assassinated her."

"I stretched the truth. I could've cut her off cold."

Greg's last night on the ward before he took off to go home was a very busy one. A young PFC came in, who overdosed on alcohol and drugs. This time, El Guru was called to help out Greg and Buck on the ward. Dr. Hall, a pathologist, was on call as MOD that night, and he came up to the ward a couple of times but it looked like he was doing the minimum to get the kid out of danger.

El Guru thought that Hall was rooting for him to die. Buck added that he thought Hall reminded him of Frankenstein, and asked them if he ever went to one of Hall's autopsies.

"Yeah," Greg responded, "and I had to leave halfway through it. He was slicing up a lady who got killed in a car accident, pulling her organs out and teaching the medical audience with a big smile on his face the whole time."

The kid made it through the night and lived, but they sent him to Landstuhl for evaluation of possible brain damage. It was discovered that he had smoked two bowls of hash and then bet a guy $10 that nothing would happen to him if he could chug a fifth of Seagram's 7 and pop a few Mandrax pills. It was amazing that he lived.

The next day, Greg caught an Air India flight to New York from Frankfurt. The plane circled London for over two hours, and there was some trouble with the plane that caused another three-hour delay on the ground. They re-boarded for 30 minutes at one point; then they were told all passengers were to get off and wait in the Heathrow Airport terminal. They re-boarded again two hours later. They got into New York six hours late and everyone who had connecting flights missed them. Air India put passengers up at a Ramada Inn near La Guardia Airport and Greg got the last room, which had a broken lock on the door. He had a 6:00 am flight to Albany, and at 4:30, he paid a jitney $5 to take him to the airport. When he got there, the American Airlines clerk said there was no such flight and it was probably leaving from Kennedy.

Greg screamed, "You got to be bullshitting me, man!" He told the clerk about all of what had happened to him the previous day in a hostile tone of voice.

"Go back to Air India and bitch to them. I can't do anything about it."

Air India apologized and told him to go to the Mohawk Airlines desk, which happened to be in the terminal next door. Greg was furious, but he hustled over to Mohawk, loudly told the clerk the whole story, showed him his tickets, and the clerk, who was seemingly hung over said that he would get him on the next flight out at 7:00 am to Albany. Greg got a seat on the plane, but they didn't take off for another hour because the stewardess didn't show up until 8:00. She looked ragged when she got on the plane, with a frozen smile. "Probably was getting balled all night," Greg thought, disgustedly. He arrived home 13 hours overdue.

El Guru spent the weekend in Luxembourg. He had four days off and he met a wealthy Dutch lady named Hannah who was in her 20s and was friendly with two of the DJs on Radio Luxembourg. She told him that via the DJs, she met an aspiring young Greek female singer El Guru had heard about earlier in the year, which intrigued him. Hannah wasn't quite as attractive as he would have liked, but she was amused by him, liked to share a bowl of hash or some wine, and knew people he really liked. She got him into a lively party of about 30 people, a few of whom were European celebrities. After that weekend, he vowed to spend more time in Luxembourg, even though he felt he was kind of using Hannah.

Greg had more bad luck. The day after he got home, he woke up with a sore throat that morphed into a monster cold and 100 degree fever for a few days. A week later, he was able to meet up with Van who was Greg's only friend left in the area, and he was married. So, Greg just hung out at Van's house, talking and listening to music instead of going out anywhere.

To add to Greg's troubles, there was the matter of his income tax filing for 1970. He spent all of 1970 in Vietnam, and according to the IRS statement he received earlier in 1971, he owed $144 in taxes. He figured this must be a mistake, and forgot about it for months. Then, a couple of days before he left on leave, he decided to go to the JAG's (Judge Advocate General) office and the JAG financial officer said he had to pay it, but he might try to resolve the situation by going to the IRS office in Albany while he was home on leave. Greg went down there and the IRS agent said that with interest, he now owed $162, and if he didn't pay by January 31st, he'd probably be in a military jail. The agent asked, "Don't you have some things you can sell?"

"Look, man, I am a soldier. I don't have a damn thing right now. I spent a year of my life in a combat zone in a war this country never should have gotten into and never should have extended beyond the last two or three years. And I'm supposed to pay?"

"Well, you made rank fast enough, so you should be able to afford it. I'm sorry - that's the law and if you don't abide by the law, you take the consequences."

Greg turned around and stormed out of there, cursing.

El Guru called a few days later from a phone they never disconnected in the nurses' station in the abandoned ward upstairs from the former Psychiatric Clinic. He laughed about Greg's Air India experience. Then they talked about sports and how Roberto Clemente of the Pirates was dominating the World Series. Greg said he went to the IRS and they told him he now owed $162 in taxes. El Guru, angrily said, "The IRS and the JAG can't send you to jail for that. You and I will write to every major newspaper in America, or at least the *International Tribune* if they try. Don't give in."

"My facial appearance is getting like a normal civilian's. I'm getting a little growth under my lip too. We'll talk about the IRS when I get back."

"Come back at night so I can take a picture of you. Luxembourg is still great. When I see you, I'll tell you about a new chick named Hannah I met there, and a good surprise that benefits me, but I have to hang up now and get back to work."

El Guru returned to Luxembourg for another two nights and spent them with Hannah. He had a good time, but something felt slightly off for him. He thought, "She's really like somebody I only want to do a bowl with, or go to a café and have lunch and a glass of wine with more than anything else. I could never get seriously romantically involved with her." But he did like the group of her friends he had met, a couple of whom he briefly encountered in the past year.

Greg had to catch another Air India flight out of New York, leaving on the night of the 26th. That morning, he drove his brother back to New Hampshire, 125 miles away, using his father's car. On the way back, he was admiring the last of a long autumn foliage season when suddenly, at the New York/Vermont state line he noticed a fine-looking young chick on the side of the road and a guy in a field about 30 yards away. Greg thought, "They can't be together," and when she stuck out her thumb and smiled, he quickly slowed down, when suddenly, "RRRRR-SMASH!" His car was rear-ended and flew into a ditch. Later, Greg's father came, and as expected, he was livid, screaming at Greg all the way home. But Greg thought, "I deserve this from him. I will never stop to pick up a chick hitch-hiking again."

Once Greg got to New York, a couple of interesting things happened. First, the Air India flight was 45 minutes late. Secondly, when he checked in, he was told there was no such non-stop flight to Frankfurt. They had to write him a separate ticket for a BOAC (British Airlines) flight connecting from London. "Here we go again," he said to the clerk. But he got on the plane OK, and an attractive, well-built young lady saw that he had an empty seat next to him and asked if she could sit there. "We were both on the same flight a few weeks ago, and I saw how upset you were with the flight and the hotel room. I really felt sorry for you."

They talked for much of the flight. Her name was Nadia. She was from Egypt and she was applying to go to graduate school for a psychology degree in Australia. She was temporarily doing administrative work for Air India in Cairo. Her father worked directly under Nasser (Egyptian president in the 1960s). Greg thought, "He's probably anti-American."

Then she said that she had just visited her sister who had married an American and lives in San Francisco. "My mother said 'This will never, ever happen again!'" Again, Greg thought, "Both of her parents are probably anti-American." But it was enjoyable to discuss topics of psychology with someone for the first time in months.

At the end of the flight, Greg quickly boarded the BOAC flight to Frankfurt. He slept almost the whole way. When the plane landed, he retrieved his baggage and on par with the rest of his trip, he just missed the train back to Bad Kreuznach. He had to wait at the station for two hours and 20 minutes for the next train. At the moment the train arrived, he realized that one of his bags was missing - a small one that had his regular glasses, his shaving stuff, and about $20 - he was still wearing his blue shades to look cool. He then remembered that he stowed the bag in the overhead bin on the BOAC flight. He decided to forget about it.

Hardly anyone was around when Greg got back to hospital barracks room early that evening. As he got his keys out, El Guru called to him from down the hall.

"Man, you look great - like Tarzan with a Fu Manchu and blue shades!"

"I lost my glasses and I only have these, and the half assed military ones I left here."

"You can get another pair at the Optical Shop tomorrow. Let me get my camera."

Greg went into his room and recounted the rest of his trip from hell, and after El Guru took his picture, he delivered the final blow. "Well, Greg, I'm afraid I've got some bad news for you that's actually good news for me. Next week I'm getting stationed at a little out-patient clinic affiliated with the hospital over at Prum - about 15 clicks from the Luxembourg border."

"What the hell? Are you falling in love with this chick?"

"Not so much that. It's a 9:00 to 5:00 job, essentially, and there is one doctor with five medics and a secretary. I always liked small towns. There are two trains in and out of there every day with good connections to the places we like to go to. And it's close to my favorite city in Europe - Luxembourg."

El Guru suggested to go downtown for the last night of the Weinmarkt Festival. When they went into the nearest Weinmarkt tent, they talked with a few locals they knew - "Paesan," who ran the best pizza shop in town; Herr Walther, who was the hospital's public relations coordinator; and Greta, who ran the snack bar at the hospital during the day. They all invited El Guru and Greg to sample some wine with them. When they got back to the hospital, El Guru suggested to Greg to get some kind of haircut at noon "when all the hospital brass is at lunch."

Things finally got slower on the ward and there was a little Halloween party at 9:00 pm on the 31st. Greg dressed up as Dr. Goodman, the psychiatrist who left several months ago. His costume consisted of a white coat, John Lennon glasses, and hair washed and down to the middle of his ears. Buck Williams dressed up as a college professor. Eileen, the civilian charge nurse, dressed up like a cheerleader. Another medic, who happened to be a patient, Rainier, got into the spirit of things and dressed up like a baby. Greg called El Guru to come up and see this. Red Cross workers brought up cookies, brownies and soda and everyone was having fun— patients and staff. El Guru laughed but he had to get back downstairs. It was his last night and they were having a little party for him as soon as they could finish the report. Dave Wilson, who was not working that night, suddenly arrived dressed up as Father Time, but soon got carried away. In his dramatically loud voice, he told a patient named Arlen, who had suffered a heart attack recently, "Time is running out on you and I'm coming to take you away." Eileen and Buck told him that was uncalled for and to get out of here ASAP.

Greg stopped in to see El Guru and said, "I know you're leaving bright and early tomorrow morning. Good luck with the job. I got your number at the clinic over there. I'm pretty broke right now but maybe we can spend some weekends in Cologne or Dusseldorf, OK?"

"Yeah, that'll be great. Call me. I can't wait to see how this'll work out."

Chapter 7

Greg Gets His Old Job Back

Nㅤew nurses were assigned to Greg's unit at the beginning of November. As he came into the nurses' station for report a few minutes early, he checked to see who was on duty that evening and he asked Buck, "Cpt. Conn? Who's Lt. Graham?"

"Buck said, "Wait till you see Lt. Graham."

The supervising nurse, Cpt. Sara Harrison, introduced the new military nurses to everyone present but she seemed to slight Buck and Greg by just saying their last names and pointing at them. Greg and Buck politely mumbled hello, but then they turned away, a little perturbed at their intro duction. They felt like a screwdriver and a wrench instead of people, even though ordinarily they both liked Sara. They both agreed that Lt. Graham was attractive.

For the first few weeks, Cpt. Conn was all business - all military and everything "by the book." But Warren called her on some of her rigidity and he had a great manner of loosening her up, the same way he did when Mary Lynn one busy night said to the staff, "Calm down. We are all here to work together as a team."

At that time, Warren went into an animated tirade and gestured wildly: "Team? I'll tell you what the hell a team is! We got over 30 patients now and some of these people are sick as hell and some others faked it to get in here. We have some medics ghosting for an hour at a time and one guy was even AWOL the other night, but if he showed up, he would've done more harm than good, so nobody wrote him up. We don't always have the right equipment to do treatments, anyway. So, you learn to do the best you can for yourself and do the best job you can with what you got. That's what a team is at this place!" Mary Lynn was shocked, but all the rest of the staff, who knew Warren well, started laughing. Even Warren started smiling at himself, and it "broke the ice" with the new staff on the unit.

But Cpt. Conn and Barbie Doll clashed right from the start. Barb had a wonderful, calm, humorous manner in relating to the patients, and although Cpt. Conn was competent, her approach was frequently the opposite. Cpt. Conn seemed to "play favorites" among patients and certain staff. Barb herself, had to be hospitalized for an intestinal problem a few weeks later. Greg and Buck felt Cpt. Conn could've treated her more humanely.

Buck said he would tell Warren to talk to her because Conn seemed to like him. Greg said maybe Sandy could because she is "Minnesota nice."

Buck said, "She's your favorite nurse. You smile more when she's on."

"On the surface, she's everything I'd want in a woman right now. We have several nurses on this ward now to fantasize about."

"Jim Owens is scheduling you and her a lot lately."

"Yeah, and you with Barbie Doll. And both of us with Eileen when Barb and Sandy are off. Too bad they're all married."

Lt. Lesley Graham was soon promoted to Captain. Buck got a kick out of her and liked her because she was very competent. Greg's first impression of her was that he she alternately tried to be domineering and seductive, although she was highly intelligent and insightful when it came to treating the patients. She would tend to manipulate them into doing things, or running errands that they didn't want to do. Buck felt that she had good ideas but they needed to be phased in instead of starting a revolution. They both wondered how she would last if she made enemies out of Sara, Cpt. Pam Keller, and Cpt. Conn.

Buck said that he liked her and so did all the civilian nurses. Greg remarked, "She's only been here a few weeks and wants us to do everything her way. But she can be down to earth and funny though. The other night we were all talking about urinary tract infections and catheterizations, and said she wondered if it would be easier to catheterize a man with an erection. I said, "I bet you'd want to try it here." She said, "OK, let's all of us take off our clothes and we'll catheterize each other. But she laughed at herself for the comment."

El Guru really liked his new job. He was working in the treatment room of the small clinic, got along with the guys and the physician well, and it was low pressure for him. He spent much of his day giving shots, administering minor medical treatments to adults and children, and charting notes. He went to Luxembourg the first two weekends of November, stayed with Hannah, and hung out with various people they knew, even smoking a little bit of hash with her and her friends. Life for him was at its best, lately.

In the meantime, Greg was still recovering financially from October and he wanted to save up for upcoming weekends away. He stayed close to the barracks, sometimes drinking a can of cheap American beer with Kent Stone, a new, friendly guy from North Carolina who worked at the Registrar's office in Finance. A few times Greg retreated to the EM Club if the food at the mess hall was lousy.

In the middle of the month, Greg called El Guru and they agreed to meet in Aachen that Friday night. Greg was the first to check in at their usual hotel (Hotel Hospitz). He didn't want to hang around at the Hauptbahnhof because it was windy and cold. The desk clerk, who spoke broken English, remembered him.

"Mr. Tailer, Guten Abend. Wo ist Mr. Horning?"

"Mr. Horning kommt very soon. I will wait here in the lobby for him."

El Guru showed up about a half hour later. After greeting one another, they went up to their room, recapped what had been happening to them over the past few weeks, ate dinner, and then got changed for their evening bar hopping jaunt. They began at what appeared to be an upper middle-class tavern and toasted each other as they drank their beers at the bar. An attractive blond in about her late 20s sat down next to Greg and smiled at him. Greg asked, "Entschuldign Sie (Excuse me). Sprechen Sie Englisch (Do you speak English)?"

She said, "Yes. I speak English very well."

She seemed sophisticated. Greg asked if she worked in Aachen.

"I work here."

"Uh, oh," El Guru whispered as he turned his head away.

Just then, an expensively dressed, 40ish big man came up to her, kissed her on the cheek, and she said to Greg, smiling, "Excuse me. I have to go to work now." And she put on her coat and went out the door with him.

El Guru laughed, "You are to prostitutes as shit is to flies."

Two men, German and Moroccan, saw the interaction at a nearby table, smiling. Greg asked them if there was a good discotheque in Aachen. The Moroccan told them to go to the Scotch Club, and gave them walking directions—the club was a few blocks away.

They finished their beers and went there. The place was packed, and they ordered beers at the bar. A lot of people were dancing. They danced with a couple of ladies about their age - Helga and Ingrid. After the songs were finished, Greg and El Guru went to their table and tried to talk to them but they spoke hardly any English. Greg pulled out a pen and a note-pad - this worked with Marlies; El Guru drew some pictures. Apparently, it was Ingrid's birthday, and both girls lived at home with their parents. Some friendly German guys the girls knew approached their table, and one of them, Okie, revealed that he spent two years at a high school in Pittsburgh, so he served as the interpreter while he and Greg talked about their times living in Pittsburgh.

Another girl, Siegrid, came by, and she seemed awestruck at the fact that two Americans were at the table. El Guru liked her right away and danced with her. As soon as she found out that he and Greg were in the Army however, she was turned off. Later, Okie and the others left with Ingrid to go to a party for her. Before leaving, Ingrid said she would be back again next Friday night. On the way out, Okie thanked them for the chance to practice his English. Greg and El Guru were grateful that they had found a night spot where there the women were not bar girls or hookers and the music was good.

The next morning, they returned to the Cathedral with the Charlemagne exhibit, and spent an hour looking at all the exquisite artifacts. This time, they paid the 2 DM entrance fee. "Look at all the incredible gold and bronze stuff from over a thousand years ago," El Guru said.

"If you remember your world history from Catholic school, he was crowned Emperor of the Holy Roman Empire here, and he had this cathedral built."

"I thought that was somewhere in France. But he's buried right here."

"It was called Aix-La-Chapelle in those days, but it is now known as Aachen."

"The Cathedral and these separate chapels - I bet they didn't have to restore much stuff from World War II. It looks like a lot of it made it through unscathed."

"I'm glad we finally saw it—and got the price right," Greg stated.

El Guru decided that he would go back to the hotel, check out, and take a train to Luxembourg to see Hannah. Greg agreed to leave with him, but he decided to go home to the barracks. They agreed they had a good time in Aachen.

El Guru slept for much of the train ride, even though he had to change trains soon. He checked his bag at the station and ate at a sidewalk café, dragging out some coffee and a glass of wine for almost two hours. Then he walked around trying to remember where Hannah lived—the times he had been with her, she drove. It got dark, so he went to Black Bess, a popular bar, thinking that he'd give it an hour and if she wasn't there, he would get his bag, go to a cheap hotel, and go back to Prum early Sunday morning. After one beer at Black Bess, Hannah came in the door with four other people. She was happy to see El Guru and he was even more thrilled to see her. They all spent almost three hours talking and joking and he wound up spending the night at her place, which was actually not far from the train station.

When Greg got back to the hospital, he learned there had been an Emergency Mass Casualty Drill the afternoon that he was on the way to Aachen. Right after the drill was over, Deputy Dog thought that Dave Wilson's roommate, Bernard Richlieu, was Wilson and he ordered him to get a haircut immediately. Richlieu argued that he wasn't Wilson, but he got the haircut anyway. Deputy Dog was upset, wondering where the hell Wilson was (Wilson actually was downtown - he was off for three days - and he didn't come back to the hospital until early evening.). On Monday morning, Deputy Dog saw Greg in civilian clothes and thought that he was Wilson (the third time that this happened) and said that he was going to write him up for an Article-15, threatening to bust him to PFC. Greg convinced him that he, in fact, was not Wilson, by showing him his military ID. Wilson became extremely pissed when Greg related all of this to him later. He stormed into Deputy Dog's office and yelled that he was going to take him to a Court Martial if he tried to give him an Article-15. Col. Lindberg got wind of this, and ordered Wilson, Cpt. Harrison, and Deputy Dog into his office. The whole thing was eventually straightened out, but Wilson kept referring to Cpt. Harrison as "Sara," which annoyed Lindberg that an officer would be regarded so informally. She told Lindberg that she scheduled Wilson for a few days off, and Deputy Dog was confused about the situation. Lindberg grudgingly agreed to dismiss this as a misunderstanding, but he ordered Wilson to get a haircut and if he ever got into any controversial accusation against higher ranking personnel, he would be busted down to Private E-1. Later, Greg spent over an hour calming Wilson down in his room.

On Greg's ward there were more psych patients coming in. Rumor had it that there was pressure on Lindberg to re-open the psychiatric clinic. Greg and Buck spent as much time as they could with these patients. There was a military psychiatrist, Dr. Holland, who came from a clinic in Mainz to see them when he could, in exchange for getting out of any on-call duty there. Buck told him that Greg used to work for Dr. Goodman, and Dr. Holland and Greg started discussing these cases privately on the unit. Cpt. Graham, Barbie Doll, and Sandy encouraged Greg to talk with staff about these patients, and any other suggestions from Dr. Holland regarding treatment.

El Guru called Greg a few days later. He told him to go up to the vacant ward upstairs from the old psychiatric clinic at 5:30 and pick up the phone - Greg would be on his dinner break then. He went there and the phone rang.

"Hey, El Guruissimo! What's happening?"

El Guru told him that their MD said the Psychiatric Clinic would be re-opened ASAP. Greg replied that he would love to be back there, but he never got the 91G Secondary MOS. Buck Williams had told him they sent it in to Heidelberg, but he hadn't heard anything. El Guru asked him if he could talk to Goring or Lindberg, or even Barry Thompson to find out what the true story was. He said that Thompson was getting out of the Army in two weeks and they've been calling him up to the ward from Preventive Medicine to see patients almost every morning. Greg knew nothing about this.

El Guru continued, "They don't want you off the evening shift up there. The other rumor is that many guys will get out of the Army several months early because there are too many troops in Germany and not enough time to send them to Vietnam."

"That won't affect me, though. I have over nine months left. I really got to run. I'll have to ghost it and get something quick to eat if I can before the mess hall closes or pay someone to get me some food from the EM Club. Call me next Wednesday on the ward. No military nurses are on that night."

That Saturday, Dr. Jay Robbins was the MOD and he happened to be in the treatment room on the ward about an hour after Greg's shift started. He overheard Greg getting into a brief argument with Cpt. Conn and Charlie Brown (another female civilian nurse) regarding how to deal with one of the psychiatric patients. As Greg walked by, Dr. Robbins said, "Hey, James, come here."

Greg walked into the treatment room and Dr. Robbins closed the door and asked, "How much longer have you got to go here in Germany?"

"Doc, my ETS is not until September, but the way I feel at this very minute, I would try to get out of this command if I have to stay on this ward much longer."

"Would you like to get your old job back?"

"You mean at the Psychiatric Clinic?"

"Well, don't get your hopes up yet, but you must know Thompson is leaving in a few weeks and we need a replacement for him. Right now, there is nobody else with any experience in mental health here, except you. The idea was put to Col Lindberg in a meeting a couple of days ago to at least re-open the clinic on a part-time basis with Dr. Rubenstein or Dr. Holland coming in from Mainz a few times a week until we get a full-time psychiatrist again."

"Wow! How soon could I possibly start?"

"I'll talk to Col. Lindberg and I'll see what I can do. Again, don't get your hopes up. So, you're definitely interested, then?"

"I sure am, Dr. Robbins. Thank you!"

"This might take some time because Master Sgt. Greene has said it'll leave a hole if you're off the ward and Col. Lindberg will want to see you first. It might be as long as a month. But I had a chat with Dr. Holland the other day, and he and I both think you can do the job. Do NOT tell anyone about this for at least another 10 days or so yet."

"Yes, Sir! Thank you very much again, Dr. Robbins."

From that moment on through the rest of the month, Greg was in a good mood on the ward. No arguments, conflicts, or griping, even though there were times when it would have been appropriate. One evening, for example, Cpt. Pam Keller, was stressed and she accidentally left a needle on a patient's bed who was an angry psychopath. The patient pointed it out to Pam. Greg overheard the conversation, as he was right near the door. After Pam's brief confrontation by the patient, Greg took her aside and talked with her very supportively. She looked like she was about to cry. He was glad he didn't pull a shithead move and walk away laughing. Instead, he gave her a lot of support as he talked to her privately. She thanked him and she calmed down.

But a couple of nights later, in a meeting off the ward after report, Buck, Charlie Brown, and Wilson had a discussion for 20 minutes regarding putting together a list of what had to change to make the ward a less stressful place between the military nurses and the rest of the staff. Not much came of it, although the next night after the opening of the shift, they "cleared the air" with some of the military nurses, and the staff seemed less tense with each other.

El Guru called Greg that Wednesday around 5:30, but Greg was so busy on the ward he couldn't talk, but told him quickly, "No news." Spec/6 Hull was on duty as the mess hall and he greeted Greg with, "Hey, James - rumor has it you're gonna start back at the Psych. Clinic again. I overheard some of the brass saying it's your job to lose."

Friday morning, around 8:30, Master Sgt. Greene knocked on his door. "James, I was hoping you'd be here. I heard you might be going somewhere up north because you got a four-day weekend. Get a haircut right now. You better look military because Col Lindberg wants to see you in his office at 11. I think you know what it's for."

"Thanks, Sgt. Greene. I'll go to the barber shop right now."

Greg had the barber give him a real short haircut known as a "Princeton" in the early '60s. He shaved off his moustache and sideburns and put on his dress green uniform. He reported to Col. Lindberg's office at 11:00 and saluted him.

Col. Lindberg said, "This is informal, James."

The conversation was about the Psychiatric Clinic re-opening, but their talk was fairly brief. After a few minutes, Lindberg said, "James, I didn't think you were interested."

"I am very much so, Sir, and I feel I can do the job."

"Well, if you feel you can do the job, you can have it - if you want it."

"I want it, Sir."

They shook hands and he said, "Congratulations - it's yours. You can start December 13th. As you know, we moved Preventive Medicine to the suite of offices where you used to be, and you'll have an office there. If you need any help, don't hesitate to call Dr. Holland."

Greg thanked him and walking out, Lt. Col. Goring came over and shook his hand and said, "I know this is what you wanted. You'll do a good job, James."

Then several lifers appeared: the new hospital Director of Nursing, Sergeant Major Dennis, Deputy Dog (who still didn't realize who Greg was until someone told him), and Master Sgt. Greene. Greene shook his hand and said, "Geez, I can't get over how military you look. A month ago, you looked like a hippie."

"Thanks. I really want this job. Now I'm going up north this weekend to celebrate. I can play the Army game, if I need to."

"It's not an Army game. It's serving your country. By the way, the Sergeant Major thought he saw you and Guerrero near the Cathedral in Cologne last month. He said it's good that you guys go out and socialize with the German people."

"We might as well make the most of what Germany has to offer."

Greg thought, "Has that old bastard actually been spying on us? I was told to steer clear of him, but Kevin Monday told me once that he really does care about the troops here, or Monday would've got 212ed (Undesirable Discharge) for all the fights he got into downtown."

Greg went back to his room, changed his clothes, thinking this was again the step in his Army career that would help him beyond military service and would facilitate getting into a Masters program. He went up to the ward, saw Eileen in the hallway, grinned and said, "Hey, I got the job!" She smiled and gave him a hug.

"I need to use your phone."

He called El Guru. "Artie, I got the job!"

"Wow, man, that's great news."

"Are you planning on seeing Hannah tonight?"

"No. She had to go to Amsterdam to meet her family there."

"Let's celebrate. Can you meet me at the Dusseldorf Hauptbahnhof around 7:30?"

"I got a couple hours of time off coming. I'll meet you there at 6:30."

Chapter 8

Is the Friendship Over?

El Guru walked right by Greg at first when he got to the Dusseldorf Hauptbahnhof until Greg called him. El Guru looked shocked.

"Wow, man! Did you prostitute yourself to the lifers for the haircut, and no moustache?"

"It's only temporary. I'll start looking more like myself after the first of the year. I really had to do this, or I'd be miserable working on the ward until the end of the summer."

They checked into the Hotel Continental. After getting changed, instead of bar hopping, they only went to Lord Nelson's to drag out three beers. They didn't seriously try to meet any people, although they briefly did dance with a couple of ladies to a couple of rocking tunes after about an hour there. Greg talked at length about his meeting with Col. Lindberg and all the events leading up to it, as well as what was happening on the ward and in the hospital. El Guru talked about how he loved his new job, about Hannah, and all the people he was meeting in Luxembourg. They also talked about politics - El Guru asked if Nixon actually wanted to go to China next year with ping-pong players. They talked about football - El Guru hoped that the Cowboys wouldn't make it to the Super Bowl because he felt they were an ultra-conservative organization ("The Minnesota Vikings are my team now."). They rapped about music - El Guru said he never gets tired of hearing "Shaft," by Isaac Hayes. Greg asked if he heard

"American Pie" by Don McLean—the story of the last 12 years in America, metaphorically. They wandered back to the hotel just after midnight.

The next day, they took a long stroll through the Lofgren—the large, beautiful public park. Then El Guru suggested they go to Aachen. After arriving in Aachen, they checked into their hotel (The Hotel Hospitz). The desk clerk gave them a big smile. "Mr. Horning and Mr. Tailer - good seeing you again!"

As they went up to their room, El Guru said to Greg, "We have to stay here all the time. This guy likes us, and he gives us the best room he's got for a cheap price."

They took a nap for a couple of hours, got washed up, changed, ate, and went to the Scotch Club. They both got shot down by women right and left for the first hour or so, attempting to dance with them. Around 11:00, a cute, short brunette sat down several stools down from them, and ordered a beer and a shot of something. She downed them both in five minutes and stared ahead with a blank look on her face. Greg thought she looked depressed. El Guru persuaded him to check her out because her because a young chick at the table right ahead of them had just looked over and smiled at him. He said, "I'm gonna go and try to rap to her."

Greg walked up to the cute brunette and asked her if she wanted to dance. She said, "Nein." He asked her if she spoke English and told her that he was an American, upon which she gave him a big smile and told him her name was Gretchen. Admittedly, she spoke almost no English, but she was able to communicate that she wanted to know all about him, America, and what he was doing here. They communicated by drawing pictures, which was Greg's "go to" method, as he always kept a pen and a spiral notebook with him. About 20 minutes later, she agreed to dance with him to a slow song. At the end, he kissed her, and she smiled and put her head on his shoulder. El Guru saw them walking off the dance floor and came over to Greg and said that he was going to pick up this girl. Greg said that he would probably get to take his girl home, and that she lived in an apartment not far away. He told El Guru, "Do me a favor. Please don't do a bowl at the hotel. We could get into big trouble and never get to stay there again."

El Guru left with his chick and waved to Greg as he was leaving. Greg asked Gretchen if she wanted to go someplace quieter, and she said she did. However, just as they got out the door steady rain mixed with snow started, and then she said she wanted to go to her place. It was a small and sparsely decorated but neat apartment on the second floor of a four-story brick building. Their clothes were fairly wet. After they took off their coats, Greg sat on the loveseat couch, and Gretchen smiled as she pulled out a bottle of Jägermeister. "Oh, hell, I know what this stuff is," Greg thought, and he smiled. They both took swigs, and when she got the bottle back, she started humming and dancing to the old song, "The Stripper," by David Rose. She started taking off her clothes and flipped her bra into the air, as she fell into Greg's arms laughing. They went into her bedroom and had sex for about a half an hour before they both passed out. In the morning, in spite of their hangovers, they had an encore. Fifteen minutes later, she said she had to be at work in Cologne by 8:30, and they quickly got washed and dressed. She said something to the effect that she had a great time, and really needed last night, but that he would probably not see her again. But he got her address, and said he would write to her, and would try to be back in 3 weeks.

Meanwhile, El Guru took the young chick (Giesela) back to the hotel—luckily, he thought, the desk clerk wasn't in the lobby, so they went right up to the room. He wanted to do a bowl of hash with her. She spoke broken English and she said that it might be dangerous if they got caught with the smell of hashish leaking out into the hallway. But she said that instead they could stay on the bed, listen to music, and have a good time.

"Let's get Radio Luxembourg on your radio (she had a transistor radio in her purse)."

Kid Jensen was the DJ. He played a seductive song almost right away ("for all you lovers on the continent tonight") – "Je T'aime" by Serge Gainsbourg and Jane Birkin.

The mood was suddenly very romantic. They had sex, but he could tell she wasn't responding well, no matter what he did or tried. He asked if he was doing something wrong. She told him no, but she had to go home, and that she lived with her parents. Also, she was concerned that, "Your friend may come back here at any time."

If he's not back by now, he won't be coming back."

"I have to go," she said, as she got dressed.

"What? I don't believe this!

She gave him a quick kiss, and went out the door fast.

In the morning, Greg came in as El Guru was leaving the room. They swapped "war stories" as they ate breakfast, but they agreed that it was time to go back to their Army barracks.

During Greg's last ten days working on the ward, it was busy with at least 30 patients every night. There would be hardly any four-day weekends with the new job, but the trade-off would certainly be worth it, Greg thought. Furthermore, Buck was getting out of the Army fairly soon. Barbie Doll, Charlie Brown and Eileen were leaving in a few weeks because their husbands were also getting out of the Army, and Sandy was getting a job at the military's elementary school as the school nurse. Mary Lynn was about to take a position on the OB ward, where she wanted to be in the first place. With big changes on the ward, Greg was glad to be on the way out, as well.

El Guru saw Hannah in Luxembourg for the next two weekends. She was probably the best woman "on paper" he had met all year, but he kept saying to himself that he felt he did not have it in him to get emotionally involved with her. He was afraid of committing to her because he was sure that there would be someone more "right" for him out there. During the second weekend, they went to various places shopping, hung out at cafes, took walks in the park, talked about international politics or music with friends, and had plenty of sex. On Sunday evening, he had to get back to Prum. She talked about the possibility of his meeting some of her family members the following Saturday which made him feel somewhat uncomfortable. He thought, "She wants the two of us to get closer. I don't really want to do that. Besides, from what she tells me, her family members are probably conservative." So, he told her that he could only see her Friday night and that he was on call for the rest of the weekend. In reality, he was on call for the clinic once a month, but not until Christmas weekend. She seemed sad initially, but she perked up when he agreed that they would make plans for New Years' Eve the next time he saw her.

Greg's last night on the ward was Saturday. He started getting in a grumpy mood while changing into his work clothes. All he could think about was that the hospital brass was ignoring any problems with drugs and sometimes violence, and there had been more fights lately around the hospital. Also, there was a racial problem starting, and most of the medics were never told that they were doing a good job or seldom got any praise from the higher-ranking people. Shortly after the shift report, he saw SFC Jim Owens, who came by to get something out of his office. Greg asked if he had a minute and after being told they could talk privately; Greg went into a tirade about what was bothering him. Owens listened to him and reminded him that it was his last night on the ward, things would get better for him, and some things probably wouldn't change. But the hospital brass was aware of the problems and would be working to alleviate them. Just as Greg calmed down, Cpt. Graham wanted to know what all the yelling was about as she walked by.

Greg said to her, "We are human beings first. We aren't goddamn machines. What are you going to do when Buck Williams is gone? He does the work of two people and you get upset when he doesn't bust his ass. Why don't a lot of the civilian and military nurses get along better? That's one reason we're losing good civilian nurses lately."

Owens said to her, "Go easy on him - it's his last night here and you're not that busy."

Buck saw him a minute later and, laughing, he said, "I overheard all that. Thanks for saying those things."

Greg went back to work. Later, he apologized to Cpt. Graham and Cpt. Pam Keller. He said to Cpt. Graham, "I didn't mean to act like a shithead, but there are problems here, and from what guys tell me, tension among staff is happening in other parts of the hospital too."

On December 13th, Greg came to work as the NCO-In-Charge of the Psychiatric Clinic and was welcomed by the Preventive Medicine staff, who put him in his old office. The staff consisted of Dr. Stromberg, a pleasant guy, 30ish; Sgt. Buddy Tillman, who was a young lifer in his late 20s with an easy smile, but reportedly had a quick temper; Cpt. Julie Hanks, a friendly nurse in her mid to late 20s (Greg already knew her casually); and Ingrid, a German secretary in her 20s—nice, very helpful, and very efficient by reputation. Greg spent most of the day talking with the staff, organizing his desk and office, and reading all about what he had to do with administering the new drug testing and rehabilitation program.

That day, Buck Williams was volunteering at his old stomping grounds, Personnel, helping out a new guy being assigned to that section, when the news came down from Heidelberg that most of the guys who had an ETS date before December, 1972, would get 90 to 150 day drops off their tour in the Army! News spread through the hospital like wildfire. Greg went down to Personnel after lunch and Buck was there.

Greg inquired, "What is this wonderful news I'm hearing?"

"They're pulling troops out of Germany because we have too many here. They don't have enough time to send them to 'Nam and it'll cost too much to send them stateside, so it's cheaper to get a lot of them out. Port of Call orders are coming in on the teletype now—three in the last hour."

He asked if Buck had to work on the ward that night and asked about the Preventive Medicine staff. Before Buck could respond, he glanced at the teletype and suddenly grinned, "Wow - this is yours coming in. You're leaving here April 13th instead of September 5th. Congratulations!"

Greg called El Guru with the news when he got back to his office. El Guru said that he was happy for him, but he wouldn't be around for a lot of fun next summer. El Guru doubted that his own ETS would be early because his discharge date was exactly one year away. Greg replied to him that he still had four months left to do what he came into the Army for in the first place, he could now apply to graduate schools for next September admission, and still have fun in Europe most weekends until he left.

"We've got to celebrate. I'll break my date with Hannah. Let's go to Dusseldorf Friday night and go out partying."

"OK. I've got to get out of here. The barracks are turning into a jungle. Half the guys are walking around drunk or stoned at night. Racial trouble is starting among some of the newer guys. Windows are even getting broken. More women are going in and out of guys room, including a couple of dependent wives. Somebody walked down the hall singing, "Wilson's got a broken door. Stone's got a broken door. A mirror's broken in the bathroom, E-I-E-I-O."

El Guru laughed and said, "I'll meet you at the Hauptbahnhof around 8:00 and you can tell me all about it."

Dr. Stromberg spent the rest of the week showing Greg what had to be done with the mountain of reports sent to Heidelberg and forwarded to Washington. He said that if mistakes were made or reports were late, the brass would get upset but Greg should not be intimidated. He also said that Greg would not see any out-patients for a while, although there would be in-patients on the ward and Dr. Holland would help. Finally, he said that after New Year's, Dr. Rubenstein would be there a day a week to provide psychiatric coverage. Sgt. Rex, a nice guy at the Registrar's office, also provided help with Greg's administrative duties.

Ingrid seemed like a terrific secretary. She was smart, friendly, and a fast, accurate typist. She spoke fluent English and German and would cover for Greg and Dr. Stromberg whenever they wanted. Buddy Tillman didn't get along with a lot of the people in the hospital but he liked the fact that

Greg was a Vietnam veteran. Julie reminded Greg of a cousin of his from Rhode Island. He met her back in May when she was new and was walking around the hallways to see parts of the hospital and whenever their paths crossed, they made quick "small talk." Greg thought he was in heaven working in the Preventive Medicine section, compared to the last six months on the ward.

That Friday night, Greg met El Guru at the Hauptbahnhof. They checked in at the Hotel Continental and went out for a night in the town. They went to bars called Ici, the Esquire Club, Lord Nelson's, and the Sing-Sing. Good music and attractive women everywhere, but they got shot down by ladies at each location.

At 1:30, El Guru had the idea to try to get into a private club called the VIP Club. He rang the buzzer and a woman appeared behind the shutters. In his broken German, he asked if they could come in. She hesitated, looked around, and then smiled as she opened the door.

Greg went right to the men's room, while El Guru checked out the place—a large, long bar, with tables along both sides. In the back of the bar there was a big living room. The whole place looked like a scene from a 1928 speakeasy in an old-time movie. People were drinking, smoking, talking, and a few were playing chess of backgammon. When Greg got back, one of the other barmaids was angry. Greg asked El Guru, "What the hell's going on with her?"

"She yelled, 'Who let these American assholes in? I'm not serving them. So, I cursed at her in Spanish."

The other barmaid said to them, in English, "It's all right. Don't cause any trouble people. Some people hate Americans here because of Nixon."

El Guru started talking with guy next to him at the bar who spoke English very well, and he started introducing him and Greg to several people who got the two of them beers. For the next half hour, these people - men and women in their 30s and 40s - started talking about topics from the Vietnam war to Nixon to Elvis Presley to the Joe Louis-Max Schmeling fights many years ago. Then one of them brought El Guru and Greg over to the parlor in back of the bar to meet "Big Boss" - the owner of the place. He was a big guy in his 50s, smiling, dressed in a black suit and very friendly. He wanted to know all about where they were from, where they were staying, if they were having a good time, and said that any drinks they wanted were on the house. He was drunk and uttered the phrase familiar to El Guru, "Mexicans bring me good luck."

El Guru whispered to Greg, "Thank God! I only have five DM left. The rest of my money is back at the hotel. How much do you have?"

"I have eight DM and the rest is at the hotel too. I don't see a cash register here and nobody is running a tab for anyone. We got it made in the shade here."

After a minute, Big Boss called over the barmaid who served them and the woman who let them in and asked if they wanted to spend the night with them upstairs. They both declined and Big Boss ordered someone to bring in a taxi driver. He told the taxi driver to take them to the Hotel Inter-Continental. Greg and El Guru thought he was taking them to the Hotel Continental downtown, but 15 minutes later the cab driver stopped at the Inter-Continental which was the biggest, most expensive hotel in Dusseldorf. They told the driver about the mistake but he laughed and said Big Boss probably thought you were two young rich American businessmen. He drove them to the Continental at no charge. They tipped him with most of their money.

The following day they got to the Hauptbahnhof and as they were deciding whether to go home, El Guru said, "There's a train leaving for Aachen right now."

"We don't have time to get tickets. Look at the lines at the window."

"Vamos! Let's pull a Bad Munster Special all the way there!"

"It's an hour away. We'll get caught."

El Guru ran to the train and got on. Then Greg decided to go with him. Greg said, "Artie, we can't stay here. We're only a couple of cars away from the engine."

"It's a really long train. We can just keep moving back, then."

They almost got caught but managed to get off at Monchengladbach. Once inside the station, they burst out laughing because the Bad Munster Special worked again.

The next train to Aachen was not for another 45 minutes. This time, they paid the fare. The checked their bags at the Haupbahnhof. Because it was getting cold, they went to a small crowded restaurant a few blocks away that served bratwurst and fries and ate at the bar. El Guru was rapping to the young barmaid who seemed interested in him. A few people came over, heard Greg speaking English, and after he told them he was American, they started discussing Vietnam. El Guru said that Vietnam was horrible. Greg jokingly said, "Come on, Artie, it wasn't that bad EVERY day."

El Guru became irate and yelled at Greg, "Fuck you! Don't listen to this asshole. He wasn't really in the war over there."

"No, I didn't see all the action, you did, and I respect that, but I did see a few bad things. You had bad luck, I had good luck. Don't hold that against me. Don't insult me in front of these people!"

Greg was angry and walked out of the bar. El Guru went out and called him, saying, "You aren't going to pull a crybaby act, are you?"

Greg went back, grabbed him by the collar, and said, "Listen to me, you little son of a bitch—never embarrass me like that again!"

"Get your fucking hands off me."

"OK. Are you going to apologize for that?"

"Bullshit I will. I never apologize to anybody!"

Greg yelled, walking away, "Have yourself a Merry Fucking Christmas. Don't call me."

Greg went back to the Hauptbahnhof, got his bag, and went over to Gretchen's place. She was happy to see him, and hugged and kissed him. He asked if he could stay, and she said, "Ja!" After he sat down on the couch, she brought over the rest of the bottle of Jägermeister they shared a couple of weeks before, and they had a long talk for two hours. Apparently, she had been the girlfriend of a Medical student in Cologne for several years and they had broken up not long ago. She was moving back to Cologne right after New Year's. She rarely went out at night, except to go ice skating with a friend of hers once a week. Even though she was almost 26, she had just gone back to get her high school diploma. It was a more relaxing evening than earlier and Greg stayed the night. He thought, "I don't need to pal around with Artie. It would be nice to have a girlfriend who lives in Cologne, but how do I tell her I'm leaving in the spring?" And she is very nice, but not intellectual at all, and I don't know what she expects of me. I wouldn't want to get someone like her pregnant."

El Guru did not stay in Aachen. He took a train and made connections to go to Luxembourg. He happened to run into Hannah and her friends at their hangout, Black Bess, and he spent the night with her, as they made plans to spend New Year's Eve together by going to a big party where most of the Radio Luxembourg DJs would be on the night of the 31st.

Chapter 9

Start of a Busy Winter

Several of Greg's friends were getting out of the Army a few days after Christmas. At the hospital, Greg had still not seen any outpatients yet, but aside from his administrative duties with the drug screening program, there were several patients he saw in the back section of the Medical-Surgical Ward with help from Dr Holland.

Off work, Greg started hanging around with Kent Stone, who was getting pulled into the "heads" camp by several of his neighbors at the barracks. Actually, he liked to drink more than smoke dope, but when he did both, he would turn into a laughing idiot. With a couple of exceptions, almost all the guys Stone worked with at the Registrar's Office were "juicers" or alcoholics, but unbelievably they never missed a day of work. Instead of going out, Kent and Greg would have a beer in Greg's room most nights. Kent was one of the few people who was interested not only in mental health, but also in all areas of medicine as well as most of the hospital operations, and he and Greg frequently batted around ideas on how the hospital could improve. Kent was friendly with everyone and well-liked by both the GIs and civilians who worked there.

The year ended for Greg with a call from Gretchen, but he never got the message until 7:00 pm New Year's Eve. She had just written to him and told him her moving date to Cologne was January 1st, and she gave him her new address. Greg didn't do any drinking that night; he and Rabbit listened to Radio Luxembourg's countdown of the hits of 1971 in Greg's room.

El Guru left work early that Friday so he could see Hannah to exchange Christmas gifts on Christmas Eve morning before she went back to Holland to be with her family. She got him a shirt; he got her a cassette player. They celebrated by sharing a bottle of wine and had sex for an hour at her place in Luxembourg.

On New Year's Eve they went to a big party in Luxembourg. There must have been about 75 people at one of the Radio Luxembourg DJ's home, wandering in and out. People from England, Holland, Belgium, Luxembourg, France, and Germany were there; some were European celebrities. Many people were drinking or doing drugs and getting very high, and there were only a few who were totally straight. Everyone seemed happy, though - a lot of music, a lot of dancing. After about 10:00 pm, El Guru started making his way around finding out where people were from and inquiring about their political orientations. Hannah was walking with her friends and another couple, but she was trying to watch what El Guru was doing across the room. After 45 minutes, she tried to join him in conversation with some people who were speaking some Spanish, and El Guru became instantly agitated.

"I told you I'd get back with you later. Hell, it isn't even 11:00 yet. Don't hover over me," he emphatically stated to her, turning away from the couple.

"You said 'in a few minutes.' Why aren't you calling me over and introducing me to your new friends? Don't be a jerk. I got you into this party."

"Don't be a bitch. Go back to your girlfriends. I'll be there in a little while."

"Look at me - are you getting fucked up? Are you drunk or stoned?"

"I'm having a good time. You will, too, if you give me some space for now."

Just as she walked away, one of the Radio Luxembourg DJs told El Guru he wanted him to meet an attractive brunette, Nicki, who was the rising European singing star El Guru had heard about. The DJ said that she was coming out with a new song, and she was going to represent Luxembourg in the Eurovision Song Contest.

El Guru was immediately smitten. "I bet your voice is as beautiful as you are."

She thanked him for the compliment and wanted to know all about him. He told her he was a civilian working the US Army in Germany and that he spent time in Luxembourg because he had made a lot of friends there, some of whom worked for Radio Luxembourg. She said that she was Greek, but had spent time in most of the European countries and Japan. He got flirtatious and asked her jokingly, whispering in her ear, if she ever had a boyfriend who spoke fluent Spanish. She laughed. Then he asked her if she wanted to go into one of the bedrooms where they could talk more privately.

Just as Nicki was turning down his offer because she had come to the party with another man, Hannah appeared, snatched El Guru away, and angrily said, "You heard her. She came with another man and I came with you! Either we both get out of here now, or I'm leaving alone"

"Why you bitch! You eavesdropped! You're not going to ruin my good time."

"Go have a Happy New Year alone, you asshole!" Then she threw a glass of wine in his face. El Guru turned around and Nicki was gone. He started to look for her, and then turned around to see Hannah going out the door, crying, with one her friends accompanying her. After the New Year rang in, he wound up passed out behind a couch. At 4:30 am, he woke up and almost everyone was gone. He went outside, peed in the bushes, walked to the train station, and took the first train home at 6:00 am.

In early January, Greg's workload really picked up with in-patients, drug rehab program reports, and he was also starting to see some out-patients. Lt. Col. Goring told him he had to clean up two rooms next to the Preventive Maintenance section and get furniture for them because Dr.

Rubenstein would be coming one day a week. Julie, a real sweetheart, helped him do this and they decorated the rooms appropriately.

More fights and destruction of property went on in the hospital barracks, and SFC Jim Owens called a meeting of the residents of the barracks. At one point he sternly said, "You guys don't know how good you have it. Cpt. Bolling is a nice guy. 1st Sgt. 'Deputy Dog,' as some of you call him, is a complete idiot whose bark is worse than his bite. MSG Greene will always listen to you and he rarely gets angry. Sgt. Major Dennis is hard-nosed, but even though you may think he's starting to get senile; he has been trying to take on a caring, grandfather role lately. I've been in the Army for 20 years and this hospital is the opposite of every unit I've been affiliated with in the past. What'll you do when they leave? In most other places, anyone with the rank of Master Sergeant or Captain or higher comes down hard on the lower ranking men. I have been told they need medical and support personnel at some 8th Division clinics and also for support at the 509th Airborne. These are bad jobs in bad places. Don't blow a good thing while you have it, or I may not have your backs 100% of the time. Also, if you screw up, the brass might even start to give out Article-15s, bust people in rank, or get them out of the Army on 212s, which WILL affect you in civilian life. The stockade in Mannheim is not a nice place either. So, get yourselves under control unless you want to deal with the consequences."

The speech was totally out of character for Owens, who was one of the nicest lifers anyone would want to encounter. He always had the respect of the great majority of men. Things did get generally quieter in the barracks for the next month. However, Cpt. Bolling toughened up when a few guys kept screwing up and he gave out a few Article-15s with reductions in rank. Two druggies got 212ed out of the Army.

Work was still going great for El Guru but a couple of guys he knew and liked were getting out of the Army earlier than expected and their replacements were really green and inexperienced - right out of Ft. Sam Houston, the Army Medical Training Center in Texas. Other new guys seemed lazy and resentful that they were sent to such a small-town area. Part of his job was to give Greg figures regarding positive drug tests for the troops in his area, and it just so happened that he had to verbally communicate this information to Greg. Remembering their last encounter, El Guru was hesitant to call Greg, but dialed his office number.

"Greg, it's good to talk to you. I'm giving you figures for the guys who tested positive over here - 11 total. Three for Opiates, and eight for Amphetamines. That's it."

"Thanks, Artie. I'll send it in with the next monthly report," Greg said coldly.

"You sound impersonal. Maybe we should get together for a few beers. I'm coming over there TDY for a couple of days next month."

"This call is strictly business, Artie."

"You shouldn't feel that way." El Guru hung up.

Off duty, Greg either started to read or apply to Masters programs to continue his education in September. One night a week, he would go downtown to a new bar, La Cueva. One Saturday morning, he decided to take a train up to Cologne to see Gretchen. As soon as he got out of the Hauptbahnhof, he noticed that Sgt. Major Dennis was outside the Dom (cathedral). He quickly ducked into a men's room at a restaurant, wet his hair and slicked it back, combing it in a "DA," so it would look more military and went out and made brief small talk with Dennis, who was happy to see him traveling. He got to Gretchen's new place, which was similar to where she lived in Aachen. They went out, split a pizza, and had drinks at the lively Santa Cruz bar. He tried to talk with her about more intellectual things, such as politics in Germany or what kinds of things she liked to read, etc. But she was more interested in hairdressing, TV comedies, and German celebrities. After breakfast the next day, he caught a train back to the hospital. He wondered how much longer this romance would last. "We like to drink and have sex, but there really isn't much else we have in common," he thought.

El Guru went to Saarbrucken one night and tried to pick up a waitress who spoke Spanish at one of the clubs. She kept calling him "Senor," and smiled. After a few beers around midnight, he tried to make his move on her, but he only got to walk her home (a few blocks away) with a quick hug and kiss goodnight from her at her door. As he started to cross the street from her building, he saw two cops and their dog nearby. The dog barked and looked at him. "Oh, shit," he thought - he had hash and a small pipe in his pocket. He hurried back around the corner and threw the hashish and the pipe in a sewer, which threw off the scent, apparently. He ran into a nearby crowded bar, quickly almost "low-crawled" his way into the Men's room, and locked the door. After about 5 minutes, he jumped out the window, ran to the train station, and caught the last train out of there going anywhere (it was to Strasbourg, France). He spent the rest of the night sleeping in the train station there, but he made it back to Prum the next morning.

For the rest of the month at work, Greg had a daily routine that kept him busy. For the first couple of hours, he got the schedule ready for the day, made phone calls, and made ward rounds. After that, until noon, he either saw out-patients and charted notes or caught up on other paperwork. After lunch at the mess hall, he saw more out-patients, and did correspondence, if needed, on his old Royal typewriter. Otherwise, he made phone calls at the end of the day. Greg quickly learned never to schedule any out-patient on the 15th or the last day of the month because the drug rehab statistics and reports were top priority. Dr. Robbins, Dr. Stromberg, Julie, Ingrid, and even Buddy Tillman helped him at various times. Dr. Rubenstein's arrival at the clinic also helped him greatly. Thanks to learning from him and Dr. Holland, Greg started to see some positive results from what little counseling experience he had. In addition, some nurses on the ward were giving him positive feedback. Not only was he doing what he wanted, but he was also getting a lot of respect from people around the hospital. Things were going great for Greg.

El Guru was starting to have some problems at work. A new MD, who had been based at USAEUR Headquarters in Heidelberg, took over the clinic in Prum. He was very "by the book," not only with medical procedures (which El Guru thought was good) but also with military regulations. Medics who worked there had to wear starched "whites" with the maroon caduceus, like personnel on hospital wards instead of fatigues. They could not wear them for more than two days in a row without getting fresh, clean and starched ones. Hair, moustaches, and sideburns had to be "military," which reportedly was not the case with other small clinics throughout Germany. Any staff had to submit a written request to him before taking any leave time, including comp time. He thought Nixon, Agnew, Mitchell, Kissinger, etc., were doing a wonderful job running the US and he disliked Democratic politicians like Ted Kennedy, Muskie, McGovern and McCarthy who he thought were all "commie leaners." El Guru was ten minutes late one day and "Dr. Prick," as El Guru referred to him, threatened to write him up until after they had a loud argument and El Guru agreed to work overtime and close down the clinic. El Guru, however, did not want to transfer back to the hospital because he was not far from his favorite city of Luxembourg. Moreover, the MD was actually an excellent doctor who taught his staff many new procedures and techniques and El Guru appreciated the medical knowledge he acquired. It also did not hurt that "Dr. Prick" went away every weekend. He also periodically went to Frankfurt; he was trying to get transferred because he did not like being in a small town.

That weekend, Greg was about to take off for Cologne when, surprisingly, Kent Stone said, "Wait. I'll go with you."

He had never been out of Bad Kreuznach before. They arrived about 6:00 pm, put their things in a locker and changed dollars to DM. "Jeez," Kent said, "it's down to 3.15 DM to a dollar now! It used to be 3.43 when I first got here. They checked into the Hotel Flandrischer Hof on Hohenzollern Strasse. Later, they went out and saw a lot of people dressed up in costumes for Fasching season. Greg knew that Fasching, which was like

Mardi Gras in New Orleans, was a big deal in Cologne, Mainz, and Munich, as well. It started at 11:00 on the 11th day of the 11th month, and slowly built up on weekends until the night before Ash Wednesday which fell in mid-February in 1972. Stone was fascinated with the whole scene.

They hit a series of bars, drinking either one Kolsch or Pilsner at each place. Kent became animated in communicating with the locals, talking not only to people in various costumes but also those who were conventionally dressed. There was hardly any anti-Americanism at all in Cologne. At 1:00 am, they returned to the hotel and Greg decided to get some shut eye. Kent, on the other hand, said he was going downstairs to ask the desk clerk for a map and that he would be back in a few minutes. At about 3:30 am, Kent burst into the room and said, "Guess what, Greg - the desk clerk knows some of my relatives in South Carolina!"

"Dammit, Stone, we gotta get out of here by 10:00!"

"Aw, come on down and talk to this guy with me. He'll let us sleep in later."

"No, he won't. There will be a new desk clerk. I'm sleeping off a hangover."

Kent came back just before 5:00 am and said loudly, "Greg - you gotta come down and taste this shit we're drinking – Jägermeister - it'll knock you on your ass!"

"I know Jägermeister. You are drunk as shit and I am hungover. Get your ass to bed now! And I hope the hell you don't snore!"

Just before 8:00 am the desk clerk was getting off his shift and woke them up for last call for a continental breakfast.

Greg yelled, "Go away!"

Kent yelled back, "No, we'll be right down!" He said to Greg, "Come on. I want you to meet these people here. They're really nice."

"I met them all last month when I stayed here with Artie. Oh, what the hell, let's get washed and dressed and go down there."

Kent added, "We can always sleep on the train."

"You can go back to the hospital. I'm gonna see if Gretchen is home and stay at her place. You know how to change trains if you need to? It's not hard to figure out. And don't fall asleep and forget to change trains at Bingen to get back to Bad Kreuznach."

They had a stale continental breakfast, but the staff at the hotel were all friendly. The daytime desk clerk remembered Greg and they spoke briefly. They showed Kent where to get a taxi to take him to the train station. Kent thanked Greg for showing him a good time in Cologne.

Greg went to Gretchen's place. She was happy to see him. He told her he needed "schlaf" (sleep), not sex, not food. She was OK with this. She put him in her bed, started cleaning her apartment, and joined him later. They both woke up later in the afternoon and started having sex. After it was over, they decided to eat at Alt Koln downtown, near where she worked. Halfway through the meal, she started crying inexplicably. Greg was perplexed; he didn't know what was up with this sad behavior. She spoke only in German to him, all of which were words beyond his grasp of understanding. Suddenly, she pulled out a piece of paper from her purse and wrote about six sentences in her child-like handwriting.

"Sie verstehen nicht," ("You understand nothing,") she said.

"Nein. You're right. Let's go home."

They tried to talk for a couple of hours, while he explained his situation to her that he was leaving to go back to the U.S. in April. She got tearful again and wanted to know if he would be working at a different hospital in the U.S. temporarily. He told her that he was leaving the Army for good. Sadly, she indicated that she felt a breakup might be coming, but not this soon. They went back to sleep, and early the next morning he went back to Bad Kreuznach. He told her that he would try to see her again in a few weeks.

On Monday, Ingrid translated what she wrote. She said, "This girl is falling in love with you. She has never been treated so well by any man except for her last boyfriend, who was some kind of doctor. Anyway, she wants to get married and have children with someone in the future. She hopes you will stay in Germany, but she will understand if someday you will leave."

"I like her, but we don't have too much in common. She's getting emotionally involved and I only have a couple of months or so left. I hope I don't break her heart, but this can't last much longer."

"You have a difficult decision to make."

Chapter 10

Friends Again

El Guru called Greg for a quick report on positive drug tests; Greg kept the conversation business-like even though El Guru mentioned that he was going to Dusseldorf that weekend. After he hung up, Greg decided that he missed El Guru's companionship. It was not the same going out bar-hopping alone or with Stone. El Guru had almost all of the same interests that Greg had and was a good travel companion. Since they had some great times last year, Greg called him back later that day.

"Artie, I don't have much time to talk. You want to go out together and hit the night life in Dusseldorf Friday night?"

"Oh, man, thanks for calling. Sure, Greg, I'd love to do that. Let's cut loose."

"I'll meet you at the Hotel Continental. But when we get there, I want us to sit down and talk about things between us."

"OK. I'll probably get there around 7:30."

They got to the Hauptbahnhof on different trains within a few minutes of each other, and El Guru called Greg outside. They shook hands and smiled. They talked for about two hours after they checked in. El Guru again said that he would never apologize for anything, and they couldn't change what happened. Greg told him that he had to be conscious of how he affected other people and, "Somehow, someday, it will definitely cost you."

After arguing again briefly, they both agreed that good friends can get on each other's nerves when they are drinking or under stress at work, or both.

"Let's both agree to let it go. You only have a few months left here unless you get a European out," El Guru said.

"I won't try for the European out. I want to go to grad school and start a career in mental health. I've decided I really like this field and I really love my job right now. But I can't do anything like this in civilian life without a Masters degree, so I've applied to about seven schools. But I'm really grateful to you for hammering into my head that the best way to cope with Army life in Germany is to do the best possible job you can at work and then to get out of town as often as you can to talk with the European people, learn the cultures, and party, but try not to go overboard."

"Thanks. You're the only guy I've met who likes to travel and has all the same interests that I do. I don't get out until the end of the year. I don't know what I'm gonna do. If I go back to school it will be September of '73, but I don't know if I have it in me."

"The only alternative to being a medic might be to work in hospitals as an orderly because civilian jobs aren't the same. You really ought to get all the education you can. You'll get the GI Bill. I bet you'd like Political Science as a major in college."

"You're right, but if I don't do that, maybe I can help change the system in other ways."

"The bottom line is, we've got to get serious about our lives in the next few years, but we can still have good times."

They wound up going to a Chinese restaurant, and talked at length about what was happening at work and elsewhere for several hours. Greg had to laugh at El Guru's New Year's Eve fiasco. They both agreed that Gretchen was getting, as El Guru put it, "dangerously emotionally involved" with Greg and he would have to commit to her more seriously or leave. El Guru said Hannah was "gone for good," but he was glad he had good times with her while it lasted. Before they went to sleep, they agreed to go to Cologne for Saturday night, because Fasching was really building up there on weekends.

They stayed at the Hansaring Hotel in Cologne, and got a good room with a private bath for only 45 DM. When they went out that night, they stopped into a place nearby for a quick beer, but they each had only one 50 DM bill. The bartender said he only had bottles for 6 DM each. El Guru wanted to get out of here, but Greg wanted to stay for one beer. Sure enough, a few minutes later, a mid-30ish, well-built brunette came over to the bar and sat next to Greg, giving him a big smile.

"Guten Abend, Herr."

"Here we go again. Finish your beer and let's split this dive," El Guru said.

Then Greg told the lady, who stroked his arm lightly, "I'm sorry but I don't understand any German."

She said, "Ah, but I speak English quite well."

El Guru turned his head and said to no one in particular, looking up at the ceiling, "Why the hell does he always draw these bar girls and hookers?"

Greg told her, "I can't buy you a drink. We have to go."

"But you are a handsome young man and I am sexy!"

She then stood up, opened up her whole dress with no bra or panties on, and said, "See, don't you agree?"

Greg, El Guru, the bartender, a couple of people at a table, and even the lady all started laughing. Greg and El Guru left the rest of their beers and hurried out the door, as Greg said, sarcastically, "We'll be back at midnight - bring a girlfriend."

Places were packed that night. After a beer at each of the first two places, and seeing lots of people in costumes and joining in singing, they met two American GIs who bought them a beer in exchange for information about Cologne and what to see and do. Greg and El Guru told them all they knew and then El Guru said, "American GIs have not had a good reputation for a long time. Speak as much German as you can. Try to make your appearance as European as you can, even though you have short hair. Be polite. Do the touristy stuff. You may never get the chance to see this country again. Don't go praising Nixon, either. They don't like him here."

Greg said, "Get to know how to read the train schedules. Change money at the train station or a local bank, never at the hotel. It helps if you can make a German friend or get a girlfriend. If anyone under 25 says they don't speak any English at all, they're either lying or stupid. All the kids that started school in the 1950s were taught English for several years."

They then went to the St. Marlena and the Jet Set. They got shot down everywhere trying to rap or dance with ladies. Greg said, "Do you want to have one last beer at the Santa Cruz?"

"If it's not good, let's go back to the hotel and eat a decent Sunday dinner tomorrow without being hung over."

"Or we could always go back to the first bar we went to tonight - I wonder if Miss Show and Tell has a girlfriend waiting for us," Greg laughed.

At the Santa Cruz, lots of top 40 type music was being played and there was a dance floor downstairs. They started dancing and rapping with a couple of chicks who worked at the university, and they were hitting it off well. But El Guru came on too strong trying to pick up one of them, and they left. After they went back upstairs, a friendly, well-dressed young guy named Jürgen started talking to El Guru and Greg. Jürgen spoke English clearly and wanted to know what they were doing in Cologne. He had a management position with a company downtown with international clients. Behind them, a guy in his late 40s with big glasses, emitted a big "Ha, ha ha!" He had a big, ugly woman with him and a very tall, muscular man dressed in a Viking costume with a shield, sword, and sandals. El Guru asked Jürgen about a girl at the end of the bar who had just winked at him and Jürgen said that she was, as you say in America, "a real space cadet. Don't get involved."

The guy behind them, who was obviously listening, laughed again, "Ha ha ha!"

El Guru asked Jürgen, as he gestured behind him, "Who the hell are these people? Are they friends of yours?"

The Viking barked out a couple of German expletives as El Guru, Greg, and Jürgen looked at each other in disbelief. The guy with the big glasses laughed again, "Ha ha ha!" Then they all laughed except for the Viking.

Greg asked the guy with the big glasses, "Herr, Sprechen Sie Englisch?"

"Yes, I do! Ha ha ha!"

El Guru whispered to Greg, "Are we that fucked up?"

Greg asked the man, "Where are you from?"

"Banladish," he said with a big smile.

"Yeah, and I'm from Mars," El Guru said, as he spoke some Spanish to him.

"Ha ha ha!" He started buckling over with laughter.

Jürgen, El Guru and Greg all looked at each other, smiling. The Viking just grunted. The big, ugly woman then went downstairs to dance.

El Guru said, "Wait - Bangladesh!"

"Yes!"

Greg, El Guru and Jürgen congratulated him on his country's recent independence. Greg wanted to buy him a drink. The man said, "No, no, it is my treat." He put his arms around Greg and El Guru and said to the bar maid, "These are my brothers -get them whatever they are drinking." He also bought a drink for the Viking and Jürgen. Jürgen saw a woman he knew and went over to talk to her after he got his drink.

El Guru whispered to Greg, "Ask him what he's doing in Cologne. Everybody in Bangladesh is supposed to be starving to death." Greg asked him and he said that he was there for a big furniture convention. Apparently, he had a monopoly on every furniture store in Bangladesh.

El Guru turned away laughing and whispered to Greg, "This guy must be one corrupt son of a bitch. Let's ride this train - this is interesting."

The big, ugly woman came halfway up the stairs and called for all of them to come down.

Jürgen also came down with the beautiful woman he picked up. They sat at a table near the bar downstairs, except for the Viking, who stood behind the table like a bodyguard with a scowl on his face. Mr. Bangladesh ordered a bottle of Jägermeister and he proudly said to the bar maid, "These are my sons."

As everyone was getting drunk, they started discussing international politics. The big, ugly woman just wanted to dance. They started playing some '50s rock and roll songs and Greg almost fell into a table as he jitterbugged with her. Then she grabbed El Guru and the same thing almost happened to him. Jürgen and his beautiful woman started making out and left. The Viking went to the men's room and somehow disappeared from the place. Mr. Bangladesh and the big, ugly woman helped El Guru and Greg back upstairs and paid for their cab ride back to the hotel. They got in a 3:00 am and woke up in time to check out of the hotel and catch their trains back to their respective Army towns late Sunday.

El Guru was seeing more kids and teenagers at the clinic, which he enjoyed. He was on CQ there several times until the end of January, but the good news for him was that Dr. Prick was going to be sent TDY to Frankfurt for the next ten months. Dr. Prick pulled some strings to get this done - rumor was that he had a lady friend there and didn't want to be stuck in a "hick" town. Medics at the clinic celebrated. In the meantime, El Guru was reading biographies of past revolutionaries - Karl Marx, Che Guevarra, the Chicago Seven, and even Martin Luther and Robespierre. He wondered if he could get a group of people to influence changing the way the Army did things by using their tactics or even promoting change in America.

On February 1st, Greg got a couple of calls from officers in Heidel-berg bitching at him for submitting his reports late. He was working at least an hour overtime every night with all his responsibilities. He needed help, and more than Dr. Rubenstein one day a week. After he got his reports fin-ished, he wrote to Gretchen and told her he was coming up to see her Sat-urday (to break up with her, he thought). When he got there, he found out that she had a date with a professional boxer a few nights ago. The boxer had a fight in Hamburg that night and was staying there until Sunday after-noon. Greg and Gretchen agreed that this would be their last night together; her brother had encouraged her to break up with Greg, anyway. They stayed at her place, watched some of Nixon's visit to China on TV and he slept with her until 4.00 am, taking an early train home.

After he got back, Greg was set for an easy week at work. There were only a couple of out-patients to see, no new in-patients on the ward, and not much data to be compiled for the next round of reports. The next after-noon, just as Julie left his office after a short friendly chat, a GI with a brief case trotted in and asked, "Specialist James?"

"Yeah, can I help you?"

"This is the right place. I'm taking over your job."

After an instant shock, Greg thought that this must be a new in-pa-tient, who, for some reason, did not get to the ward first. He quickly remem-bered a similar situation last year with a psychotic 1st Lieutenant who proclaimed that he was a new administrator before he put a cardboard crown on his head and stated that he was the "new Burger King." Greg pulled out his clipboard and asked the guy for his name, rank, who from the out-patient clinic sent him here, and what seemed to be his main prob-lem. The guy became upset and said, "I wasn't sent by anyone. My orders were to report here and this is where I'll be working."

"Let me see your orders."

The guy thrust a copy at him. Greg scowled as he read that Specialist 4th Class Louis Wachtel, 91G20, was indeed assigned to the hospital. Greg said, "OK, Wachtel - just because the orders say you got assigned here doesn't mean that you'll be working here. The hospital has other outpatient clinics in others town with mental health slots so you could be going to any of those places. I think it's damn rude of you to come in here the way you did without introducing yourself and declare that you're taking over my job as if it were now. I'm sure Cpt. Bolling and Lt. Col. Goring would have told me you were coming, which is why I asked who sent you here."

Wachtel snapped back, "I have an interview with Lt. Col. Goring tomorrow and Sgt. Rogers at Personnel told me I would be working here."

"You've been in the Army long enough to know you can never be sure of anything. Now I would show you around but I have to go to the ward for the rest of the day. (This was crap but Greg was upset) Come back and see me tomorrow after you meet with Goring."

Wachtel got up and trotted out with his briefcase, saying nothing. "If he gets assigned here, I must have done something to piss off Goring," Greg thought. He went to Personnel where he saw Rabbit, who magically knew gossip about everybody. Rabbit knew of Wachtel from when they were briefly at the same hospital in California in 1970. According to Rabbit, Wachtel's reputation was that he was naive, tactless, and super straight. Also, he told Greg that Wachtel really was Greg's replacement, two months early. Greg told Rabbit that he called Artie earlier, and that he was going to meet him in Cologne for Fasching weekend since it was Presidents' Day Weekend and he was using leave time for Monday and Tuesday.

Rabbit replied, "No you're not. We have an IG (Inspector General) inspection in the barracks Saturday morning."

Nobody had told Greg, so he went to Deputy Dog to see if this was true. "Yes, it is, and your ass will be there with your room spotless Saturday until you're dismissed!"

Greg called Wachtel and told him that he had to help prepare for the barracks inspection and for him to stay in the office Friday afternoon, and ask Ingrid for help if anything came up. He then called El Guru, told him what happened, and they agreed to meet at the Cologne Hauptbahnhof around 6:30 Saturday night. Immediately after the inspection was over, Greg took a quick shower, snuck out the back-door downstairs, ran down the street and hailed a cab so he could get to the train station and go to Cologne.

Chapter 11

Fasching in Cologne and a Trip to Amsterdam

Greg met El Guru in Cologne. They checked into the Hotel Hansaring, ate dinner, and went out partying. The streets were crowded with people in costumes. A giggling woman with a clown-painted face ran up to El Guru and kissed him, then ran away. Greg was showered with confetti, and people 15 feet in front of him had a liter of milk dumped on their heads from a window upstairs. People were laughing, happy, having fun.

Greg asked, "Is this what Mardi Gras is like in New Orleans?"

"I don't know," El Guru said, "but I've heard this is what Fasching is like here."

"Let's go into Old Mac for a beer to start."

At 11:00, they were still there, drinking, laughing, and talking with various people at the bar. Someone left a horn near where they were sitting at the bar, and they took turns blowing it—El Guru tooting it at pretty women who smiled in return; Greg tried tooting it to the beat of whatever music was playing, as people laughed. The song "How Do You Do," by Mouth and MacNeal, was playing and everyone at the bar sang the chorus. Right after that, El Guru said, "Let's get in this line." People were singing to the German drinking song, "O-Ja-Ho-Ja-Ho." They got in the line and about 15 people sang along as they went around the bar, up the stairs, and out the door, around a parked car, and back down to the bar again. Both Greg and El Guru, along with several other people, were laughing hard. At the end, a couple of teeny boppers hugged and kissed them briefly. Someone bought them another round of beers. They tried to pick up some young chicks but were shot down. After talking to the bartender for a while about Fasching and the parade on Tuesday, things started dying down and they left.

They spent a quiet Sunday walking around parts of Cologne on the warm winter day and went to a German bowling alley. Greg hadn't been bowling in eight or nine years. El Guru said that the pins are attached with strings on top in Europe. They bowled two games, and both did relatively well - scores for both ranged from 148 to 167 for all four games. On Monday, they decided to hang around downtown Cologne to rest up for all the big Fasching festivities and parade on Tuesday.

After breakfast, they checked out of the hotel and got the last available locker at the train station. It would not totally lock but they both thought that since it was down at the bottom, near the corner, and the key pulled out, it would be OK. Plus, they would only be gone for a few hours. Greg said, "I don't know about you, but I'm joining in on the parade. I borrowed these overalls from a new guy at the hospital with my long john underwear top and I'm going into the men's room to put blotches of toothpaste on my face and slick back my hair. That's my costume. All I need is a beer glass. Are you coming with me?"

"You're absolutely nuts, man. I'll go to the bar down the street and if it's crowded, I'll try to rip off a glass for you."

El Guru did just that and was back in 20 minutes with a seven-ounce narrow glass declaring that he would be going up the street to watch him for a while, but not to march alongside the parade with him. "Go make a damn fool of yourself," he laughed.

Greg took off his glasses and walked in the street near the curb for one block, aside the parade. Sgt. Major Dennis was walking on the sidewalk near him but did not recognize him. Just then, two women grabbed his arms and hugged him. "Ah! Hackenschmidt," one said, and the other one smiled and felt his biceps. Apparently, Hackenschmidt was a famous German strong man of some kind. They said something else to him that he didn't understand, but he pulled them aside and asked, "Sprechen Sie Englisch?" They each give him a weird look—one understood some English and filled up his beer glass.

"Danke Schon," he said, as he kissed them both on the cheek and smiled. Apparently, they thought he was crazy. He turned around to look for El Guru, hoping they both could continue the conversation with these ladies, but he was gone. So, he kept marching up the street alongside the parade for about an hour, asking people on the sidelines if they would fill up his glass—a few smiled and said, "Prosit!" ("Cheers") Others got angry and told him (in German) to "get the hell out of here!" One guy was drunk and he thought Greg was "Heinz," a guy in his party of about a dozen people who were all drunk. They filled up his glass twice as Greg spoke gibberish German to them, as they were laughing. The probably thought he was as drunk to the max, as they were. The people in the coaches in the parade were dressed in elaborate, showy costumes and masks - as kings, queens, pirates, and more, as they showered the crowd with candy and trinkets. Greg caught a whistle and started blowing it. He also got a tiny bottle of 4711 Eau de Cologne. Some people shook his hand, as he marched along. He started to get a heavy buzz from all the beer, so he walked back to a bar near the train station and watched the end of the parade outside. A lot of drunks were in the bar. Greg went into the men's room and coming out, a guy named Rolf, who spoke perfect English, bought him a cognac and talked with him about America for about an hour. Greg was drunk and left the bar, walking a three-block area looking for El Guru, who was nowhere to be found. By this time, it was starting to get dark.

Greg went back to the Haupbahnhot, washed the junk off his face, and went back to his locker to find that someone had broken into it and it was empty except for his bag (which had a lock on it). He was shocked. Then he noticed his Chesterfield top coat stuffed in a nearby trash can. He pulled it out and the $20.00 he had was gone, as well as his pipe and a pair of civilian glasses. Luckily, he had a pair of prescription shades in his pocket. This sobered him up fast, but he realized he only had 10 DM left, which was not enough to make it back to Bad Kreuznach. He decided to hop on a Trans-European Express train going to Mainz, pulling a Bad Muenster Special. He moved back to the next car, when heard, "Fahrkarten, Bitte (tickets, please)!" He moved back a few more cars and then locked himself in the WC of one car until the train roared into Mainz. Greg pulled off the Bad Muenster Special successfully, but the next connecting train would only take him as far as Bingen with the money he had. So, he took a chance and bought a ticket to Bingen, knowing he'd have to pull one last Bad Muenster special. He was very tired and started to doze off once he got on the train. About a half hour later, he woke up to find a familiar face two seats away.

"Hey, Rollo," Greg called.

The guy turned and recognized Greg. "I told you my name's not Rollo, it's John," he said as he smiled. "Remember that night in Cologne last summer?"

"Yeah, and I need your help."

"You want to buy a watch from me?"

"No, I'm flat broke - 20 Pfennigs - and I want to sell you mine."

"What have you got?"

"It's a Longines - only about a year old."

"Let me see it."

He examined the watch and said, "I don't have that much money myself but I'll give you 10 DM and this cheap Pittsburgh Steelers watch so you have one. I don't know who the Pittsburgh Steelers are. Nobody does here, but some American might."

"That's not important. I'll take the deal. I don't care if the watch works or not. Thank you, Rollo. I mean John. Now I can buy a ticket to get home from Bingen."

"Any way I can help," he replied as he went back to the next car, trying to sell the watch.

Greg miraculously got to work by 8:30, and the first thing he did was call El Guru, who said he was running the front desk and the clinic for sick call and would get back to him later. Wachtel was still processing in, and Ingrid said there had been no important calls, so Greg went down to the snack bar. He saw Goring in the hall and asked him about possibly transferring Wachtel because he might be needed elsewhere. Goring said, "No, he's here to stay. Jesus, you've been complaining you need help for over a month and we got you someone. You only have two months left to put up with him, if you don't like him. Besides, a new psychiatrist is coming here next week." Greg thanked him for the information.

After Wachtel showed up, Greg discussed all the clinical procedures in detail with him: initial observation and introduction to the patients, giving the patients the initial questionnaire to fill out (this included a brief description of why they were there, chief complaint symptoms, previous psychotherapy, history of substance abuse, etc.) and the Mental Status Exam. He also told Wachtel to get a case history, and decide whether to keep the patient for psychotherapy or refer to Dr. Rubenstein after making a provisional diagnosis. Wachtel seemed minimally interested. He made a remark to the effect that Greg obviously had first-hand experience with alcohol and drug abusers and he lifted his head with his eyes downward at Greg and stated, "I'm married, so I know a lot more about couples than you do, and I'll deal with them." Greg bit his tongue and thought, "Was Rabbit ever right about this guy!" He told Wachtel to be with him when he did all the substance abuse reports. "After March, it's on you. Or the new psychiatrist. I won't be around to hold your hand," Greg said.

El Guru called in the afternoon. Greg asked, "What the hell happened to you in Cologne? I went back to look for you and you disappeared. Someone broke into the locker, ripped off the $20 I had in the pocket of my coat, which was in the trash can, and your bag was gone!"

"You were the one who disappeared. I lost sight of you after you were a block away. I went to look for you and couldn't see you, so I waited about two blocks away from the cathedral. Then I met these three American girls from Phoenix, Arizona. One spoke Spanish. I started flirting with her and wound up spending a couple of hours with her and her friends. Then I realized later that I had to get the last train out of here to go back to Prum. The locker door wasn't locked but all our stuff was still in there. Good thing we both had locks on our individual bags. You had the key to the locker. I closed the door and left your bag in there. Then I tried to find you but I had to catch a train back or I would have been stuck there until this morning.

"I don't believe this shit. This better never happen to us again. Next time we get a locker that locks all the way, even if we have to take a train to Bonn or somewhere else to get one."

Then Greg proceeded to tell him the story of the latest Bad Muenster Special and meeting Rollo, as they both laughed quite a bit.

The rest of the week was surprisingly slow for both El Guru and Greg. El Guru said he was going to Luxembourg for the weekend. Greg, after a visit to see a psychotic patient admitted to the ward, got talking with Warren, who asked Greg if he wanted to go to Amsterdam. He said he had four days off starting on Sunday, and he and his wife agreed they need a break from each other. He said, "She's OK with it if you come with me. She said I could go to Brussels because it's a dead town but I was in Amsterdam about 10 or 11 years ago and I had a blast then."

Greg said, "I would like to see Amsterdam. And I want to use up as much of my leave time as I can before I get out of Germany. Can Artie come with us?"

"She's met him and she doesn't trust him. I have to leave Sunday, though."

"OK, I'll go. I'll go into work all day Saturday to rack up some comp time. Dr. Stromberg will be cool with that. It'll be fun cutting loose in a big international city with a black dude in his 30s."

Warren laughed and said, "Yeah, let's cut loose, man."

On Sunday, Greg and Warren took off for Amsterdam. Most people there spoke English so there was hardly any language barrier. They checked into a very old hotel, equivalent of $13.00 per night each. Their room was on the 3rd floor with two creaky twin beds.

They got cleaned up, got a map and took a walk to find a good bar. They passed through blocks and blocks of the "red light" district along the canal - beautiful looking, barely dressed hookers seated in big bay windows, looking for action. They met an American couple who told them to go to the Leidsplein, which apparently was comparable to the Altstadt section of Dusseldorf. After arriving there at about 10:00 pm, they dropped into the Blue Note - a place with 20s/30s crowd. The cheapest beer was the equivalent of $5. They dragged out their beers, and got shot down rapping to some ladies who were turned off by the fact that they were Americans. Warren said, "It's because of that beer stained tie you're wearing - we're not in New York City."

Just as they were starting to leave, an attractive, tall, blondish lady in her late 20s, who was at a table with some people winked at Warren, smiled and said, "Hello, there, soul brother." Warren stopped dead in his tracks and asked her to dance. After they came back to her table, she introduced him to the people there. In turn, Warren called Greg over and introduced Greg to her. Three of the people there finished their drinks and left. The other two, a couple, watched Greg and Warren warily and made minimal small talk.

The lady's name was Yuke. She was 27, single, and lived with her parents and her six-year-old son. She related that all of her boyfriends were either black or Italian and she was obviously turned on to Warren. He came onto her with some sweet, flirtatious rap lines, but he thought that it a was a major obstacle that she lived with her parents and had a young child. He offered to have her stay with him and Greg, but at that, the couple whisked her away. She gave Warren her address and phone number, though, and said she wanted to see him after she was through with work the next day.

Greg and Warren went back to the hotel, and to their surprise the hotel bar was open all night. They talked with the bartender and his female friend, who also lived at the hotel - they were co-owners of the hotel, on a purely business basis. After a couple of hours, Warren was starting to get loud and drunk and wanted to go out to some bars but the bartender warned him, "Bullets fly low in Amsterdam at this time of night." They went to bed at 3:00 am.

At 9:00 am, Warren was trying to get Greg up and out of bed, telling him about two Swedish ladies downstairs - they were drinking Bloody Marys, as was Warren. Greg told him he would be down in a little while. A half hour later, he came back to the room and saying, "Come on, Greg! What the hell's wrong with you? We're having a blast down there."

Greg got washed and dressed but when he got there, Warren was the only person left at the bar. Warren blamed Greg for not getting down there fast enough. Greg said that Warren probably started getting loud and drove them away. They both agreed they were hungry, but Warren wanted to take a walk and get coffee first to sober up. They both put on their shades and walked into an area where there were a load of junkies hanging around, staring at Greg and Warren as they walked by. They drank coffee at a place where the counterman was the only straight dude. A couple of guys tried to sell Warren some "smack," (cheap heroin) but Warren and Greg got out of there fast.

After walking around Amsterdam for a while, they went into a bar to get ham and cheese sandwiches. Then Warren got very friendly with people at the bar, telling jokes, singing, and becoming an instant celebrity there. Two 20ish American chicks came in - they were strippers at a nearby joint, according to the bartender. Warren went over to rap to them. Greg told him he was going to take a walk and would meet him later at the hotel - he didn't want to get drunk. After walking a few blocks, an absolutely gorgeous, well built, Scandinavian woman came up to him and said, "Hello," with a seductive smile. Greg thought she was surely a hooker, so he started speaking in a mixture of several languages. She thought he was weird or crazy. Then, after five minutes, he said, "I know you cost too much and I don't pay anything for anybody." She looked at him funny and walked away. He went back to the hotel and took a nap.

Warren came back a few hours later and said, "These American bitches want us to go see their act tonight. Oh, shit, I forgot to call Yuke!"

He called Yuke from the lobby and arranged to meet her early that evening. Greg went out to eat a Mexican restaurant while Warren went back to the room and took a brief nap. When Greg came back, Warren was gone, Greg went downstairs to sit in the lobby when Yos, the female co-owner, called him over and wanted to know if he would stay with her later to watch the movie "Picnic" which was on TV in the lobby at 8:00. Greg accepted the invitation. Only two people checked in the entire time the movie was on, but at one point Yuke called the hotel and wanted to talk to Greg, which shocked him. She told him that Warren was coming on too strong, drinking all the time, and she wanted to know "what was wrong with him." She agreed to meet Warren the next day but she wanted Greg to be there also. Greg said he would be there, but he wondered what was really going on with them.

By the end of the movie, Greg had moved closer on the couch to see if he could cuddle with Yos, but she told a long story of abuse by several men and he suggested that she see a mental health counselor. She did not feel the need to do so, but she said she felt comfortable talking with him. He told her he was checking out in the morning and had to go back to Germany. Suddenly, Warren came staggering into the hotel, so drunk that Greg had to help him upstairs and into bed. Early the next morning, Greg asked him, "What's the story with you and Yuke? You know, she called me last night and wants me to be with the two of you today."

"Oh, yeah, I think I remember that. Let's get out of here, check our bags at the train station, walk around more of this town, and then we'll go meet her."

They walked around the center part of the city, in and out of some stores, checking out prices of clothes. A kid with a big smile on his face and a big tin can, walked up to them outside of a store and asked them for money to "help fight dope in Amsterdam." They laughed at him and the kid laughed, too. Soon after this, another guy asked if he could buy some smack from them. A few blocks later, they ran into Yuke and her little boy, and they all went to a small restaurant nearby. The four of them got something to eat and Warren started drinking immediately. After three beers, he went to the men's room, and Yuke told Greg that she was disappointed in Warren. Then she said, "Maybe you and I could have a good time together in Brussels or Cologne if I can get away some weekend. Or you should come back in May when the tulips are in bloom and there are boat tours of the canals."

Greg replied, "I'll think about it."

She gave him her address, and when Warren came back, Greg excused himself to go out and take some pictures, and he said he would meet Warren at the train station. Warren showed up about two hours later. He was not interested in seeing any of the museums, although he was fairly sober.

Warren said, "Let's get out of here and go home. I miss my wife and kids. I had a good time but I'm glad I'm married with a family and I got this out of my system." He slept for a couple of hours once they got on the train.

When they changed trains in Cologne, Greg said, "I got another day off. I told people at the hospital that I'd be back Thursday afternoon. I have some money left, so I'm going to Dusseldorf for the night. Can you get home OK?"

"Yeah, I remember. I can read the schedules."

"Stay sober, dammit!"

Greg could not find a cheap hotel anywhere after he checked his bag at the train station. By 8:30 he thought, "Maybe I can pick somebody up. I have to stay somewhere." After getting shot down by women at a couple of bars, he went into the Downtown Club thinking, "If I can't pick up a chick to stay with here, I'm getting out of this town and heading back, even if it's all night local trains." Just after he got an Alt beer, the guy next to him sensed Greg was an American and initiated a conversation in English. His name was Rainer; he was in his late 20s. He was with two women, Kristel and Marianna. Kristel and Rainer wanted to talk a little bit about America, but Greg couldn't keep his eyes off Marianna, who was a beautiful blonde - she just listened and smiled. Suddenly, she took out a bottle of perfume and dabbed a drop on Greg's nose as they all laughed.

Greg asked her, "Sprechen Sie Englisch?"

"Ein Kliene Bisschen (a very little bit)."

"Parlez vous Francais?"

"Nein."

"Habla usted Espanol?"

"Nein," she answered smiling.

"An biet Vietnamese?"

They all laughed. A minute later, El Guru walked through the door, and Greg, who was surprised at this, called out, "Artie, good to see you! What are you doing here?"

"You said Dusseldorf might be good during the week so I decided to take tomorrow off and come up here tonight. But hotels are all booked."

Greg said he knew that, as he introduced his new friends to him. They all smiled and said hello to each other. Rainer said he would be the interpreter. They tried to speak what German they knew, and Greg drew some pictures as well. Marianna worked as a fashion model at one of the stores in Konigsallee, and Kristel worked in the same store. Rainer said he had known them since they were 10 years old. Marianna said she would rather teach Greg some German than learn English. El Guru and Kristel, a short, cute brunette, turned on to each other right away. A 30ish guy with a big beard came in and gave Marianna a hug - she smiled and spoke with him several feet away. With Rainer's help, Greg wrote her a quick note saying that he would like to see her again, and he discretely put the note into her hand with the hospital's address in German as she smiled. Rainer told Greg Marianna had a nine-year old daughter but was married only briefly when she was a teenager after she got pregnant. Greg thanked him and told him he had to leave. El Guru pulled Greg aside and said that it was looking very likely now that he could stay at Kristel's. "If I don't go home with this lady, I'll meet you at the Hauptbahnhof in an hour."

Rainer said to Greg, "If you come to Dusseldorf, I'm always at the Downtown Club."

The next day, Julie called him into her office and said, "This new guy, Wachtel, is nice but he is weird. He left the offices wide open for an hour or two a couple of times. He left a patient alone in his office. I don't know if he left that guy alone but the patient left. Wachtel didn't tell us where he was going. When he was gone, I closed the doors yesterday."

Greg bluntly told Wachtel that he should go to the lab with him to cut down on the time for compiling statistics for the drug rehab program, but Wachtel didn't want to go. "I have other things I need to take care of," he said.

"Look, man, I have around six weeks left, so you've got to learn this crap soon. And I heard you left our offices open for hours. And you even left a patient alone in your office while you went off this unit. Where the hell did you go and why did you do that?"

"I had to see Cpt. Bolling. I had to get my wife and my living situation taken care of. That's more important than this place."

Greg's blood was boiling. He yelled, "Goddamnit! You don't just walk out of this fucking place and leave it wide open without at least telling Ingrid, Sgt. Tillman, Cpt. Hanks, Dr. Stromberg, or somebody. And you never leave a patient alone! Things get stolen out of unattended offices. Never, ever do that again!"

"I have things I need to take care of," as he got his briefcase and walked away.

Julie talked to Greg for a few minutes and said, "The new psychiatrist is here. I'm moving my office to the room a few doors down from you to make room for him."

"Good, I'll help you. Let's do it now. It'll help work off some of my anger."

Chapter 12

New MDs and More Partying

Dr. Guy Whitman was about 30 and he seemed to be quite personable. Greg made ward rounds with him the next morning and helped him get his office set up. He was from the midwestern US, and went to medical school somewhere in New York but he got drafted just before he finished his residency. "My first impression is that he seems to be the kind of guy I could be friendly with," Greg thought.

Coming out of the mess hall after lunch, Sgt. Joe Jackson, who was usually at the front desk at the OPC, ran by saying something nonsensical with a glazed look in his eyes. This was totally out of character for him, so Greg ran after him, as he made his way upstairs to the Med-Surg ward. He ran into the Nurses' station and started screaming at a couple of nurses, especially Pam; she was really scared by this. Then, luckily, somebody had called Dr. Whitman. Greg grabbed Joe by the arm and asked him, "What's going on with you, Joe? What are you feeling?"

"I'm fucked up."

Then he pushed Greg and Dr. Whitman out of the way, and he ran downstairs toward the Lab and X-ray clinic. Greg said, "Come on Doc. We've got to get this dude!"

"Let him go. He'll stop."

"What? He might do something destructive to himself or someone else! God knows what the hell drugs he might be on."

"Go ahead and look for him, then."

"I damn sure will!"

Greg thought, "I have a jerk for a psych tech and a jerk for a psychiatrist too?"

Greg looked for Joe for about 25 minutes when Buddy Tillman saw him and said he was with Dr. Whitman at the Out Patient clinic in one of the rooms there. Warren, who was just coming into work early, and another guy had seen Joe sitting on the back steps crying, and had called Dr. Whitman. He didn't admit him but gave him some meds and wanted to see him and his wife for regular therapy sessions. Joe apparently had been under a lot of stress in his job and with his marriage, but he was not taking any street drugs, to Greg's surprise. "Good job by Dr. Whitman after all, "Greg thought.

At the end of the day, El Guru called Greg to let him know that he was coming back to the hospital to spend the day on Monday the 28th for some temporary administrative duty, approved by the new temporary physician at his clinic. He would stay in one of the empty rooms on the 3rd floor of the barracks, and one of the guys from his unit would stay in the room next door, but he had no interest in partying. He said that this weekend he was going straight. "No drinking, hash, nothing."

Greg said he was flat broke until Wednesday (payday). "All I have is a couple of cans of Pabst out on the window ledge. You know, I don't believe you came up to Dusseldorf in the middle of the week, bopped into the Downtown Club, and picked up Kristel. I didn't pick up her girlfriend but I definitely like her and I want to see her again."

"Yeah, she let me spend the night with her but nothing happened. She wanted a commitment from me to see her every weekend for weeks before she'd have sex with me. I told her, honestly, I wasn't sure if I could do that. I didn't tell her 'No way,' which is what I meant. I did sleep on the big couch she had, but she wouldn't let me touch her other than a quick kiss goodnight and a quick kiss goodbye in the morning."

"I hope this doesn't ruin things for me and her girlfriend, Marianna."

"No. She said Marianna likes you. She gave me her address to give to you."

"Thanks! I'll write to her now. Maybe I can get a date with her next weekend."

Greg was working very late on the 28th to finish all the end of the month reports for Heidelberg. El Guru stopped by and said they would meet in Greg's room at about 8:30. After putting things in his temporary 3rd floor room, El Guru went downstairs to see various people in their rooms. He wound up doing a bowl of hash in the room of a guy named Stevens - a good dude who spoke Spanish and English. El Guru and Stevens were joined by McAfee, Sam Garner, Jerry (who never did go before the E-5 Board) and some German guy who hung out at the EM club. Greg got back to his room at 8:15. He met Kent Stone on the stairs who said he'd be up at Greg's room in a few minutes with a "surprise." Just as Greg opened his door, John Tombaugh yelled, "Hey, Greg, where you been?" About a minute after that, El Guru, Tombaugh, Stevens, McAfee, Jerry, and the German dude all came over to Greg's room. Stone was coming up the stairs with four bottles of German beer. They promptly lit up another bowl of hash, passed it around, along with the bottles of beer.

Greg exclaimed, "Christ - you guys can't stay here very long. If we get busted in here, I will lose my job! Who's on CQ tonight?"

"Ralph. He's cool. He knows what's going on. He'll cover. We'll get over on the lifers," McAfee said.

"OK, but I want you guys out of here by 9:30. I have to air out this room."

"Open the window now, El Guru said.

Greg took a few swigs of beer, but everyone else was smoking, drinking, and getting stoned. At El Guru's request, Greg tuned into Radio Luxembourg. A few guys started singing to 'Mother and Child Reunion' by Paul Simon. The German dude asked Greg to give him a "shotgun" from the second bowl they passed around. Greg was about to throw him and the other guys out of the room but then a song by Nicki was playing on the radio. El Guru shouted, "Holy shit! I know this broad. I damn near picked her up New Year's Eve."

"Suuure, El Guru, Jerry said mockingly, as the other guys laughed. "You are such a bullshitter when it comes to girls!"

El Guru yelled, "No, I am not bullshitting. I met her at a New Year's Eve party in Luxembourg and she sang a little to me but it was called 'Après Toi,' not 'Come What May.'"

"Now you're not a bullshitter. You're a liar," Stone said, as he laughed.

"Oh, we've had this talk before," Jerry said. "Is he a bullshitter or a motherfucking liar?"

"That's it! Everybody out of here, NOW," Greg said, emphatically.

"OK, don't get pissed. We'll go to McAfee's room," somebody said as they exited.

Greg opened his window wide to get rid of the smell of hash and left it that way. El Guru came back an hour later, looking cross-eyed. Greg asked him if that really was Nicki on the radio. He said yes, and nobody believed him, but that was the song in English lyrics. Greg helped him to his room upstairs.

Greg was having a better relationship with Dr. Whitman, but only communicating with Wachtel when he had to. He and Wachtel had some disagreements about drugs, patients who wanted to quit drugs or alcohol, and the reports. Dr. Whitman intervened a few times, and Greg informed Dr. Whitman about the reports and how he operated the clinic, "but it's yours, now."

Dr. Whitman was admitting some interesting patients who Greg saw on the ward. One was a homesick 18-year-old PFC from Virginia who had a hard time adjusting to Germany and made a suicidal gesture. Another was a 28-year-old officer who tried to convince staff he was a "plant" from Heidelberg to bust drug abusers. His cover was blown when he paced up and down the ward ranting that he was going to be promoted to Brigadier General while he was on the ward and that half the patients were addicts and half the staff were pushers, "poisoning the troops." In addition, there was a Spec/5 who was angry and depressed. He had come back from Vietnam to find his German wife having an extra child after she had an affair with someone right after he had left. Greg also saw a few motivated out-patients, soldiers, and dependent wives for short term therapy with Dr. Whitman's help, which he greatly appreciated. For the next week, he spent all of his spare time reading about psychotherapy and psychiatric diagnosis topics. He either stayed in his room or hung out in the hospital library.

El Guru went back to Luxembourg for the weekend. He found out from a Radio Luxembourg DJ that Nicki won the Eurovision song contest - an honor for her song. The record was taking off around Europe and she hadn't been back to Luxembourg.

Greg got a letter from Marianna asking if he could come up to Dusseldorf on March 18th. He wrote back quickly, saying that he would be at her house that night at 8:00. In the meantime, he was ordered by Goring to do a complicated month-by-month manpower report that had not been done for the clinic since 1968, and he had to dig through records to catch up on everything from then until now. All these statistics on clinic personnel, in-patients, and out-patients had to be in Heidelberg by March 15th. It took him four days working 12 hours a day (along with his other clinic duties), but Goring said he did some of it wrong and wanted the corrected copy on his desk by the end of the day on the 13th.

On Friday the 10th, after work, Greg called El Guru, who agreed to meet him in Trier on Saturday. They met at the train station there, and checked into a hotel for only 17 DM, at 3:00 pm. Despite the inexpensive rate, the hotel lobby and the room were very nice.

"Let's go sightseeing, "Greg said.

"Yeah. There's a lot of history in this town."

They went to the old Porta Nigra, the old Roman gate to the city from around the second century. "Wow, look how big that is." Greg said. "Probably 50 feet high of old Roman stone architecture, with all those huge open windows."

"Look, Napoleon must have built a couple of his arches at the entrance," El Guru said. Then they went to an old Roman cathedral that seemed more like a fort. It was built in the 4th century, and was re-built years later. "That's impressive," El Guru said.

"Yeah, but that twin spired Dom in Cologne is the best I've seen of the old structures."

They moved on to see some kind of famous gardens and the central market place, but El Guru was disappointed that the Karl Marx museum just closed.

"It's starting to get dark. Too bad we can't explore the ruins of the Coliseum," Greg said.

"We saw a lot in a few hours, though," El Guru replied.

The night was a different story, though. There were places that looked like military hangouts, off-limits clubs, and dirty old men's bars. They stopped into one bar and talked with an Australian dude who persuaded El Guru to do a bowl of hash with him at the Aussie's hotel room. Greg said he would meet El Guru later at the Club Boccaccio down the street. At the door, Greg thought, "Oh, shit! This is a private club." But they let him in, and some people said hello to him calling him Werner. It turned out to be a swinging discotheque - it dawned on him he got in because they thought he was "Werner." Greg talked with people in his broken German. It didn't take people long to realize that he was not Werner, but nobody complained. He had a couple of beers, danced with a couple of teeny boppers, and then he saw El Guru tapping at the window from the outside, looking pissed. Greg went around to the entrance and El Guru was yelling, "How the hell did you get in here?"

"These dudes think I'm a regular," as Greg smiled.

The bouncer turned around, went up to Greg and said, "I'm sorry, sir, this is a private club. You have to leave."

"What? You let me in here."

"I didn't know you were American. You look much like a club member named Werner."

"Aw, c'mon. We will be good. We will not cause any trouble."

"No, you must leave now."

On the way back to the hotel, Greg asked, "What happened to the Australian dude?"

"I thought he had dope with him. He thought I had dope on me. He is a bullshitter, talking about how he knows chicks form the university here, and he doesn't."

"At least we did some good sightseeing."

"Cologne, Dusseldorf, Aachen, and Luxembourg are the only places to go at night."

El Guru had an easy week and he was getting into more record keeping and administrative work for the clinic, since his new MD, like his temporary predecessor, didn't want to be bothered with that stuff. He was also serving as somewhat of a role model for some new medics who came into the clinic, as he was de facto NCO-IN-Charge, just as Greg was at his clinic. Since El Guru was getting out of the Army at the end of the year, he also did a little bit of "ghosting" and had people at the clinic cover for him, which was why he took off to Dusseldorf in late February during the week, just for the hell of it. He did use some leave time to make it look good; both he and the clinic secretary kept track of everybody's time and they were lenient. El Guru got permission from the new MD to make up the policy for taking off time. "As long as everybody gets their work done - and done well - during the hours the clinic is open, and stays on CQ one weekend for one 24-hour period once a month, and comes to work alert and sober, then if you need time off, we'll cover for you." The new MD and the medics all agreed that this unwritten pact was quite reasonable for everyone who worked there.

Greg saw a few patients a day, met with Dr. Whitman to discuss cases, and took his pre-ETS (Estimated Time of Separation from the Army) physical exam. The cooks themselves didn't eat at the mess hall one night (signifying that it was a horrible meal), so he went downtown. He was walking near the bahnhof and he suddenly noticed Peter Herkt, the German bartender at the EM club last year. Greg had tried to locate Peter in Dusseldorf on one of his jaunts.

"Hey, Pete! I thought you were in Dusseldorf making big money at some bar there. I tried to find you several times. I love it up there."

"I am still at the New Orleans Club in Konigsallee. I got married, but I should have waited longer. Can we have some drinks? This time on me. You were such a good patron at the EM Club."

They went to the new pub near the bahnhof and had a beer. They caught up on what was happening in town, with some people at the hospital, El Guru and others. Pete then insisted on going to the Big Ben - an off-limits place for Americans. The barmaid, who served them cognacs, sometimes went to the EM club at the hospital with her girlfriends. During their second drink, she waved and smiled to the MPs who were looking in the windows, and the quickly went away. Pete (feeling no pain) started talking loudly, and he said to Greg, "Watch this." The guy sitting next to Pete at the bar was talking to two women to his left. Pete took a match to the guy's drink and a big flame shot up about a foot high, scaring the shit out of Greg, the guy, and the two ladies. The barmaid threw Pete and Greg out, saying to Greg in her perfect English, "This is why no Americans are allowed here."

"Tina, I didn't do it, he did it. I'll talk to you at the EM Club some night."

"I no longer go there. Raus! Now!"

They went to La Cueva. Pete introduced Greg to a few people he knew, and one guy bought them beers. Then Dr. Holland, Joe Saxon (his social worker) and Gerry Ruff (a Spec/4 who worked with Kent Stone) came in and they all sat down at a table while each had another beer. They were now starting to sing songs to the music that was playing and getting drunk. Pete said he had to go home, as he was apparently staying with his parents. He helped Greg get a cab to go back to the hospital.

That Saturday Greg had a date with Marianna. El Guru wanted to go to Cologne on Friday night - he and Greg agreed to use leave time for that afternoon. They met at the Hauptbahnhof in Cologne, got bratwursts to eat, and checked into the Hotel Flandrischer Hof. They went over to Old Mac, and as they ordered a beer, the chick next to Greg said something unintelligible.

"Ich verstehe Deutsch nicht gut (I don't understand German good.)" he said.

She replied, in a British accent, "Don't give me that shit - your glasses give you away!"

El Guru laughed and said to her, "He's trying to be cool. He lost his civilian glasses at Fasching the last time he was here."

Her name was Taffy and her girlfriend's name was Pat. They were from Wales, cute, and about in their early 20s, and they were with a guy named Moffi - a German graduate student at the university there who was Pat's sometime boyfriend. Taffy and Pat worked for a Canadian military facility in Monchengladbach. Soon they talked about doing some hash.

El Guru's eyes lit up. "Shit, one of the rare nights I didn't bring any with me."

Moffi said, "It's hard to get anything since Fasching. The police have dogs out all over the place tonight anyway."

"I want to get high," Taffy said.

"Maybe we can just get drunk," Pat replied.

El Guru said to Moffi, "Man, you know this town, you know students—there's got to be someplace where we can score some."

Moffi said, "OK, we can try, but no guarantees."

El Guru and Moffi went out to look for someone selling hash, as Taffy gave them 30 DM. As they went out the door, Taffy called, "Come back in an hour so I know we weren't ripped off."

Greg stayed behind with the ladies.

It turned into a nasty night of rain mixed with snow and wind, but El Guru and Moffi had an umbrella that Taffy gave them. They went to a couple of places that were real super-freak type joints with loud rock music and people hanging around obviously high or stoned. A guy at the first place wanted to sell them greenies (a pill that could give people a speed trip) and at the next place a couple of people wanted to sell them Mandrax (downers) at a ridiculously low price. They were suspicious of them so they left. They couldn't find anything else.

In the meantime, Taffy was getting drunk and after dancing with Greg to a slow song, she gave him a big kiss. Greg got his hopes up, but they were dashed when she said that she had an American boyfriend who was an officer in the Army and wanted to break up with him, and the only way she would do it was if he caught her in bed with some guy. "He'll just fuck off and go away," she said. She asked Greg if he would spend the night with her and go along with this.

"That is pretty damn risky. I don't think I want to do this. Tell me about this guy."

"He's a Captain. He's from Pittsburgh. His name is Stan. He's 24; he got out of college a few years ago and majored in Psychology at one of the universities there."

"Describe him." Greg though that maybe there was a chance that he knew the guy.

"He's about your height with blue eyes and blond hair that's almost white. He has an annoying laugh that drives me crazy. I've been with him for eight months and I have to move on from him."

Greg thought. "This has got to be the guy who used to sit next to me in Social Psych class several years ago! He's a good dude."

Greg said, "Taffy, I'm pretty sure I know him - I used to sit next to him in one of my classes when I was in college in Pittsburgh. No way in hell will I do this. I like the idea of a one-night stand with you, and maybe even more, but never this way."

"All you have to do is be on your way out the door when he gets there then."

"He'd recognize me and kill me. Besides, I liked the guy when I was in college."

Just then, El Guru and Moffi came back. "We couldn't get anything that wasn't dangerous," El Guru said.

Taffy drunkenly cried, "Where's my fucking umbrella?"

"I'm sorry," El Guru said. "Somebody must have ripped it off at one of the places."

She was at the door and screamed, "You bastards - I'll get soaking wet! Pat, let's leave these stupid twits."

They left. El Guru and Moffi had a couple of beers and talked for a while. Greg decided to go back to the hotel. El Guru came back to the room an hour later.

Greg inquired, "Did you try again to score some dope with that dude?"

"No. Chalk it up to a bad night. Moffi said both those chicks can be real bitches, but Taffy does seem to like you."

Greg told him the story of what happened and El Guru said, "I get it. It's kind of a code of honor not to mess with a dude like that whom you know. Your shit luck with women continues. Hope it's better tomorrow night in Dusseldorf for you."

El Guru left at 5:30 am because he had CQ at the clinic until 8:00 am Sunday. Greg went to Dusseldorf and checked into the Hotel Continental. He took a nap, went out to get something to eat and later took a bath and got dressed. He walked for about a half an hour to Marianna's house, where she was waiting for him with a smile at her front window. Her daughter brought him upstairs, and Marianna gave him a quick hug and a big smile. She tried to speak a few words in English and spoke slowly in German to him as she opened a bottle of wine. Greg found out she was 28; Marianna though Greg was closer in age to her. She lived in an apartment upstairs from her mother. The furniture in her place was as beautiful as she was - there were many antiques, including a Victrola with a crank, and a guitar that must have been at least from the 1930s. Greg suggested they drink a toast to St. Patrick's Day.

"Toast? Das ist brot."

"No," Greg smiled. "Not what you eat with eggs. It's also a saying. Or, 'Cheers.'"

She smiled. "Ah! Ich verstehe." She then asked, "Nixon nicht so gut ist. Warum (why) ist Nixon President?"

Greg explained that the Democrats did not have a strong candidate to run against him.

"Kennedy?"

"Chappaquiddick," Greg said.

"Ah. And McGovern?"

"Vielleicht (maybe)." Greg thought, "This is great. Not only is she beautiful but she knows politics and she's apparently not a conservative."

Her friend, Jürgen, who spoke some English, and Veronica, his fiancée came by. Another couple in about their 30s, Gerhard and Dorothea also dropped in. Gerhard spoke fluent English. He spent a few years in Alabama about 10 years before. Greg liked all of them - they all decided to go to Jürgen's place, which was not far away. But no sooner had Greg got there when he went to the bathroom and his zipper broke. He called Jürgen in to help him, who got some safety pins and he laughed and said, "Maybe you won't need these later."

They stayed there for a couple of hours talking about the growing drug abuse problem and also some politics. They decided to play a game with dice and a cup - one person rolled the dice from the cup and points were scored in a manner that the next player would bid high or low from that total before shaking the dice - in other words, a 2 and a 5 thrown would be either 25 or 52. The first person declared which one and the next person would bid over or under before throwing the dice.

After the game, they went to Gerhard's house near Krefeld, which was about 35 miles away. Gerhard drove and made it in 20 minutes going about 180 km/h on the Autobahn. Jürgen and Veronica took their car and drove about as fast. Greg and Marianna were scared shitless. When Greg asked if there was any kind of speed limit on the Autobahn, Gerhard just laughed while Dorothea bitched at Gerhard to slow down. The cars they passed looked like dashes going by. Once they got there, Gerhard challenged Greg and Mariana to a game of Foosball. Jürgen said, "He does not lose in his house." Naturally he won, and Dorothea prepared some food for everyone, and they all played Parchisi. At about 3.00 am they thanked Gerhard and Dorothea for their hospitality, and Jürgen and Veronica took Marianna and Greg back to Greg's hotel. Again, they held each other tight in the backseat and Greg tried to make out with her, but he didn't get very far. She gave Greg a quick kiss goodnight as he got out of the car. Greg called her at noon, again thanking her for good time. They talked very pleasantly for a few minutes. She ended the conversation, saying she would write to him. He never heard from her again, despite calling her and writing once. "Maybe I shouldn't've told her I was leaving Germany in a few weeks. If I only I had met her six months earlier," he thought.

Chapter 13

The Whirlwind Bus Tour

El Guru called Greg just as he was getting off work the next day. "Hey, did you sign up for the Sergeant Major's bus tour to Milan and maybe Venice this weekend? He's paying for everything except meals."

"No, but I guess I could go now. Wachtel said he and his wife were going, but they had to cancel. It's my last chance to see different countries, even though there will be several lifers on board. Are you going?"

"No. Too many lifers. About 35 people are going, I hear. Besides, I wasn't impressed with Italy a couple of years ago. Switzerland is OK, though, if you're staying there."

"Tombaugh, Ole Olafsson, Mackey, and Weiss are going, so I can hang around with them. Do you know them?"

"Only Tombaugh. I met him the night we all got blitzed in your room. Did he tell you about the party he went to at a new officer's house and somebody put hash in the brownies, and that Lieutenant was still stoned the next day? The officer and his wife thought they must've drunk way too much wine. That must've been funny as hell."

"No, I didn't know about that. I'm sure he didn't do it - he's more of a straight or juicer type. Ole is a good dude who likes to party. We went downtown to Onkel Willy's new place – Treffpunkt - one night. The other two guys are very straight, but they're OK. What the hell, I'm really 'short' (GI term for little time left in the service). I'll go to Italy."

"Have a blast. I'm going to Luxembourg."

Greg talked to Sergeant Major Dennis who said, "Sure - we'd love to have you come. I know you only have about three weeks left here."

Master Sgt. Greene walked by and said, "James, you're free to ETS. Or we can put you up before the E-6 Board ASAP if you want to stay here and extend for six months, or re-up for three more years of Active Duty as part of your six-year total obligation."

"I will stay in the Army under two conditions. You station me at the R&R Center in Sydney, Australia, and promote me to Lt. Colonel." They all laughed.

El Guru had a routine week and went to Luxembourg Friday night. He went to his favorite bar, Black Bess, picked up a lady named Frieda who lived not far away, and spent the whole weekend at her place. She was slightly taller than him and slightly older (26), but they had terrific sex together several times during the weekend, and she liked to smoke hash, drink wine, and talk about politics. Frieda had a government job as a secretary dealing with environmental issues of the country, and she also spoke several languages. She knew Bob Stewart, a late-night Radio Luxembourg DJ; El Guru also knew him. She told him she had no intention of getting married or having any kids for several years, at least. This was music to El Guru's ears.

As Greg boarded the bus for the tour on Friday afternoon, he slipped into a long nap. When he woke up, the Schwarzwald (Black Forest) looked like beautiful country, and Basel (Switzerland) seemed like a modern city. They stopped for two hours in Lucerne, where he and Tombaugh changed money at the train station, went out to dinner, and walked along the lake. "This is a really cool town. Why didn't I ever come to Switzerland before?" he thought.

At 11:30, they had to get off the bus and wait an hour so the bus could be put on a train through the Alps into Italy. It was a long ride to Milan, and they didn't get there until 7:30 am The Sergeant Major went into the hotel and they told him that his reservations were actually for the following weekend. After much bitching, the group wound up at the Hotel Cincinnato, which looked like somewhat of a flophouse. Most of the group were not thrilled at this, but Greg thought, "All I need is a clean bed, a clean bathroom, and some good sightseeing here." He stayed in a room with Tombaugh, Mackey, and Weiss. They all took a nap immediately.

Two and a half hours later, Ole woke them up saying, "The Sergeant Major's arranged for a day trip to Venice, if you want to go. I'm going."

"Yeah, I'll go," Tombaugh said.

"I'm in for that," Greg said.

Mackey and Weiss stayed at the hotel.

In Venice, trying to buy souvenirs and pricing food at restaurants was a hassle because everything had to be bargained. Ole and Greg ate a spaghetti dinner outside while Tombaugh was so frustrated at the price haggling, he went to a store and bought a loaf of bread and ham. Then they hopped on a boat that took them around some of the canals (which seemed dirty), including the famous Bridge of Sighs. Ole wanted them to go back to St. Mark's Square to find the Sergeant Major and ask him if they could stay overnight in Venice and meet them in Milan the next morning ("Look at all the women and neat little bars they have here," he said.). When they arrived at St. Mark's Square, the Sergeant Major said, "You have to get back here in two hours. I just found out all the trains in northern Italy are going on strike tonight. I just told some people to tell that to any of our group who came over here."

In the train car on the way back to Milan, there was a friendly Italian soldier who said he never met any Americans before, but communication was difficult, despite attempts by Greg, Ole, and Tombaugh to speak a bit of languages other than English. He shared a bottle of wine he had with the Americans, and Tombaugh gave him the rest of his bread. The soldier's father ran a small restaurant right next to the train station in Verona, and they had a 15-minute layover there. Just before the train took off, the soldier came back with three bottles of red wine from his father's place and gave them one each! They drank some of the wine, but dropped the rest of it off at the hotel in Milan because they wanted to go to a little restaurant a block away to get sandwiches.

Greg and Tombaugh got up early to tour Milan. They saw the big "Vota Communista" sign over the train station. "I wonder how El Guru would react," Greg thought. They saw the Sforezesco Castle, a Renaissance structure that was partially frescoed by Da Vinci. Then they walked to the Duomo, the largest Gothic church in Italy - very impressive. Tombaugh wanted to go in, but a priest wouldn't let him in because he wore shorts, as it was almost 70 degrees out. They later walked to the San Maria Delle Grazie, where Da Vinci used to hang out. Da Vinci's original "Last Supper" was painted on one of the walls - it mostly survived a bombing in 1943, with only a little bit of restoration. They were in sheer awe of this faded painting, and took pictures. On the walk back to the hotel, they saw kids playing soccer, winos stretched out on benches, and women walking with their children.

That evening, Greg, Tombaugh, and Ole went out to get a beer at a bar. There were prostitutes all over the place. The Americano bar looked like a rough joint, and they drank their beers there fast, as a fight started breaking out between two guys. Unfortunately, the only places that looked inviting were private clubs. A guy who spoke English said, "You need a car and wear a sport coat to get into any good lounge." On the way back, a prostitute tried to flirt with Greg - she had a German accent. They talked to her in broken German, but she spoke some English. Ole asked her where she was from.

"Dusseldorf."

Tombaugh asked, "Why are you here?"

"Too many girls give it away there," she said, smiling.

"I told you guys you should take a trip up there," Greg said. A car came by and picked her up immediately. After eating at a cheap restaurant, they went back to the hotel, and the whore from Dusseldorf followed them in, along with three guys, giving Greg, Ole, and Tombaugh a wave and a smile. They heard moans for a while from the room on the floor directly below them.

"She's sure making a lot of Lira (Italian money) tonight," Tombaugh said.

The next morning, the bus took off at 8 am. It was a beautiful, clear day, but the temperature must have dropped at least 40 degrees from the time they got on the bus until the time they got to the Italian-Swiss border in the Alps. A foot of snow blanketed the ground, as the group went out to take pictures. Later they pulled into St. Moritz, which is a popular winter resort for wealthy people. Greg and Ole couldn't get into a couple of restaurants because they weren't dressed well enough despite the old sport coats and sweaters they were wearing, but the prices were outrageous, anyway. They joined Tombaugh and huddled around an outdoor bratwurst stand where you had to roast your own, across the street. It felt good to be around the fire, though, because it was so damn cold and the bratwursts came out just right, with help from the vendor.

They gazed at the alternately snow-covered mountain peak scenery of the Swiss countryside while on the bus for the rest of the afternoon. By 4:30, they stopped for a half hour break at Vaduz, Liechtenstein - a quaint town of about 5,000 people. Greg and Tombaugh went to a café and had drinks with a couple of friendly locals who told them they should try to visit the Duke's castle. Unfortunately, there was no time for that, but they did get a glimpse of the impressive structure in the distance as they left Vaduz. Tombaugh drank half the liter of wine he had left over from the stop in Verona, and he was feeling no pain by the time they stopped into a small town gasthaus in Austria to eat dinner. He and Greg were the last ones in, but the place was full, and they had to stand up and wait a while until a small table became vacant. Tombaugh started singing songs loudly - first, a verse from "Beautiful Sunday," by Daniel Boone, and then to a waitress, "I've Never Been to Spain," by Three Dog Night. A few people laughed at him - nobody spoke any English except for the bus tourists. He and Greg ordered dinners, but instead the waitress gave them beers. Tombaugh laughed and guzzled his beer, but then she brought only one Weiner Schnitzel dinner.

"Hey, I didn't order this shit," he said.

"I didn't either," Greg chimed in.

Tombaugh started eating the Weiner Schnitzel; Greg took a bite and gagged.

"You're gonna puke if you eat this crap, John," Greg said.

"I don't give a shit, I'm starving. You can have my roll."

Greg was pissed - he never got his Cordon Bleu dinner and the bus was leaving. He threw 5 DM on the table and said, "That's all I'm paying for."

As they got to their seats, the Sergeant Major asked, "Who ordered the Cordon Bleu and didn't pay for it?"

Greg said, "I did because I never got it."

"James, you go back there and explain what happened. See if you can get it to go."

The waitress was outside and was angry and screaming something in German at Greg, who screamed back at her in English about what an incompetent bitch she was. Tombaugh was yelling out the window about what a bullshit meal he had. The owner said Greg could not get the meal to go, but he had to pay for it. Tombaugh threw a 10 DM bill out the window at Greg and yelled, "Here! Tell him to wipe his ass with it! Get back on the bus - we want to go home!"

For the next half hour, Greg went to the front of the bus and talked to the Sergeant Major and MSG Greene about what happened, and he apologized to them over and over again about how he did not mean to screw up any German or Austrian-American relations. The Sergeant Major was upset, but he accepted Greg's apology. Master Sergeant Greene and his wife actually chuckled at some of Greg's story.

Tombaugh was snoring away. Later they had a five-minute bathroom stop at Worms, but Greg and Tombaugh couldn't wait for the public men's room to empty out, so they walked a block away and urinated on what turned out to be Martin Luther's statue. For the rest of the trip, Tombaugh was groaning about what a hangover he had. When they got back to the hospital, the Sergeant Major gave everyone permission to report two hours late.

Chapter 14

Greg Gets Out of the Army

During the last several days of March, Wachtel finally started taking an interest in seeing how all the reports were done, and Greg explained everything to him patiently. Dr. Whitman took over Greg's few outpatients and also took on the technical operation of the clinic. None of the in-patients seemed like blatant personality disordered, psychotic, or hard care drug abusing people. Greg felt relieved that finally things were going smoothly for his last few weeks at the hospital. El Guru called him late in the afternoon on Tuesday, and Greg told him all about the trip to Italy as El Guru laughed a few times.

He said he wished he had gone on the trip and asked if he would get to see Greg one last time. Greg said he had hardly any money. El Guru said that if they met in Cologne, he could subsidize Greg, but only for Friday night. He was seeing Frieda Saturday night, anyway, but he also said she was curious about Greg.

"Does she have any friends?"

"Her best friend is in love with some guy from Liège. The other few I've met seem like a bunch of bitches. That could be a problem for us down the road."

"OK. I can scrape up about 25 DM - enough for a round trip ticket up there, a bratwurst and a beer. The rest has to be on you. We don't get paid until Monday."

"I'll meet you at the Hauptbahnhof at 7:00. My goodbye present to you."

Greg had just arrived at the Hauptbahnhof Friday night when El Guru came by looking "shell-shocked" as he dropped his suitcase, and his hands trembled.

"What's up, Artie? Are you all right?"

"You won't believe what happened to us from just past Bonn to a few miles away from here. There was a UFO, or a flying saucer, or some kind of goddamn thing that came out of the sky like a flash of light and hovered over the train for about 10 minutes. All of us on the train were scared shit-less - people started praying and I even started praying."

"What kind of shit have you been smoking?"

"Fuck you! I saw it with my own eyes and so did 20 or 30 other peo-ple. Look around at them right now. See they're all nervous as hell and talking so fast. People are trying to calm them down. Let's get our asses to a hotel."

They checked into a hotel nearby and later walked to a pizza parlor. El Guru could only eat one slice of pizza.

"Maybe we should have a few beers at the places we usually go to," Greg said.

"Let's walk there. I'm coming down from this but I need to calm down 100%."

As they ambled along, El Guru started talking about Frieda and some future plans, and said that he would try to get a European out in December because he spent so little time in America that he didn't know if he could adjust to the changes in society after all the time away. Greg remarked that he, too, would have an adjustment after spending only a lit-tle more than one month out of the past 27 in the U.S.A., while having some great times in Europe. El Guru suggested that Greg come back that summer because there were cheap flights via Air Iceland to Luxembourg.

Greg replied that all of the money he sent home from Vietnam was set aside for furthering his education, and that the GI Bill would probably pay for tuition, but not more.

The bars were fairly empty, which surprised them. At Old Mac, they had a beer, and as par for the course, a prostitute tried to pick up Greg.

Greg remarked, "Hookers never hang out here. What the hell is going on tonight?"

El Guru said, "Now I remember. I think it's Good Friday. I bet that's it."

They asked the bartender, who affirmed what El Guru believed. They chatted with a couple at the bar who were from Dusseldorf who knew Pete Herkt from the New Orleans Club in Konigsallee. El Guru wanted to hop on a train to see him, but they said he has a weird schedule and he rarely works weekend nights any more. El Guru and Greg then tried to get into the Jet Set but it recently had turned into a private club, and Suzi didn't work there anymore. Even the Santa Cruz was dead. They decided to go back to the hotel. They left the next morning, and Greg hoped they could get together one last time for an evening trip closer to the hospital "We can't end our last trip like this," El Guru said. "Call me Wednesday or Thursday."

Greg began the ordeal of properly processing out the next week. Things got so busy at the clinic and on the ward, he had to buy his own one-way train ticket to Frankfurt in advance instead of getting one at the hospital. One night the EM Club wouldn't let him in because he didn't have a club card for the month. He got pissed and told the new doorman about all the business he had given them last year - some guys at the bar were yelling at the doorman to let Greg in, but to no avail. Inside, Sam Garner said, "Screw this place. If you won't let Greg in, I'm out of here too." A few others left with Garner. Greg called El Guru the next day; he told Greg he couldn't get away, but he was coming over to the hospital on Monday night to stay over until the next day, for meetings and other business, and they could go out that night. Greg spent a quiet last weekend, taking pictures downtown and hanging out in various guys' rooms, saying goodbye. He was going to Ft. Dix, NJ, with Garner and McAfee, and he was to meet them in Frankfurt Thursday night. In the meantime, El Guru spent another enjoyable weekend with Frieda in Luxembourg.

El Guru didn't get to see Greg until he was locking up his office at 5:00 pm. They went to the mess hall to eat dinner and Ralph joined them. After exchanging some pleasantries with El Guru (Ralph had worked with him at the hospital for a year), Ralph said to Greg, "Hey, home, we gotta go out one time before you go. Let's all go out tonight. I wanna get fired up with you dudes. Y'all always used to have a blast downtown or away from here."

El Guru said, "Home, I'm gonna have a chick with me."

Ralph laughed, "A-ha-ha! A-ha-ha! You pullin' the same shit these dudes upstairs getting' away with! I shoulda known. You slick, Artie."

Greg, shocked, asked, "What the hell - is Frieda with you here?"

El Guru said she had a meeting in Trier and that she said she would meet him in Boppard tonight around 8:00. She wanted him to get on a train and bring Greg along - it was supposed to be a surprise. He planned on staying up there with her, and taking the first train back to Bad Kreuznach so he could get a ride to Prum in the morning.

Greg exclaimed, "Wow! I could only stay for a couple of hours and I'd have to get the last train back tonight."

Ralph said, "Hey, home - I got a car - remember? Let's all bop on up to Bop-pard and Artie can meet the broad at the station at 8:00. Let's get changed after we eat and leave. I got a map - take about an hour to get there."

Greg said, "Yeah. Let's all get changed and bop on up to Boppard."

They got there at 7:15 and Ralph parked at the wharf. They walked around part of the town and Ralph rapped briefly to a couple of other soul brothers who were stationed at Hahn AFB, not far away. They saw a sign that read "Diskotek," where some well-dressed people started to enter.

Ralph told El Guru, "James and I will be here. Pick up your chick and bring her over."

"OK, home. She might want to eat someplace but we will be there."

"Right on, home."

Ralph and Greg strolled into the upscale disco. Immediately Ralph got an empty table next to some young ladies and he said to them with a smile, "Hey, sweet things - me and James here just bopped on up to Boppard tonight to have a good time. We got the Guru man and his chick comin' too. Maybe we can all have a good time."

Two of the girls looked at him like he was crazy and split. The other two started laughing; as did Greg.

Ralph asked both of the remaining two to dance and they shot him down, leaving abruptly. A few minutes later, El Guru came by with Frieda. She was an attractive, dark-haired, dark-eyed, slender lady with a big, seductive smile, slightly taller than El Guru. "Just his type - on the surface," Greg thought. He introduced her to Greg and Ralph. Ralph said, "Ooh, you got a fox here, home! A ha ha, a ha ha!"

She suggested somewhere else down the street for them to go - a popular casual bar. Although the place was packed, they got the last open table. Ralph bought a round of drinks, "On me, home - it's James' last night. Guru get the next one." Then he saw some other black dudes at the bar and he yelled out, "Hey, homes!" He went over to them and made comments, laughing, to a few ladies along the way.

Frieda grimaced and asked El Guru, as she watched Ralph, "Is this your typical Negro American man? I have only met one in my life and he was not like this man at all."

El Guru smiled and said, "Don't worry. He's harmless. He likes to laugh and have fun just like us."

"Greg added, "You get to know him and he will make you laugh but he has a serious side to him, too, when he talks about work."

Frieda said, "He is strange, and he is your friend? What is he like when he smokes a bowl of hash with you?"

Greg and El Guru both laughed and said they never did the stuff with him. Then Ralph came back and said, "The brothers say we should'a gone to Koblenz. Be a miracle to get any pussy here."

Frieda seemed turned off by this remark. El Guru, finding it amusing, took her out to the dance floor. A minute later they were playing a new song from Deep Purple's new Machine Head album, "Smoke on the Water," and Greg got up and danced with a young chick and he suddenly saw Ralph dancing with her teeny bopper friend. For the duration of the song they were all having a good time. Then the two girls went to the ladies' room, and Ralph was waiting on the dance floor for them to come out through the next few songs.

"What the hell'd these bitches do - sneak out the back door?"

"Give it up, home, move on to the next broad," Greg said, walking back to the table.

"They can't be both takin' a crap - ha ha ha, ha ha ha," Ralph laughed.

El Guru and Greg both cracked up laughing, but again, Frieda was not amused. She turned her attention to Greg and wanted to know all about him, his job at the hospital, and why he was not opting to stay in Europe and maybe work at a civilian job there. He, in turn, asked about her, why she was in Luxembourg, and why she had meetings with various groups in Trier, Strasbourg, and Brussels with her job. She said she spoke several languages, but she was very vague when it came to offering information about her work. At one point, after she learned that much of Greg's work was in mental health and drug abuse, she half-accused Greg of trying to "psycho-analyze me." Greg told her that he was not working right now. She ignored Ralph, who was alternating talking to El Guru about their methods of picking up European women, and talking about various people at the hospital. Suddenly Ralph spoke up and got serious.

"Black folk are at a disadvantage here. Same with Mexicans like El Guru. We got to make our own breaks. Older people, freaky people, white rednecks, cons - they all want to turn on the black man. James is a good dude. There are a lot of whites who are good dudes, but more and more in the Army at the hospital there are ones that ain't. And a lot of the new young brothers see what's goin' on right away, and they don't trust. And it ain't like it used to be at the hospital now."

El Guru said, "From what I've seen over here, black and all minority GIs have it a little better in big cities and GI towns. Once you're out of work, it helps to get out and meet the locals. Me, I like small towns and small cities, generally. Greg likes the big cities where there are no Americans and we have had some good times there."

Greg said, "I think you guys are both right, off what I've seen. I really do feel more comfortable in places where there are few, if any, American GIs around. I try to come off as being more European than American as best I can, but it doesn't always work."

Suddenly Ralph said, "Ooh - there's a chick I like. I'm gonna give it a shot."

"Play it cool, home," Greg said.

El Guru, Greg, and Frieda started talking about politics, Vietnam, devaluation of the U.S. dollar in the past year, traveling in cities in Europe, etc. Ralph seemed to be hitting it off with the chick, a tall, thin German lady in her early 20s who was with another couple. Frieda asked Greg to get Ralph's keys so that she, him, and El Guru, could do a bowl in his car. Greg said he would never do such a thing, and Frieda seemed to get turned off by this.

El Guru said, "She just wants to see if you're some kind of narc."

"I wouldn't even do that with my own car," Greg said.

At 11 o'clock, Frieda wanted to leave. El Guru whispered to Greg that he was getting horny, anyway. Greg went outside with them briefly.

El Guru said to him, "Look, man, it's been great - the times we had together, all those weekends. I'm gonna miss you. Please stay in touch. I want to come and visit you sometime by the end of the year, or even better you could come back here for two weeks. You know my address. Write to me sometime in the next two weeks, OK?"

"I sure will. We will definitely stay in touch with each other."

They shook hands, Greg told Frieda that it was nice meeting her. She replied, "Very nice," gave a quick, frozen smile, and led El Guru away.

Greg started thinking about all the good times he and El Guru had traveling and bar hopping, the times they pulled off the Bad Muenster Specials, all of the discussions they'd had about politics, sports, and their futures and life in general. He hoped El Guru would follow through on his plans to go back to school and eventually get a satisfying career.

Ralph was trying hard to pick up a lady whom he introduced to Greg as Inge, a local girl. She was fascinated by Ralph at first because she said she never met a black American man before. Unfortunately, she was with her cousin and his girlfriend who were making out on the couch in front of the table across from Ralph, and he took it as a signal that he could make physical moves on Inge, but she promptly resisted. Then Inge and her cousin and his girlfriend decided to leave.

Greg told Ralph because it was 11:30, they'd better go home. Ralph agreed but mentioned getting a nightcap at Onkel Willy's. Greg said he wanted to be dropped off at the hospital because he had to finish all his processing out in the morning. He also reminded Ralph that he was driving after drinking four beers and that he better be careful on the way back.

Ralph said, "You right, home. I really had a good time. I gotta bop on up to Boppard more often."

After leaving, El Guru and Frieda checked into a hotel. El Guru was horny but Frieda was not in the mood at all. She said, "I just want to sleep. Tonight, was good in some ways. I think your friend Greg is interesting. But I don't trust him. And your friend Ralph is - how do you say it - uncouth."

"I thought Ralph would keep you laughing. Greg has been my best friend here. He won't try to get you busted for any dope. In fact, let's do a bowl right now and talk about it. I can't believe what you're saying."

"No. I have to go to work tomorrow. This was a mistake coming up here."

El Guru was suddenly livid. "This might be the last time I ever see Greg again! He's been my best friend for over a year now! If you don't like him, go fuck yourself!"

"Don't talk to me like that. Sleep on the fucking floor if you want. I'm going to sleep. Don't touch me."

"You're acting like a real bitch. Just like most of the friends of yours I met."

"We'll take separate trains in the morning, then. Or you can take a fucking bus back to your little town."

They left separately in the morning - she left before he was awake and left him a note saying that she would like to talk with him the next time he came to Luxembourg, but there would be no guarantee that things would ever be the same after last night. He was puzzled as to how things suddenly got to that point, and he spent the next few days wondering whether Freida was worth seeing her again.

Greg finished up his work at the clinic Wednesday. It took two hours the following morning for him to go around the hospital and say goodbye and thanks to everyone who helped him there. The other guys leaving on that day got a ride to Gutlet Kaserne in Frankfurt, but Greg had opted to take one last train ride. "Too bad America doesn't have a rail system like this anymore - maybe this new Amtrak system there will make it," he thought.

He met Sam Garner and Bill McAfee at Gutlet Kaserne. Some hard-ass NCO was checking people for haircuts and ordered Greg to come back and trim his moustache and sideburns to military regulations before he got an assigned bunk, which pissed him off. The NCO said he would bump him off the flight home and give him KP if they were not up to military standards.

At 7:00 am, they were at the Rhein Main airfield taking a Saturn Airways plan to the US.

"Look at this goddamn thing, with all the orange and yellow rings around it. Maybe it came from Saturn," Sam said.

"Get set for a bumpy ride, shitty food, and ugly stewardesses," Bill said.

The flight was surprisingly smooth. Greg sat next to a guy who was stationed at Augsburg, and he had been in Munich for last year's Oktoberfest. Greg told him about an older chick named Erica he met there, who worked for an American military base in Augsburg. The guy actually knew Erica, although he hadn't seen her lately.

"I tried hard to stay with her because I went there cold. No place to stay at all," Greg said. "I didn't care whether or not I'd have sex with her. I told her I'd sleep on the stairs, but she didn't trust me."

"That's too bad, because right about after that time, she started screwing a lot of GIs. Almost overnight around that time, she changed. She is one real fucked up chick."

"Thanks for telling me. I don't want to hear any more about her," Greg said.

After a stop in Bangor, Maine, they touched down in Philadelphia with a rousing cheer of GIs at 4:30 pm and went to Ft. Dix, NJ. They were promptly met by a drill sergeant who told them that due to a large number of troops being discharged, they would not be getting out until sometime Sunday morning, at the earliest. They were assigned to bunks and Greg was right near Bill and Sam. For most of the evening, the staff there went over general information about 201 (personnel) files and the final DD-214 (discharge sheet) papers with the GIs. Greg's Secondary MOS of Psychiatric Social Work Technician was nowhere to be found, nor was the secondary MOS as Lab Technician that he earned in Vietnam; fortunately, his medals from Vietnam were listed on the DD-214. Officially, his MOS was 91B20 Medic only for his Army career, which bothered him greatly.

The next day, Sam, Bill, Greg, and another guy played cards—500 Rummy and Gin—all day long. The radio station played about the same 15 songs over and over again. It got so boring, Greg took a walk for an hour by the Basic Training areas which brought back memories, most of which were bad, from 1969.

On Sunday, there was a final check of personnel records. When Greg was called, he noticed his Social Security number was screwed up by two digits. He told staff about this, but instead of correcting it on the spot they told him he had to go back to the end of the line and wait, which lasted about two and a half hours - he was furious. When he came to the final clerk, he noticed his birth date on the DD-214 was a year older than he actually was. He thought, "I'm not gonna say a goddamn thing to her. I want to get the hell out of here and go home."

The clerk said, "Hey, it says here you've been in the service two years and 11 months, counting your time on Inactive Reserve before you went on Active Duty."

"Yeah, that's right."

"Well, you know they have you down here for transfer to Active Reserves."

"But that's only for one month."

"No, they'll try to keep you on that status for at least the rest of this year. Do you really want to go to the meetings, summer camp, and all that other bullshit?"

"Hell, no!"

"We'll change that right now. Reserve Control Group, St. Louis - Stand-by Reserve."

Greg thanked her profusely; she smiled and said, "Get out of here and go home."

After getting his last paycheck, a jitney came by and Greg and a few guys paid $10 each to go to the airport. He met Sam there, who was leaving on a flight to West Virginia.

"Hey, Greg, take my dog tags (he threw them to him). I don't need 'em anymore."

"Good luck, Sam. If I ever want to change my identity, I'm you."

They both laughed. They got on their planes. It was an easy flight for Greg to the Albany, NY, airport. Just before midnight Greg was home. Free at last!

Chapter 15

An Excellent Summer

Greg and El Guru communicated through letters for a few months. Near the end of April, El Guru wrote that he went to Heidelberg to help make a presentation regarding statistical information about the drug abuse program for his clinic. Immediately after this concluded, he went to Luxembourg, met Frieda at a café, and they broke up. It was by mutual agreement with no hard feelings. El Guru stated, "I didn't want to get involved with someone who would try to dominate me and change me. That night in Boppard got me gun shy about going any further with her." He also related that he was going to be trained as a lab tech for the clinic. "Greg, I remember you said you liked doing that stuff in Vietnam for a while. It will be an interesting change of pace for me for the months I have left."

Greg wrote back right away and told him, "The day after you get out of the Army, you will be bombarded by insurance companies hounding you to buy life and health insurance. They will call you, send you info in the mail, and they might even come to your door. Pick one company fast and forget the others. One bastard even told me a guy from another company was lying and he was a rep from the same company. By the way, I got accepted at graduate schools - two in Kansas and two in Massachusetts, and I have to make a decision very soon about where to go in September."

In May, El Guru took a trip to Barcelona, Costa Brava, and Cadiz, Spain. He wrote to Greg and said, "I had a great time. I spoke Spanish the whole time I was there. Barcelona is an international city with something they call the Magic Fountain - real colorful with some shows - but the city is too big for me. I took an all-day bus trip to Costa Brava - rugged coastline, small towns, and friendly people. The long train ride to Cadiz was well worth it and I stayed for a few days lying on the beach, flirting with the girls and talking with the locals. I loved Cadiz. I see that J. Edger Hoover died. He was a shithead. And someone shot George Wallace but he didn't die - one out of two. Nixon keeps bombing Hanoi and Haiphong Harbor. He should not get re-elected but the American public is dumb. Kennedy screwed himself with Chappaquiddick. And I don't think McGovern will make it if he gets the nomination. I'm not smoking dope at all. I'm enjoying reading various books. I know you're a Pittsburgh Pirates fan, but watch out for the Mets. With Willie Mays now, they're off to a hot start. I hope you decide to go to one of the schools in Kansas. Maybe we could meet halfway from Albuquerque for a few days if I end up at home instead of somewhere in Europe."

Greg wrote back that he decided to go to a school in Massachusetts in the fall because it was close to Boston, not far from the ocean, and only several hours away from home by car. Plus, he could see the Red Sox. He said he was letting his hair and moustache grow a little longer so he could fit in with 'normal people.' He was spending time over at Van's house, converting 8-tracks and reel to reel music he recorded onto cassettes. He remarked about a great new group, Tavares, playing at Rudy's, a bar outside of Albany.

Greg continued, "I got so used to European ladies, I'm feeling self-conscious talking with American women and I don't know why. I had to go out and buy a lot of new clothes - mine from 1969 are mostly out of style. Guys are wearing different colored shirts now with wide collars. Casual pants are flare-out, almost like girls wearing bell bottoms. They're coming out with 'earth shoes" now. Good thing I got another pair of wire-rimmed glasses before I left. I still have my blue shades and I bought a beret - maybe I'll wear it sometimes. Living at home is a big turnoff, especially since I just turned 25 and I'm unemployed. I bought a '68 Ford Falcon. I get a 6-pack of German beer, usually Lowenbrau, if it's available but if not, it's back to Schlitz or Pabst. I have no desire to smoke any dope again, and I never liked the smell or taste of it, anyway. I know you'd like me to come over there for a couple of weeks but I can't afford a trip to Europe. Instead I may go to Canada for a month; I have just enough money to do it. My brother could go with me and that might cut expenses, although we'll probably fight like hell. I miss traveling already."

El Guru was notified that his discharge would now be in November. He wanted to apply for a European out but he has told the rules had changed. In a letter to Greg in late July, he stated that they rejected him because permission from the German government had to be granted now! He felt he got screwed because of that hash misdemeanor he got nailed with back in '69. What upset him more was that he wanted to live in Luxembourg, or even Spain, not Germany. He said that hash was hard to get lately, and most heads were speeding or shooting up. He saw Kent Stone who told him he was getting discharged soon to go back to North Carolina.

"I've been going to Bitburg AFB to get as much training as I can as a lab tech, and they gave me a Jeep to drive there. I went to Luxembourg one weekend and a lot of the people and some DJs I knew are gone. Even Kid Jensen is on tour with the Rolling Stones. But I met somebody else there - a 19-year-old girl who lives in Stuttgart named Ursula who speaks good English and loves Mexican food and Sangria. I went down to Stuttgart and met her parents. They are very nice people; very open minded. We didn't get to have sex this trip but I still had a great time. I really like this girl. For some reason, everyone I met thought I was from Tunisia or Morocco, and they were shocked that I was an American. A few told me, 'You're not like the thousands of GIs that are here in Stuttgart.' It pays to try to act European, like the way we did, I think. Hope you had a great time in Canada."

Greg had gone to New York City late in June and after talking with his friend Mort about plans for the summer, Mort encouraged him to go to Canada with Greg's brother, Danny, after the Fourth of July. "You can sleep in the car every two nights and stay in a motel every third night, Mort advised. Greg took Mort's advice and decided to go to Canada with Danny. He sent El Guru a long cassette tape on August 1st describing the entire trip.

"We agreed to take turns driving as we took off on July 6th, and started fighting the moment we crossed the Canadian border. All he wanted to do was smoke cigarettes and stop to eat about four times a day. We hit a couple of lobster festivals, which were delicious, cheap eating. You cannot beat the Maritimes for delicious seafood. In St. John and Shediac, New Brunswick, we did a few touristy things and then went to Prince Edward Island by ferry. When you get off the boat, you see red clay, much like some places in Vietnam. PEI is very clean and at night it is really dark - no wonder the speed limit is the equivalent of 45 mph. He drove to Nova Scotia after we took the ferry back. There were two gorgeous women hitchhiking near the ferry and I yelled at him to stop but he wouldn't, yelling back, 'Remember what happened to you the last time you tried to pick up a girl hitchhiking?' Danny wanted to spend the night in the car outside of a place called New Glasgow, and I got bitten by mosquitoes far worse than any time in my life. I told him, 'That's it. From now on I'm driving.' The next day I drove up to Cape Breton Island and the Cabot Trail which had exquisite scenery - rolling hills, cliffs, bays, and waterfalls. We were tired and stayed at the Holiday Inn in Sydney. We just wanted to cool off and get into the pool, but they had just painted the pool and it was closed. So, we both slept on our beds in the motel room for four hours and completely missed the total eclipse of the sun. There was more fighting over that and whether or not we should go to Newfoundland by ferry. He insisted we didn't have enough money to go all the way there, so we went to Dartmouth, NS, spent the night there, and after more arguing, we both decided we'd had enough of each other. He bought a plane ticket to fly home out of Halifax, which was fine with me. He's definitely the opposite of the travel companion you are.

"I went to Truro - a nice, clean town, where I had some minor car trouble. The mechanic at the gas station was a big Dodgers fan and he surprised me by saying that my Ford Falcon was actually made in Canada, making it easier and cheaper to fix.

"The next night, I was Amherst - a nothing town. After that, it was back to Prince Edward Island to Summerside, a town of about 15,000. I got a big lobster plus dessert at a fair for only $3.00! Surprisingly, the water at the beach was warm because of the current in the strait up there. I went to a bar in Cavendish where the bartender and I had a long discussion about America and Americans. I tried to convince him that the younger people, born in the mid-1940s and after, were, for the most part, not ultra-conservative, 'Archie Bunker' types (as he put it), but he was skeptical. I went back to Charlottetown and almost everyone I met wanted to talk about American politics and why the war wasn't over by now. As proof that this is a good place to live, I was told that they only have a few policemen and they mainly play cards all the time – crime is that low there!

"Then I went to Moncton, NB. They have a thing called Magnetic Hill where you put your car in neutral, go down the hill and look far away forward, and it gives the effect that you're going back uphill. The first time I tried it, I almost rear-ended somebody but I got the effect the second time. The weather got colder the next day when I was in Fredericton - kind of a dead town with a beautiful RCMP station.

"The next day I drove to Bangor, Maine, and stayed at a small Holiday Inn instead of a parking lot, and I ate at an Italian restaurant. I splurged that day. I met a cute blonde who was finishing up her degree in political science at the University of Maine - again, we talked about world politics for a while. I didn't get to score with her but at least I got my best night's sleep of the whole trip. From there I went to Montpelier, Vermont, which is another nice town of about 10,000 people. I met a dude at a small tavern who was in Bien Hoa the same time I was in Vietnam, and after we swapped 'war stories' for a while, the lady who owned the place joined us. She was from Pittsburgh, but had not been back for ten years. The three of us talked for a couple of hours and it was great conversation - there are friendly people in northern New England. Then I drove through Burlington and hung around there for most of the day. It is a modern, small city where the University of Vermont is located. I wound up spending the night in a Plattsburgh, NY, parking lot, to save a few bucks, again.

"I took off for Montreal the next day. I couldn't find a place to park in that huge city so I drove to Ottawa. I checked into flophouse downtown called the Ritz for $6.00; at least they had a parking lot. As soon as I got in, I killed spiders in the bathroom and went to sleep. I went sightseeing the next day. The changing of the guard outside of Parliament in the morning was interesting - a formal, pompous ceremony with a military inspection. Later I spent a couple of hours at an exhibit promoting Canadian tourism. 'You are going to parlez Francais,' and described the ways of life all over Canada."

"People were quite friendly there, especially at night when I went to a piano bar and a guy gave me a tambourine to play along with him and somebody bought me a beer. I picked up a cute mid 20's brunette there named Shirley Ann who wanted me to take her home, spend the night with her and drive her and her girlfriend to Toronto the next day. As I was driving, she lit up a joint and talked about having me look for a job in Toronto with them. But when we got to her house, some guy was pacing back and forth inside the big bay window. Shirley yelled, 'Oh God, that's my ex-husband! You have to get out of here.' She wrote down her phone number, kissed me quick and said, 'Call me tomorrow.' I went back to the Ritz. I never called her.

"I saved the best part of the trip for last. I went back to Montreal the next day and stayed at a cheap motel near Jarry Park, where the Expos play, and saw a major league game for the first time in four years. Bob Gibson pitched for the Cardinals, but the Expos beat them 2-1. At night, I dropped into a lively discotheque named Maxim's, but later I went to a quieter place called the Rockcliffe. Within a half hour, there was a very good looking tall 30ish lady checking me out at the end of the bar. She turned her back to the people next to her and crossed her legs my way. I asked her to dance to the first slow song that came on. French was her primary language, but she wanted to speak English better. We went to a quieter area of the bar, and talked for a couple of hours. Her name is Celine - she's 32 and 5'11! She was in a car accident three years ago, her pelvis was smashed, and she had to have a hysterectomy. Because of that, her husband got rid of her, and her divorce was about to become final very soon. She is in nursing school, and she does some modeling for cigarette commercials, even though she doesn't smoke. A lot of French I learned in school started to come back to me. Later, she said she would stay with me at my motel and sleep with me, but no sex because it had been a long time for her, and she was unsure if she was ready for that. "My bad luck continues," I thought.

At 9:15 am, we went to her place. She said she wanted to sleep longer in her bed, then she went into the bathroom. She came out naked. We had thoroughly enjoyable sex for the next hour, and we were both pleased that we were so compatible together. Later, we went to the Man and his World exhibit (The old Expo '67), the Jardin Botanique, took a walk through Old Montreal, and saw the Chateau de Ramesay museum. I had a great time, and I am thrilled with this lady. I can't wait to see her again. I would have stayed even longer, but I had just enough money to make it home. What a trip! I'd do it again if I ever got the time and money. I have to figure out when Celine and I will see each other. I'm hoping she gets a three day weekend in a few weeks, so I can spend some time together in Lake George."

El Guru sent him back a tape. "Cassette tapes are a great way to communicate, even though it's kind of one-sided both ways. It's better than a letter, and right now I don't have access to a phone call to the U.S. Hey, maybe we can go up to the Calgary Stampede someday.

"At least you're on a hot streak again. That lady Celine sounds really good. Too bad she's not 4 or 5 years younger. The beauty of it is that you can't get her pregnant, so you can have lots of fun. Ursula is coming back here in a few days. Maybe Ursula and I can start sending tapes to each other. I can't wait to see her again, too. I always preferred women closer in age to me, but she is a pleasant surprise. She's cute, she's smart, we can talk to each other about anything, and she's good in bed.

"I really don't want to go back to the U.S. with four more years of Nixon. McGovern screwed up by getting rid of Eagleton, and Shriver might've been better in the first place, but people won't vote for McGovern because of the way the whole thing was handled. So, we just keep dragging out the war in Vietnam that should've been over several years ago. I haven't heard of any great protests, so it seems like people in America are beaten down.

"I love working as a lab tech. Not only am I doing the same stuff you did a couple of years ago - urinalyses, gram stains, and CBCs - but I'm also enjoying my time as NCOIC. We have a good bunch of people in this unit right now. I found out if I can go to Ramstein AFB and make arrangements for a flight to the Torrejon, Spain AFB, then I can get an easy flight to the U.S. - all stand-by and costing nothing. I might try to do that for Labor Day weekend and tack on a few days of annual leave to see you. There has to be flights available to Newburgh or Plattsburgh, NY. I know they have Air Force Bases there."

Greg sent off a tape to El Guru right away. "I just came back from spending three days and nights with Celine in Lake George. We went to the beach, spent time in and out of all the shops, went out to dinner every night, and lots of great sex. We're communicating better verbally - I'm speaking more French, and she's speaking more English. I wound up paying the IRS $163 for the time I spent in Vietnam, plus $25 for taxes last year in Germany! The first time I'm in financial trouble after I get to Massachusetts, I am calling Ted Kennedy's office about this. My long-time friend Van is a mechanic and he has saved me money with maintenance on my car. I went to a New England Patriots exhibition game with a cousin of mine from Kingston who has season tickets for them. The Patriots stink, but Jim Plunkett and Randy Vataha are good. I also had a small winning day at the racetrack in Saratoga. Watch out for a horse named Secretariat, who will probably win the Kentucky Derby next year.

"My college roommate, Don, called me one day. He was hitchhiking around Granville or Whitehall, NY near the Vermont border, and he took a chance that I might be home. He left Pittsburgh because he broke up with his fiancée, and he just wanted to travel around for a while. I met him in Glens Falls, and he was on the road again. Unfortunately, he can't get me World Series tickets if the Pirates make it again."

On the evening of August 30th Greg was home and got a phone call from El Guru who had arrived at Sault St. Marie AFB in Michigan. He explained that he got a flight from Ramstein the day before to Torrejon AFB in Madrid, and they said he could fly standby right away to the US. He couldn't get a flight to Newburgh or Plattsburgh for a couple of days without a connection to Dover, Delaware, but he could fly standby to Griffiss AFB in Rome, NY, first thing in the morning.

"You just did this on the spur of the moment?"

"I told you I might be able to pull it off. Do you have room for me there?"

"I'm sure we will. My father can be a bastard at times, but he'll welcome anyone who is a war veteran. My mother is a nice lady. My sister is nice, too - she lives 20 miles away so we might not get to see her. My brother calls himself a prick but he will really like to talk international politics and sports with you."

"Sounds like it's OK to come then?"

"Yeah, a distant cousin might come up from New York City - he's a colorful character. If there's no room we'll get a place near Lake George."

"What about Celine? Will I get to meet her?"

"I can't see her for at least a few months. I have to save money for grad school and she's saving money for nursing school. I just got a small, one room place in Massachusetts for $30 a week with a tiny fridge and hot plate. I may to make friends fast, look for handouts on food and drink cheap beer. I will lose weight."

"You were always great at stretching money. I'll call you when I get into Rome tomorrow, probably around noon."

"OK, what a surprise. It'll be great to see you."

Greg's parents said there would be no problem with El Guru staying at the house. The next morning at 10:30, El Guru called and Greg drove to Rome. Greg got there in the afternoon, and took El Guru through Albany. El Guru remarked that part of the Hudson River reminded him of the Rhine River. El Guru talked all about his girlfriend Ursula and remarked that Celine sounded like the best lady Greg had ever met in his life, "Even if she is an oldie, she's a goodie."

"It's hard to see her when she's over 200 miles away, but I'll try to keep it going until she starts screaming that she wants me to move up there and get married and speak mostly French. There were a few subtle hints about that last week."

They got to Greg's house, and after introductions (as Artie) and having a beer with Danny, they ate dinner. Danny, who was a Senior in college majoring in Political Science, was impressed that El Guru knew all about the DIA as well as the CIA. His cousin Mart from New York talked with El Guru about the few years he spent out in Colorado and they conversed about the differences between the western and eastern US. El Guru had never been to the East Coast.

They drove to suburban Albany later to hit a couple of night spots. At Harold's Office, there were about 100 people, all in their 20s, where they met Alan, a neighborhood friend of Greg's who had just been discharged from the Army himself. Alan now spoke fairly fluent Spanish and he and El Guru hit it off well, bantering back and forth in a mix of Spanish and English. The three of them had a discussion about the growing racial problems in the Army.

Greg said, "Let's all go to Rudy's. They have that great new group there called Tavares that I told you about. I bet there'll be about 200 people there. It's on the order of Lord Nelson's in Dusseldorf, only bigger." They enjoyed the music and danced briefly with a couple of ladies. Tavares sang a spellbinding a capella "Ol' Man River" to thunderous applause at the end.

The next day, Greg took El Guru for a ride around some of the town in the Adirondack region, as well as Albany, Schenectady, and Troy, and into Vermont. El Guru was impressed with the smaller towns and cities. He liked Saratoga Springs and Lake George, especially the Revolutionary War battlefield at Saratoga. He wanted to watch as much sports as he could on TV. They watched parts of Yankees, Mets, and Red Sox games. The NHL Team Canada played the Russians for the first time ever. Pre-season pro football games were on TV, too. The Olympics were also taking place. El Guru exclaimed, "Those Israeli athletes got gunned down like it was the St. Valentine's Day Massacre!" El Guru was in heaven watching all these sports.

The next day El Guru talked a lot about international politics and violence with Greg and Danny. They discussed whether what had happened at the Olympics could happen in the US or elsewhere in Germany, or in England. Danny said, "We're too civilized for that to happen here. If anything, it'll be blacks versus whites in a big city."

Greg said, "If it's one thing I've learned in life your never say 'never' or, 'it can't happen here.' Look how the world has changed since Kennedy got shot."

El Guru said, "The whole world had to change because people thought that we would go along smoothly because nothing happened with the Cuban Missile Crisis. But then, the whole racial thing built up and you had one segment of people who didn't want to change and another big segment of younger people who did, or else they would rebel. People worldwide generally are still uneasy or angry. There's a gang in Germany now called The Baader Meinhof who believe that terror is the only way to create change."

El Guru left early in the morning. Greg drove him to Griffiss AFB. He couldn't get a flight out until 6:00 pm so they went to the Baseball Hall of Fame in Cooperstown for several hours. El Guru was in awe of the place and wished he could stay longer.

"Thanks a lot for taking me here, Greg. Never in a million years did I ever think I'd get to see the Hall of Fame and it's even more than I dreamed it would be. I love this whole, unique, small town part of New York. I'm so glad I made this trip. Can you imagine if they had trains running here like they do in Europe?"

"That's because gas here is still 30 cents a gallon and not 10 times as much as it is over there. The Interstate Highway System killed the railroads."

"They could probably coexist, though."

"They're trying with Amtrak between larger cities, but I don't think it'll last. It's kind of expensive. I think that's the only way to go to New York City though."

El Guru later got a flight to Dover AFB, from there to Torrejon, Spain, and by the next night he arrived at Ramstein AFB and back to Prum.

Chapter 16

Greg Goes Back to School and El Guru Gets Out of the Army

Greg mostly hung out with Van until it was time to leave for his new tiny apartment in Worcester, MA, a few hours away. His first impression of Worcester was not good. He got two parking tickets, one of which was written as he got in the car and was about to drive away. His landlord had a PO Box and when he went to the Post Office to the mail clerk to pay his rent, he was ordered to go outside and put it in the mailbox. Also, in Massachusetts, you have to go to a separate liquor store to buy even a six pack of beer.

One good surprise happened after the first weekend. Greg was walking downtown when he turned a corner and suddenly saw his old Army friend, Buck Williams.

"Buck! What are you doing here? Great to see you, man!"

"I'm going back to school here to finish my degree and get a double major in Pre-Med and Political Science."

"You had only one semester to go, didn't you?"

"Yeah, but like I told you last year, I'm gonna try to go to medical school. It'll take almost two years of coursework and I'll graduate with about 170 credits, but it's really what I want to do. I'm working at St. Vincent's Hospital on the evening shift. I'm an orderly but they're letting me do some other things - TPRs and BPs. The head nurse for the evening shift is great. She's like a 32-year old brunette Barbie Doll. Did you decide to go to grad school here?"

"Yeah. I start classes tomorrow. Most of them are late afternoon or evening. I hope that you can be a support system for me. You must know a lot of people here."

"They're all gone. They've all graduated in the past few years. I have a sister who's a Freshman, but she has her own friends."

They went to a Holiday Inn bar, talked for almost two hours catching up on what had happened in their lives in the past nine months, and exchanged addresses. Buck was renting a room in a private home. He had a phone; Greg couldn't afford one until his first GI Bill check came. Greg agreed to call him a couple of times a week to get together when Buck wasn't working or studying for an exam. Buck agreed to stop by Greg's apartment when he was free.

El Guru sent Greg a tape around the first few days of October. "I'm pretty broke, but it was worth the great time with you in New York. Ursula is coming up every few weeks. Col. Lindberg, Sgt. Major Dennis, and Master Sgt. Greene came over the hospital for a surprise inspection of our clinic while I was working in the lab, just as I was on the phone telling Ursula that I was short of cash. Lindberg overheard this and asked me if I was selling drugs! I told him I never did that, and just as I said it Greene accidentally hit my arm and the tube of urine I had in my hand went all over Lindberg's shoes. Greene and I thought it was funny, but embarrassing. They got out of there fast. Ursula and I spent a day in Aachen. As we walked by our old hotel, the desk clerk, who was coming to work, smiled and said, 'Guten Tag, Mr. Horning!' I had to explain to Ursula about my alias - she thought it was weird.

"I got a letter from a cousin in New Mexico who said that Albuquerque has just about the highest crime rate in the US right now - drug busts and murders, believe it or not. He told me a few old friends didn't make it back from Vietnam. He said Mexicans, Indians, blacks and whites don't interact as much with each other. My Port of Call is now for November 1st, and a few days later my ETS will be at Ft. Dix. I want to come up there and see you and Buck Williams. Wasn't that good luck you saw him on the street? I always liked Buck."

Greg did lots of studying, and he volunteered to give a case presentation in one class concerning one of his patients in Germany because he hoped it would help his grade for the course. The other classes involved writing lots of papers. The first round of exams were take-home essay questions but had to be turned in to the department by 9:00 am the next morning. Going back to school after several years away was both anxiety evoking and motivating. He and Celine wrote to each other about every two weeks and called each other occasionally once he got his phone. She came down one weekend. He showed her around the area, they went out to a club dancing, and generally had a great time.

Greg and Buck unsuccessfully started looking for a place together. One landlord told them, "Absolutely no visitors." Another person was ready to rent to them until he found out they were "students." A third couple said they would raise the rate by $100 from what was listed in the paper because there would be two people moving in instead of one. Buck liked his job, and Greg was getting more comfortable back in school after his mid-term grades were mostly A's.

On the night of November 2nd, El Guru appeared at Greg's place, still in uniform. "I didn't have time to call, so I flew to Boston. A guy I met on the plane gave me a ride," he said.

Greg hugged him, saying "Artie, get out of those dress greens - look at all the medals from six years! You're a civilian now. I can call you 'Mr. Guerrero' now. How does it feel?"

"Great, but I will really miss Germany and Ursula. Let's call Buck Williams."

"He's either working or asleep but we'll go over and see him tomorrow morning. I thought you would be going home to New Mexico."

"I am, but I can spend a few days here if it's OK."

"Of course, my pad is a little cramped. Take my bed and I'll sleep on the floor. I'll buy an air mattress somewhere tomorrow."

They saw Buck the next day and El Guru caught him up on what was happening with the Army in Germany. Greg later had to go to the school library to research some professional journal articles for a paper he was writing. El Guru wanted to go downtown and walk around for a couple of hours and Greg said he would meet him back at the apartment.

At 5:00, El Guru came back to Greg's place and said that a couple of girls told him about a place called the Peacock Club. Greg said that it was not too far from his place, and they had a band and dancing. He warned El Guru that Worcester seemed like a cliquish city. Greg also mentioned that regarding meeting women, Celine would be hard to beat, and he showed El Guru her picture. El Guru wondered why she was in Nursing school when she could make a lot more money as a model. Greg replied that, "She's just a student like me and Buck. I think she understands that I don't have a lot of money now and can't go up to see her."

"I just got paid. Let's go bar hopping tonight."

At 9:30, they went to a bar called Sir Morgan's Cove. There was a good band playing a set of Beatles' songs - rockers. Greg had never been there before but they really liked the band even though they were loud. Somebody at the bar told them the name of the band was Aerosmith. Then they decided to go to Will's - a bar with a jukebox, where at times some people danced on the sawdust floor. A Boston Bruins game was on TV. El Guru remarked that he was never really interested in hockey but he liked the bar. Greg said that it was the closest bar to his apartment; a place to watch a game, listen to good music on the jukebox, and had good bartenders.

El Guru remarked, "A couple of these older babes look good. Watch this."

There was a late '60s song playing on the jukebox and a couple was dancing. He asked two different ladies to dance. One shot him down, the other didn't even pay any attention to him and a big guy standing nearby told him to leave her alone. He came back to the bar and said to Greg, "Let's get out of this place. I don't deserve to get treated like shit." He gulped the rest of his beer and they went out the door.

They went downtown to The Office, another fairly good bar that Greg had been to once. El Guru wanted to get a table because he thought it would change his luck, and he did dance with an attractive girl to a couple of songs. At the end of the second dance she started getting angry at him as they were walking off the floor and she stormed back to her table. Greg asked him, "What the hell happened?"

"The small talk went good. I started complimenting her on her hair and her body and I told her she must work out, and she could work out with me. She said she just turned 21 and liked guys even older than me and giggled. I told her 'Hey, you don't have to ball a father figure - how about me?' She got pissed off."

"You got to watch your mouth, again. Women's Lib is in full force everywhere. I know it's hard for you to get used to, but this ain't exactly 1966."

Just then, the girl came by on her way to the ladies' room and yelled at him, "And I'm not looking for any father figure, creep!"

Greg decided that they should go home to avoid the possibility of getting a DWI.

They met Buck for lunch the next day at a sandwich shop, and El Guru ordered "a roast beef sub." Buck told him that here it was "called a 'grinder,' and they will toast it." El Guru thought that was weird, but he enjoyed it. After talking a little bit about the upcoming Presidential election, El Guru suggested that Greg and Buck should get a place to live together. They both said that they were trying, but after the first of the year was more likely.

That night Greg and El Guru went to the Peacock Club to see if they could find the girls El Guru had met the day before. The girls didn't show up; there were mostly couples there, and the few unaccompanied ladies shot them down.

"These damn women in this town are probably so conservative that I bet the place closes at midnight so they can all go to church in the morning, "El Guru said.

"It's your first weekend out of the Army and you're pissed. You should be celebrating."

"I was hoping to have sex, but the chicks here are a bunch of tight-asses."

"You sound like a baby in a high chair with a hard-on crying, 'I want to get laid! You can't try to score with a chick after a few minutes of rapping any more. It doesn't work like that now, for anybody. It's an adjustment coming back to America in a lot of ways. I'm still feeling it. Why do you think I took off for Canada this summer? Why do you think Celine wasn't a one-nighter? She's kind of foreign, in a way. As it turns out, though, she's probably better than any American lady I've met in a long time, even though she's older."

"You're getting too damn conservative now."

"You use that line for anybody or anything you don't agree with. Let's go home."

The next day, they took a ride into Connecticut, but the fall foliage was gone everywhere. They met Buck for a hamburger at Gino's later on. El Guru declared that maybe he was more of a Western guy than an Eastern guy. Buck told him that adjusting to America would take months, maybe, but El Guru would be OK. He echoed Greg's words that, "The '60s are long gone."

In the morning, Greg gave El Guru a ride to Logan Airport in Boston to catch a plane to Albuquerque from there. They didn't think that they would see each other again for at least a few years unless one of them won money in a state lottery.

Greg said to him, "I hope you have a good time in New Mexico and get a car, a job, a girlfriend, and a good place to live soon. Bottom line - that's it's all about. Maybe you can persuade Ursula to come over."

"Yeah, you're right, now that we're out of the Army and getting on with our lives. Good luck with Celine. Let's stay in touch by tapes. Hey, I'm sorry if you thought I was a pain in the ass. It just hit me this morning when I got up, how I should've acted a lot better and I shouldn't have said some things I said."

Greg was busy with exams and writing papers for the rest of the month. At the end of the month he got a tape from El Guru. "I got my own place, like yours - small, weekly rent. The car I got is a '63 Chevy. Load of miles on it but they made them good that year. My cousin was right - there is crime everywhere and police are everywhere. I want to speak more Spanish but the girls here only want to speak English and I don't like that. Nobody is talking about Nixon and Watergate here. Since he got re-elected people forget so damn fast.

"Hey, who sang 'The Pope Smokes Dope' that you played for me up there? Send it to me on tape if you can. People here don't believe there is such a song, probably because they're all supposedly Catholics. It is a catchy tune, actually. I started reading *The Interpretation of Dreams*, by Sigmund Freud, and it's fascinating. You should read it.

"It's been really cold here lately. They even got a few inches of snow here yesterday and these damn people don't know how to drive in it. I was laughing at them at first, skidding off the road, but then I thought, 'Wow - what if I get hit?' It's rare that we get much snow here. I could never live where you live because of the ice and snow in the winter. I miss Ursula."

Greg responded a couple of weeks later, "Welcome back to Christmastime in America. Why don't you try to go back to school next semester, or is it too late to apply? I'm just hitting the books with all the tests and papers. Buck helps me with the typing when he's available and I buy him lunch but he eats like a bird. We are moving into a place together right after the first of the year in a shaky part of town. It's a big 3rd floor apartment. The landlord seems like an old drunkard. Celine wants me to go up there for Christmas but I can't because I'm broke. She's probably going to get rid of me. I have just enough money to buy people in my family some cheap presents for Christmas. David Peel and the Lower East Side does 'The Pope Smokes Dope.' Even Buck hums it. I got it from Van, my friend from back home. I think I've finally adjusted to being back in the academic world. I will send you a Christmas card from me and Buck with our new address."

Around Christmas, El Guru replied with a tape. "It is hard getting adjusted to living here. I tried to open a bank account and they wouldn't accept a passport as an ID! I threw a fit, and I demanded to see the manager who gave me a line of crap first. He apologized but it was too late. I wonder if it's my beard, the way I was dressed, or because I'm letting my hair grow, but I have rights. I went to another bank and everything was OK. This would never happen in Europe.

"Nightlife here is pitiful - all country music. Unemployment checks are coming inconsistently. I'm optimistic things will get better, either here or someplace else, but it's frustrating living here again. Merry Christmas and Happy New Year. Anyway, I think both of us have had a really good year and thanks for being part of the last two years and all the great times we had together. I hope I can move on with my life at least as well as you and Buck are doing."

Chapter 17

Another Shocker From El Guru

Greg was at his parents' house on New Year's Day. After he took a shower and got dressed at 10:00, his mother told him, "Your friend Artie is on the phone."

"Hey, El Guru, Happy New Year. What's up - did you score last night?"

"No. Roberto Clemente got killed in a plane crash late last night."

"What! Clemente! What the hell happened?"

"He was on a cargo plane delivering relief supplies and his plane went down in the Gulf of Mexico."

"Whoa! I am stunned! Thanks for telling me. Are you doing OK otherwise? Are you looking for a job?"

"I can't find a job, and you can milk unemployment benefits only so long. I might not even stay here - maybe I'll go to El Paso or California. I don't have enough money to go back to school, even with the GI Bill."

"Something will break for you. It's a big city there. Why don't you go to a junior college and transfer to New Mexico later? The GI Bill would cover that."

"No. I'd have to work part-time or full-time, anyway. Look, I gotta run. Stay in touch. Say hi to Buck for me when you get back to Massachusetts."

"What a way to start the year," Greg thought.

After Greg arrived at the new apartment, Buck told him several things he learned from living there for a week. He overheard one of the people downstairs saying that the landlord never gives a security deposit back. "The oven doesn't work right and the landlord won't fix it—at least I have a good toaster oven for us. There is a psychotic lady on the first floor who yells at night periodically. The girls who live on the floor below us are hookers and they have a pimp called Pee Wee. The bathtub drains really slow. There's no lock on the back door, just a night latch on a chain. To top it off, snow removal on this street is poor. We might not stay here more than six months if we can't stand it anymore. At least the lease is month to month."

"Time will tell if we made a mistake."

Greg took barely a full credit load because two required courses were offered at the same time and there were no electives which interested him, which meant he would have to enroll for two courses that summer. He started working 20 hours a week selling women's shoes (which he did for a year in college) because the GI Bill only paid for part of the academic expenses.

In February, he went to see an IRS agent who strongly recommended that he file amendments for the taxes he had paid the two previous years, along with copies of his military pay vouchers (fortunately, Greg had saved all these documents), and he declared that Greg deserved a refund. Buck, who was turning out to be a good roommate, did lots of studying, sleeping, working, and talking about sports. There were no difficulties sharing expenses. Greg and Celine still called each other every few weeks. He thought for sure she would have dumped him by now but they both wanted to continue the long-distance relationship. Strangely, he had not heard from El Guru - he had no response from a tape he spent at the end of January, asking his thoughts on the final ending of the Vietnam war. A letter to El Guru in early March was returned to him stamped: "Moved, Left No Forwarding Address."

Finally, a tape from El Guru arrived on March 18th with an APO address. El Guru said, "Well, I decided to go back in the Army on Groundhog Day because I wanted to get back to living in Germany. My life was going nowhere in New Mexico. I think I can help change the Army system with the young guys, and now that there is no more war, things should get better. There were too many hard-core drug addicts in Albuquerque, and girls there are cliquish and they don't want to speak any Spanish. My direct approach with them doesn't work anymore - they either want to be romanced or are turning into Women's Libbers instead of straight-shooting types who want to discuss their opinions and look at all sides of the issues.

The corruption and favoritism politically are sickening in the US, and it trickles down from Tricky Dick in the White House. I hadn't gotten an unemployment check in over a month. You asked me to sit down and write my philosophy of life now that I'm turning 25. Well, I'm too upset to do it right now, and I have at least 40 more years left to look back and do that. I've been going through changes for a few months now.

"This time I'm in Bremerhaven. I met a 23-year old lady named Ingrid who is the most mature female I've met in a long time. I told Ursula I was back, but we kind of decided not to see each other again because the distance is just too far, and that's probably what will happen with you and Celine someday. Maybe I can move in with Ingrid some point soon. I had a great time with her on my birthday - she's really into pleasing a man. She wants to learn Spanish from me. She really makes me feel special.

"Nobody works very hard here at the hospital, unlike central or southern Germany. I'm working the day shift of a Med-Surg ward right now. The census has been low. One problem with this hospital it that it's far away from Dusseldorf, Cologne, Aachen, and especially Luxembourg. Let me know how you and Buck are doing."

Greg called Buck over to listen to the tape. "You won't believe this shit. Artie went back into the Army!"

"He did what?"

"Listen to this! I'm shocked and pissed at him right now. How could he be so dumb?"

"Where the hell is he, anyway? Not that far away from here, I hope."

"He's in Bremerhaven, Germany - way up north."

"Germany again. Did his old girlfriend move up there with him?"

"No. He broke up with her and found another woman that weekend."

'Let me listen to the tape."

Buck listened intently to the tape. He thought it was a good move for El Guru to get out of Albuquerque, but to surrender his freedom to attempt to heroically change a military system was asinine. Greg thought El Guru didn't give himself enough of a chance to even try to get a job as a lab tech. They both agreed they might not see El Guru again for years.

Greg wrote El Guru a letter expressing his displeasure with the rash decision, but he hoped they could remain friends. El Guru wrote back that it was his choice and that life in America, at least in New Mexico, was a dead end for him. El Guru said, "Right now the establishment and lifers in this system screw over American Indians and Chicanos as much as young blacks. There is a lack of promotions for enlisted men, no decent assignments in the system open to them, and the system comes down harder than it should for punishments. That has to change if everybody cooperates. I can try to help turn that around." He also said, "I quit smoking anything, but if someone offers hash to me wanting to talk about politics or race relations, I will do it. A lot of these 18 and 19-year-old guys are hard to relate to, though. They seem like they're sullen, even angry at times. What's that phrase you used to say - 'passive-aggressive.' That fits the description of most of these kids. They look at their time in Europe as a jail sentence instead of all the great things they could experience."

Over the next couple of months, he sent Greg a few tapes bitching about Nixon, Haldeman, and Ehrlichman, how the American public is dumb regarding Watergate and how ignorant most American GIs in Europe are about politics in the US. He said, "Maybe a revolution is what we need. I'm in for that if that's what it takes but it has to be non-violent in nature. You know, if people learn as many languages as they can and try to communicate with people of all ages, races, and nationalities without making quick judgements, they would be far better off because those things would mature them as human beings. One thing I have learned from you is that we are all human beings first." He said his favorite song was 'The Cisco Kid' and he really likes the group, War (ironic name). The lifers there wanted him to go up before the E-6 Board, but he refused. He said, "I don't want to be classified as establishment until things start changing here for lower ranking enlisted men. Buck would be proud of me for that."

Celine came down to see Greg at the end of April. She met Buck and thought he was a great guy. When Buck left for the night shift at the hospital, Greg tried to make up for lost time sexually, but he overdid it. A few times in the next 8 to 9 hours was a bit much for the both of them. She didn't want to take a shower together this time. Greg went to work at 10, and later in the afternoon, she drove to the department store where Greg worked. He introduced her to Claudine, a French lady in her late 30's who was a beautician across from the shoe department. When business was slow, sometimes Greg would have conversations with Claudine. Greg's boss gave him permission to leave early because Celine was there, and things were getting slow.

Celine said, "Your amie, Claudine, is tres chic."

"She said the same thing about you when you went over to see the dresses," Greg replied.

"Claudine likes you. You know she is married - avec children."

"She is no threat to you."

"Let us see where 'Love Story' was made. Allons-y."

They drove to Cambridge and had a hard time finding a place to park, but after they did, they walked around and disagreed regarding whether or not it was a great movie. They had a late dinner, and Greg suggested that they go out dancing for a couple of hours. Buck was just leaving for work when they got back. More sex. He thought, "It was really worth the six months wait."

On Sunday after Buck left for work, Greg wanted her again, but just as they got started, she wanted to stop. She said, "Tonight we sleep!" After breakfast, she told Greg as she was leaving that he was, "pas charmante - not like last year." However, she still wanted him to come to Canada to meet her friends and family. Both would be not be through with their coursework and internships until December, but she felt they could make time to see each other after the summer. As she left, Greg thought, "I bet she'll get rid of me. I don't know where this is going." He asked Buck what he thought of her, and he said, "She's a cool chick, but too bad she's not 5 to 10 years younger."

Greg and Buck decided that they had to leave their residence after their semesters were over. The psychotic lady started a fire in her kitchen, but everyone in the building was safe, thanks to a rapid response from the fire department. One night the landlord caught the girls downstairs in the middle of an orgy, and he evicted them in May. Needles and syringes were outside the door.

El Guru sent Greg cassette tapes several times during the summer. He mentioned that there were racial problems and major drug problems in most military bases in Germany. "The stubbornness of the lifers and the brass is reflected in their massive denial that anything is wrong with the system. They enrolled me in this NCO course for a month - it was a pain in the ass getting up at 4 am. Remember Brent, the black dude who lived off grounds who used to call you 'Jimmy James?' He's here TDY in the NCO class with me, and he said that the problems with the younger GIs in Bad Kreuznach are the same as they are here. He says 'hi' to you and Buck.

"If Nixon isn't impeached, he could turn into another Hitler, but it looks like John Dean and Butterfield really blew the whistle on him. Ingrid is a great cook, sex is good, but there's not a lot else we have in common. Sounds like things could be better with you and Celine, too. Go up to Montreal and see her, or try to meet an American woman. I'm missing Ursula again.

"It's anybody's guess who will get into the World Series. The Pirates aren't the same without Clemente, and Steve Blass can't throw a strike. The Dolphins won't go undefeated again; the Vikings look like the best team in the NFL. The German DM has now dropped all the way down to 2.50 to a dollar, which I think started when Nixon had that wage-price freeze a couple of years ago. More and more, it's looking like I made a big mistake going back into the Army. I definitely want to go back to school when I get out."

Greg and Buck couldn't find an apartment together, so they got two separate places a mile away from each other. Greg spent a good part of the summer doing an internship with six to nine-year-old kids. He organized a Monopoly tournament and a whiffle ball league, as well as playing with trucks and cars, making things in sandboxes, and painting pictures with the kids. Although he liked the kids, working with the parents could be frustrating. In one case, he swore it was the fault of the first-grade teacher that the kid was even in the program. As a result, he decided that he wanted to work with adults only, if he were to have a career in mental health. The other graduate students in the program there - Dick, Ben, Peggy, and Paul - were all very likeable people and Greg car pooled with them. But he stopped receiving a GI Bill check for several months and he was low on cash; he had to go to Senator Ted Kennedy's office in Boston at the end of July to get it straightened out. At least he got paid back with interest for his IRS amended claims of the prior 3 years, which helped him make it through the summer financially.

Gas prices started rising and almost doubled. Greg got a part-time job selling shoes again at another department store in late August. He called Celine to see if he could visit her in Montreal, but she told him she was moving into a new apartment and it would be better for him to come up there at another time. He offered to help her move, but she rejected that idea. "Another bad omen for this relationship," he thought.

El Guru called Greg early in October. "Greg, I got to talk to you. It's important."

"Artie, this is costing you your ass. What's up?'

"No, it's costing the hospital. I found an open line they never disconnected at this place, exactly like a few years ago in Bad Kreuznach, so I can call once in a great while when I work evenings or nights if I don't get caught ghosting. Otherwise, we keep sending tapes. But that's not why I called. We're on alert to go someplace far away TDY, and it could be dangerous. That's all I can tell you. I just wanted to let you know."

Oh, man! Are you gonna get involved in that Israel-Egypt flare-up?"

"Like I said, I can't tell you."

"What a mental error is was for you to go back into the Army! From what I've read and saw on TV news, it seems like Golda Meir and Moshe Dayan control the United States."

"Israel does not control the United States! The United States controls Israel!"

"Isn't Sadat the good guy is this thing? It looks like he wants to open up the Suez Canal, that's all."

"You are so fucking naïve! I think he wants to destroy Israel."

"You know, gas prices keep going up over here because of this crap."

"You're talking out of your ass! This could lead to another World War."

"Is that what they're thinking over there?"

"This is Nixon wanting to avoid impeachment. It's not about the Arabs and the Jews."

"He wants us to get involved in their crap so it's a distraction for his problems. Start a war. We can't support the rest of the world anymore. People in Europe should know that."

"You're right about that. We're out of Vietnam now. Somebody would assassinate Nixon if we started a major involvement anywhere in the world. But I can't tell you what kind of operation this is—it's classified information."

"This might be 1967 all over again, or a lot worse. Just cover your ass and stay safe."

"If I don't go anywhere, I'll send you a tape in a few weeks. I have to cut this call off."

Chapter 18

A Bad Ending to the Year

Greg got a call from Celine asking him to come up for Canadian Thanksgiving weekend and her 34th birthday. He couldn't go because he had just been notified that the department store where he was selling shoes was going out of business in October, and his hours were being cut to 10 per week. This meant he would not have enough money for the trip. Since she was a full-time student herself, she couldn't make the trip to see Greg. There was some arguing over the phone. Greg thought, "This has got to be the end for us. This would last longer if I had a regular job."

Late one night, around the end of October, a dude who was stoned slammed into Greg's car and totaled it. His passenger ran away just as the police showed up ("Probably had a lot of dope on him," Greg thought). Two minutes later another car crash happened 20 yards away from Greg's. It took over an hour for the police to sort everything out. At least Greg wasn't hurt more than a whiplash, but he had to buy a cheap used car ('67 Mercury Comet), which cost him $350 and it also needed ball joints and newer tires. To top off October, one afternoon Greg bought a winning lottery ticket for $50 but a minute later it blew out the window into traffic! At least Greg was able to limp home to NY with his Mercury Comet and Van, a great amateur mechanic, repaired what was needed. This wiped out his GI Bill money for November until the insurance check for $500 came through just before Thanksgiving. Buck was so busy he and Greg rarely saw or called each other.

El Guru sent Greg a tape on November 3rd. For two and a half weeks on the "Top Secret" mission (during the Arab-Israeli War) he had been sent down to Landstuhl where he worked in an ER and on a surgical ward with hardly any time off at all. He was upset that they sent him anywhere because he was not a Special Forces medic. When he got back to Bremerhaven, he was informed that he and some other medics were going to be isolated in a room for a week with their meals brought to them because they might be needed back at Landstuhl. In typical Army fashion, they didn't go anywhere. He was angry; Ingrid said that she couldn't tolerate such crap anymore, and she dumped him. He said in the tape, "Ingrid really didn't surprise me. I still miss Ursula more than ever, though. I will try to see if I can get transferred to Stuttgart to get back with Ursula. I have some leave time coming, so I could try to go down there and look her up." He was only able to get a newspaper twice that month and had no access to a radio.

Greg heard from El Guru again in mid-December. "A bunch of guys are being sent elsewhere. One Spec/4 was sent to Stuttgart because they suspected he was a hash dealer and he wasn't. I wanted to trade places with him to get back with Ursula, but Personnel wouldn't do it. Maybe I'll try to get back with Ingrid to get through the winter. It's cold and snowy every few days and I hate being in these cold barracks. I still have a little old VW Bug, but gas prices are going way up here and we can't buy gas on Sundays now.

"I still think the Vikings will get into the Super Bowl and win. I bet you spent all your money going to the last two Patriots games. I'm sending you a pipe for Christmas—no, there's no dope in it—but with a can of Rum and Maple tobacco, like you used to keep in your room. At least you don't smoke cigars any more. Tricky Dick ordered those Special Prosecutors fired six weeks ago and he still didn't get impeached yet. It looks like he'll pull it out of his ass and Americans will be stuck with him for another three years. Have a Merry Christmas; your time in Worcester should be up soon. I hope you graduate in January and land a job pretty quick."

Celine sent Greg a Christmas card with a letter saying she wanted him to come up to Montreal for New Year's Eve, so they could do some serious talking, ("parler serieux"). It took him a few days to respond back, saying he couldn't make it and would try to call her sometime after the first of the year. He had a job interview in northern Vermont and he told her if he got the job, he could see her more often. They would never hear from each other again, but he knew that this was the end anyway. The language difference, the physical location difference, the age difference, and lack of money were all too difficult to overcome, from his perspective.

Greg spent a great deal of time on a required research course which was difficult for him but he really like the professor, Dr. Angie Varney, personally and professionally. She guided him through his research project - simulated gambling was the main topic. The end result was to do an experiment and write a paper good enough to submit for publication in a professional journal. Greg met his friend Ben coming out of a building on campus after the last of the final exams. Ben said, "Hey, man, it's all over except for the Comprehensive Exam."

"I still have to write up and type the experiment for Dr. Varney."

"Good. Let's celebrate and go to the Plaza (restaurant). Everybody knows me there. I was raised on good Italian food."

The Plaza looked like Italian restaurants in big cities - dimly lit booths along the sides, with overhanging Tiffany-like lamps, and several tables in the middle of the room that could be combined for big parties. Four older Italian men in the back-corner table stopped what they were doing and stared at Greg when he walked in the door. They all brightened up when they saw Ben behind him. Suddenly, almost everyone inside got up and gave Ben smiles, handshakes, hugs, and wanted him to introduce his friend. Greg felt a little uneasy with this and the questions they asked him, but the Italian meal was probably the best he ever had.

Ben grinned and said, as they left, "Good thing you're half-Italian. Hey, I might see you out partying somewhere tonight. This celebration isn't over for me yet."

Later that evening, Greg dropped into Flannery's for a beer and there was Ben dancing with a lady on the crowded dance floor. Ben suddenly glanced over at the bar, saw Greg, and waved with a smile. After dancing, Ben called him over to the table where he was with several ladies, and introduced Greg to a girl named Carole, whispering, "This is your type of woman. I'm gonna take my chick home."

Right away, Greg had a couple of slow dances with Carole, an attractive, mid 20s blonde secretary. She insisted on going home with her girlfriends, but she gave Greg her address and phone number. Greg left immediately, and when he got to his apartment, he spent the rest of the night revising the entire experiment. He called Carole the next morning and she surprisingly agreed to type most of his paper for him that night. She told him to come over at 7:30 when her small kids were in bed. Greg thanked her profusely as he left her house at 9:30. He asked her out for Saturday night but she shot him down. However, she said she would like to meet him at Flannery's Friday night with her girlfriends. He told her he had a job interview for a counseling position in northern Vermont, but when he got back around 10:00 pm he would go to Flannery's.

Greg went home and made a load of mistakes typing the last few pages. He called Buck who came over to help him type up the rest of the experiment.

Buck asked, "What time does this have to be in tomorrow?"

"Midnight tonight."

"Jesus Christ! You didn't tell me that!"

"I screwed up. I thought I could do it myself, but I'm exhausted."

At 11:45, they zoomed over to Dr. Varney's office and arrived at midnight. They got a janitor to open her door and get put his paper on her desk, but there were no other papers there. Greg said to Buck, "Damnit, looks like she came and went. I hope I don't get an Incomplete for the course, which will look like hell on my transcript."

The nightmare for Greg continued the next day. At 10:30 he took off for a small college in Vermont for a job interview. He thought that if he got this job, it would kick-start his career. Up in Vermont it started raining and snowing intermittently, it became very foggy, and he was almost an hour late for his interview. He accidentally walked into a room on the campus where some administrators were discussing which 10 faculty members to fire. When he arrived at the correct building, he slipped on the ice and fell into a snowbank. Once inside, he saw two people playing cards. The guy said, "Are you the Greg James we've been waiting for all afternoon? It's miserable out there why did you bother to come? Here - have a glass of wine. I'll call Barbara (the department director who lived on grounds with her husband) and maybe we'll go over to her place to see if we all feel like interviewing you."

The interview went fairly well, Greg thought, but her dog did not like him and kept growling and barking at him most of the time while she giggled. "For $7,000 a year I could stay for two semesters and move on," Greg thought. An hour later, as he was leaving the campus, it started sleeting. He picked up a Biology prof hitchhiking at the campus entrance who asked if he could have a ride to Montpelier. The prof had just been fired, and as Greg dropped him off, he said, "You really should start looking for another job because this college is in financial trouble."

A few blocks away, Greg's car skidded on the ice and knocked the ice off a pickup truck. They guy he hit was irate, cursing about people from New York. He was drunk, and yelled at Greg, "This will cost $150 and you will pay for it, you son of a bitch!"

"Bullshit! It's a little scratch."

Just then a cop arrived. He took statements from Greg and the other guy, whose brother also showed up, encouraging them to "get the whole thing settled and get out of here because it's snowing like hell now."

The cop said, "This isn't even $50 worth of damage. I'm not even going to report it, and it's not even worth reporting to an insurance company."

The drunken guy said, "So, the people of Vermont get fucked over by incompetent cops!"

"You give me any more trouble and I will pull you in for a blood alcohol test. Remember I let you go last summer at that fight outside of town. Get in your truck and go home!"

The cop called Greg over and told him to be on his way, and that gas stations in Vermont were closing at 6:00. As Greg started to drive away after the cop left, the drunk called out to Greg, "You better pray, baby, you better pray!"

He followed Greg down I-89 for about 40 miles, through the driving snow before Greg lost him. Later, Greg neared the New Hampshire state line and skidded down the exit ramp. He made it to Hanover, NH, where his car stopped dead at a gas pump. Then he drove on through sleet and fog with no one going faster than about 35 mph. He wound up at another gas station near New London, NH., after which he skidded down a hill. Then he unfortunately took a wrong turn and didn't get home until long after Flannery's had closed.

He called Carole the next morning who said she had waited for him with her friends, but they left after 11:30. When he told her what had happened, she didn't believe him. He called his landlord right after that to notify him that he was moving out immediately, even though his rent for the month had been paid. Greg packed his things and drove to his parents' house in NY. On the way out of town he couldn't find Buck, but he dropped off a Christmas card at his place, saying that he would be back to see him in February when he had to take his oral comprehensive exam. Greg hoped that December would not be an omen for the coming year.

Chapter 19

El Guru's Best Year and Greg's Worst

El Guru sent Greg a tape a couple of weeks later after Greg related his tale of woe in a tape. He said, "Wow, I didn't know whether to laugh or feel sorry for you with all the crap you went through at the end of the year. You had those car mishaps, Celine is gone, and you blew it with that chick Carole? You are the mental health dude, but I can't help but think you might be psychologically punishing yourself somehow.

"Let me tell you what's happening here. Thanks for the Christmas presents. I'm having some trouble with the VW Bug I bought so I may sell it and go back to trains and buses because gas prices are soaring, anyway. I called Ursula and she seemed happy to hear from me, but Stuttgart is almost 700 clicks (KM) - over 400 miles away and I wouldn't trust this car for that long of a trip. Besides, she is really busy with coursework, even though she wants me to stay in touch. I did go to Dusseldorf this weekend because I was feeling lonely. I only went to Lord Nelson's and danced with a couple of chicks but I thought about Ursula. At the Hotel Continental, the desk clerk remembered me as Mr. Horning.

"On the train back to Bremerhaven, I was reading *The Making of a Psychiatrist*, by David Viscott. You read that one last year and it's an interesting book. I know you recommended *What Do You Say After You Say Hello?* by Eric Berne, so I'll try to read that one next.

"The young black GIs here seem to have chips on their shoulders. One of them mouthed off to white guys, 'We will get even with you for what you did to our ancestors hundreds of years ago.' They don't believe how much Mexican-Americans have suffered for years. I've always felt like an outsider with most groups, and you told me that a lot of times you don't feel like you fit in with a lot of people, even though you're white and educated. For me, this is difficult to discuss with most Americans. I can talk with you and Buck about this, but not somebody like Dave Wilson with his hard-headed streak. The Army brass ignores the racial problem, and heroin is worse because hash is hard to get. I'm working at the OPC now - it's better than the ward. But most medics here aren't half as competent as they were at our hospital three years ago."

Greg mailed resumes to about 20 places in New York and New England. Some sent him rejection letters, some ignored him. He got rejected by the school in Vermont where he had interviewed on the nightmare trip just before Christmas. His grades came and he was pleased at his final very high GPA, 3.7. El Guru called when Greg was home alone one day at 2:15 pm.

"Hey, Amigo! Que pasa?"

"Artie - you're on the secret phone at the hospital?"

"Yeah, I'm working nights this month and I just got up a little while ago. It's about 8:15 here and it's colder than a witch's tit. We got a new NCOIC at the OPC and he's a real lifer - 20 years in the Army. The new Clinical Director told us no more 10 days on and four days off. A lot of the GIs here are useless. They just want to hang out in the barracks; they don't even want to go downtown. I took a train to Cuxhaven Saturday - it's a nice town and not far away."

"That's a shame. All the good times we had a few years ago and some were as close as downtown, only a mile from the hospital. Now you're back in Germany and it's not the same and I'm stuck living at home, unemployed."

"At least school went well for you. I should have gone back to school. Do you get your Masters degree after you're done with this last oral exam?"

"No. They say it will be at the graduation in May. Unemployment is higher in the past year, and rising gas prices don't help. I hope I find work someplace. Living at home is like I'm 17 again, dealing with my father. He was just diagnosed with cancer in his eye and they have to take out his eyeball. He's a bastard to live with right now. The only times I get out are if I drive over to see Van, or with Danny. Danny graduated from college last year and he just found a job selling men's clothes. At least he's employed."

"Sorry about your father, but I know you had conflicts with him down through the years. I have to go. Send me a tape and tell me about the exam. Say hi to Buck for me."

Greg took off for Worcester and stayed with Buck. The next day, he went on campus at 8:30 but was told his exam had been postponed until 11:00, which made him anxious. Greg thought he came off poorly and the examiners seemed to concur with his reaction, although he got more confident during the last quarter hour. Suddenly they said, "OK, that's enough. Have a seat outside." Greg could hear them arguing briefly and thought, "Damnit, maybe I didn't make it and I'll have to go through this shit again in April." They called him back in and told him he had passed.

A wave of relief washed over him. Both professors thought he wouldn't pass after the first half-hour but then they said, "You did very well after that. Research and theory are your bag." This was the opposite of what was said to him in 1968 by a prof back in Pittsburgh.

He saw his friends Frank, Scott, and Vicki outside, and they all met for lunch about a mile away. Greg related to them all the areas and questions they had asked him and why it took one hour. After Vicki and Frank said they were both done in about a half an hour, Scott added, "Jesus, I never heard of anyone taking such a grilling. We saw Ben and they asked him three questions, gave him a case, asked for his diagnosis, and let him go with an A. He was done in 15 minutes. You went through a ball-buster."

Greg hung around with Buck at his place and went to bed early because he had an interview in Blackstone, MA, the next day. He didn't think he came off very well in the interview, which was for a counselor working with kids. As he got into his car, however, he saw five unopened cans of Schlitz in the snow near his left rear tire. "This wasn't a total loss of a trip," he thought. He never heard from the interviewers at Blackstone. But at least after taking the GREs the next weekend, he wound up getting a 1200 total for the Verbal and Math sections.

In the middle of April, in a tape, El Guru said, "The Army is going back to the way it was in the 1950s and I don't like it. I'm still refusing to go up for E-6 until the system starts changing. When I tell our 1st Sgt. this he tells me to watch my mouth about my opinions. I'm starting to play softball on the hospital team. I have to - I'm overweight and out of shape. I called Ursula. She is begging me to come down to Stuttgart. I miss her. She is really into Women's Lib now but I'm finally adjusting to that. Nixon may be toast now with all that's coming out.

"Hey, you got a few interviews but no offers. It must be depressing. Maybe you should try Canada for jobs. From what you said, all you're doing is sending out resumes, playing chess with your brother, and recording music with Van. Are gas lines that long everywhere there?

"You are right - music is terrible right now - some stupid nun singing 'Our Father' is in the Top 40! The only song I like is 'Eres Tu,' by Mocedates, but maybe because it's in Spanish. I'm glad Hank Aaron hit the 715th homer. He's a great player who never got hurt. I can't believe the Padres' owner got on the PA and told the fans his team was playing stupid baseball - all he knows is how to sell hamburgers. Money is really taking over professional sports now, more than ever, it seems."

At the end of the month Greg got a part-time job for about 12 hours a week, working a one to one case at the home of a man his age who was blind and brain damaged from the time he was three years old. It was frustrating, but his parents were nice people and the job was funded by the county. In May, he went to his Masters' graduation and he was curious to see if other people were as frustrated as he was regarding employment.

Many grads he spoke with were unemployed too, or working at menial jobs, or living off their husbands or wives, so he didn't feel so bad about his situation. After the ceremony was over, Buck suddenly showed up.

"Hey, Buck, thanks for coming! I was gonna call you later. How'd you know I was getting my degree today?"

"I saw it in the paper. I wouldn't miss it. I was hoping we'd see each other again."

"That's really nice of you to come. Wow - you grew a moustache I see! I would buy you a beer but I'm broke and you're not a drinking man anyway."

"Thanks for the offer but it's your day. Besides, I just got off the night shift and I have to get some sleep before I go back in. But I got some good news. I got accepted at a Medical School in North Carolina for September."

"Congratulations! Better than me - I just got shot down after interviews at more places. The only good thing that's happened to me this year was that I got great GRE scores."

Greg had to hurry back home because of the gas shortage. Lately there could be almost a two hour wait in line at some gas stations; Greg knew he'd have just enough gas to make it home. Some stations had signs for no gas; at times there were fights in the gas lines which delayed people more. Nixon dropped the speed limit down to 55 mph and State Police were nailing speeders on the Mass Pike and the NY State Thruway.

In the next few weeks, Greg gradually developed a nagging sore throat, low-grade fever, and weight loss. He stopped smoking and drinking, but neither of these alleviated the problem. Strangely, none of his family members were sick, nor the family of the brain damaged man he was working with. He heard from El Guru by tape in mid-June.

El Guru went to Spain for two weeks and had a great time. "I invited Ursula to go with me, but she couldn't make it. Instead, she said she would come up to see me in July. While I was in Spain, I didn't speak any English at all and it was wonderful. I read *To Kill a Mockingbird* while lying on the beach in San Sebastian and what people say is true for this one - the book is even better than the movie. I was really surprised about how much people there knew about American politics. I wanted to go to Portugal, but I couldn't get in because of a military coup taking place. Instead I went to Valencia - gothic architecture and the quaint 'old town.' Then I went to Seville. I saw flamenco dancing and even a bullfight. It did me a lot of good to get away from Bremerhaven, but the first thing they did when I got back was give me a drug test! I haven't even smoked any hash since last year.

"I wish I could get discharged tomorrow but I signed a contract. Nurses are all rank-conscious - authoritarian is the word, I think. Buck got his dream to go to medical school. Will you ever see him again? Sorry to hear you're sick. You should go to a doctor or the ER or do something. Let me know if you finally get a decent job. Keep on pushing. Hold your head up."

Greg told El Guru, via tape, "I had another interview in July but it was on a day when I didn't feel well. I can't shake this sore throat, and I'm still losing weight. In the meantime, I connected with an organization offering openings for state jobs in Wisconsin, and I'll go out there because I'm going nowhere here. I was too embarrassed to go to my high school reunion. I'm getting bummed out."

El Guru responded with a tape in August, "I am having a pitcher of Sangria to celebrate getting rid of shithead Nixon. He is a pitiful human being who had a chance to make things so much better in the world, and he screwed things up royally instead. Who knows if Ford will be any better? I asked to be reassigned to the mailroom and I start tomorrow. Almost all of the medical people here don't care about their jobs except for a few rigid nurses and a couple MDs.

"Ursula is here now. She is staying downtown, and I am falling in love with her all over again. We talked for four hours straight after she got here and concluded that this was a new beginning for us. I think I want to marry this woman, and she seems to feel the same way. No woman I've ever met is this good - we are clicking intellectually, emotionally, sexually, and with hobbies and interests. I don't even want to look at anyone else. One other thing - she's getting more religious and we discuss religion, philosophy, and psychology, and I really dig it. I don't even curse as much anymore. I don't want to smoke anything again. I am just so happy right now. It's sad that she has to go back to Stuttgart to finish school, but we will write to each other, call each other, and even send tapes to each other. I wish I was out of the Army or could transfer down to Stuttgart.

Greg and El Guru's lives were 180 degrees away from each other. El Guru was trapped in the Army but otherwise he was really happy; Greg was a free, well-educated civilian, but he was trapped living at home with no decent paying job, and he was a mess physically. In mid-August, Greg decided to drive to Wisconsin because he had a few interviews lined up in Madison and Milwaukee. His car broke down outside of Valparaiso, IN, and he had to get it towed to a garage and stay at the cheapest motel he could find, walking a few blocks with his duffel bag. He could not afford to make it to Wisconsin, but he had enough money to go to Bucyrus, Ohio, where he was contacted for an interview. Halfway through, anxiety took over and he blew the interview.

As he drove home to NY, he thought, "Why am I self-destructing?" He made it home a few days later, feeling physically and mentally miserable.

By mid-October, Greg felt he had to get some kind of a job somewhere, even part time. He started working selling men's and women's shoes 20 hours a week in Clifton Park. He liked the manager, the other employees, the customers, and he also got a salary plus a good commission. He thought, "Maybe I should change careers to sales." Two weeks after he started working, his physical symptoms started to go away.

El Guru sent him a tape in early November. "It was good to hear from you and at least you got some kind of a job despite all your bad luck. Maybe you'll meet some chicks selling shoes. Interesting that your physical problems went away. Maybe you were that depressed and didn't know it. I went to see Ursula in Stuttgart. We had a wonderful time. I even went to church with her twice. It was sad for us to say goodbye. If we can hang in there for 14 more months long-distance, I will try for a European out again. I haven't asked her if she would consider going to America. Now here's the shocker: we got engaged, and we plan to get married in the summer of '76. She will be out of school and working, and I will be in college, most likely. Also, we are convinced right now that the only way to get squared away personally is through Jesus Christ. I'll be going to Mass every Sunday now.

"The Pirates didn't even make it to the World Series. Are you more of a Patriots or Steelers fan now? Both teams are looking good. Maybe you should go to church or start reading the Bible for things to go better. Maybe you're being tested by the Lord."

Greg told El Guru in a Christmas card that he was still sending out resumes but got no interviews. He didn't go out of the house much, except for work and to see Van. El Guru sent Greg a Christmas card, saying he was still into religion and prayer. He went to Stuttgart again to see Ursula, and they talked about the possibility of living in Spain after he got out of the Army. He liked his job in the mailroom, but was resentful of what the "new Army" was becoming. Still, he thought 1974 turned out to be one of the best years of his life because of Ursula. Greg chalked up 1974 to being one of his worst ever.

Chapter 20

El Guru Turns Radical

The next year got off to a better start for Greg. He started dating a lady from Albany. Even though he felt the relationship probably would not "go anywhere," after seeing her after several dates, it felt good to be out socially again. He started working as a psych tech on a mental health unit at a local hospital. The staff on the unit seemed to be very competent. He finally got his own apartment at the end of the month. Over in Europe, El Guru still had a good work ethic, but he ignored requests to go before the E-6 Board again. He cared about religion and Ursula, sports, music, and traveling, but not much else. One year to go before he was to be discharged seemed like an eternity to him. Greg got a tape from him in early February.

"I started thinking about my life and how it's evolving while I was lying in bed last Saturday. The religious stuff is fading away. Maybe I forced it on myself, but it's really not me. Don't get me wrong - I needed that period at the end of last year to give me some discipline in my life, but I felt isolated, and the Jesus freaks here are phony people. I was stagnating. I wasn't improving as a human being, except for developing respect for God and the Church, but right now I can make a more satisfying life by trying to make some positive changes in this system or in the world, however I can. For me, it might have to be political, if anyone will listen. America isn't getting any better, even with Nixon gone. I think a revolution is really needed to wake people up. I want to meet more human beings from other countries and to see how they feel about the world situation and their personal lives. I want to take a leave to go to Greece, Turkey, Israel, Egypt, or maybe even Russia.

A lack of finances, power, and maybe higher education might stop me from accomplishing what I want. But the old El Guru is back. By the way, I'm glad you finally got some kind of job.

"Ursula is now saying 'we can't go on like this. We're just too far away. Can't you get a transfer to Stuttgart?' But I keep trying and I can't. Now she's subtly pressuring me to get married this year. I hope it's not over because I really miss her when she's not around. I'm taking a course downtown in conversational German. She doesn't want to meet me in Luxembourg. She likes Dusseldorf, but it's too far for her. She mentioned the possibility of taking a semester off and taking some courses up here that could transfer to her university and I hope she's serious about that.

"Anyway, I'm getting back into shape physically so I can play fast-pitch softball on the team here like I did briefly last year. I haven't met anyone who likes sports, music, politics, traveling, and going out at night like you and I did. A few people will talk about one of those things, but that's all. Speaking of politics, Ford pardoned Nixon, which pissed me off a little, but we knew he would do it. Now Ford wants to cut GI benefits so he can spend the money saved on active duty military, but that will never get past the House or the Senate. I'm getting very interested in Socialism, not Communism, because Communist leaders become too selfish and turn into dictators - not just in Russia, but in places like Yugoslavia or Cuba."

Greg's tape recorder broke, so he wrote El Guru a letter. He felt that Ford had a chance to be a great president if he hadn't pardoned Nixon. He thought Ford had a good, sincere manner of talking to people and he meant well, but his conservative politics were not in tune with most Americans, except for maybe old farts and Korean or WWII vets who were stuck in the 1950s.

Greg also wrote that he liked most of the people at the hospital. However, a lot of staff on the mental health unit didn't like each other. There seemed to be "cold war" type factions, not just in terms of unit procedures and mental health treatment, but also personality clashes. The mental health unit was split into several treatment teams, and Greg felt that his interdisciplinary team members were quite knowledgeable clinicians. He was about to go on the 11-7 shift for a month, which meant that he would be on call for the ER, and any kind of social life would die.

At noon on a late April day, when he was still working nights, Greg was surprised to get a phone call from El Guru.

"Artie, I was still asleep. Tonight's my last night on 11-7. Did something bad happen?"

"I took a chance thinking you'd be off today. Well, Ursula and I broke up. A few weeks ago, she decided to come here and take two courses to see how we could function as couple being with each other a lot more frequently. It was great at first, and we discussed maybe getting married and even moving to someplace like New York City next year. Gradually she got more pissed over my political leanings - she claimed it was all I talked about, and she didn't agree with Lyn Marcus, the leader of a new Socialist party that I really like. We got into some long arguments, and she felt that I should be caring for her more, and giving her more support for a difficult math class she was taking. Then she wanted me to move in with her after the courses were over and get married. She thought I would be a distraction if we lived together while she was taking that class. It came out during the last argument we had, that one night after a class she went out to a bar downtown. Some German bastard who used to work at the hospital picked her up, brought her to his place, and fucked her. And she said that it was like when we first met - relaxing, joking, and he made her feel special. It really broke my heart."

"Can you get some help as a couple - try to get back with her?"

"No, I'm gonna throw myself into Socialist politics. I came over here originally to try to help make changes in the system, and it's like tearing down a brick wall with a little hammer. I'm better off trying to influence a new movement that could be taking off world-wide, and I will try to help make changes for what should be right in the world. Sure, losing her will hurt a lot, and she already told me she's going back to Stuttgart in two weeks. I can't just go crawling back to her to give her that power over me."

"Breaking up with Ursula will hurt because you were in love with her. Please be damn careful with the Socialist thing. There could be worse consequences for this than getting busted for hash like you did six years ago. Don't think somebody undercover at the hospital, like a CID (Criminal Investigation Detective under the guise of an enlisted man) doesn't know about your radical leanings."

"What do you think of Lyn Marcus and his EAP group, and what were you able to find out about him?"

"He sounds like a charismatic, radical cult leader. An asshole, but I know you don't want to hear that. Socialism isn't all that bad per se - like they have in the Scandinavian countries - but we probably won't see changes like that incorporated into American society during our lifetime."

"There is a lot of peer-group pressure to conform to a more conservative America, and I won't stand for it if I am able. People have to be educated toward what is right morally and as human beings helping each other."

"But is the radical Socialism you're looking at the way to go?"

"Damn right, it is."

"You always said you don't advocate violence, overthrowing governments."

"I don't, and it won't happen overnight, but just maybe the time is ripe for some gradual, major attitude changes to start taking place. And I'm willing to be a part of a revolution."

"What do you think of Arafat and the PLO group? Does Palestine have a right to exist?"

"Yeah, but Arafat wants to do it violently. I don't advocate that at all. Nothing will come of it though, because the United States controls Israel."

"Anyway, now that Ursula is gone, what are your plans for the summer?"

"I don't know. I'd like to come over there and talk to you about this situation."

"OK, but it won't be one constant bitch session about radical politics."

"Just listen to me in person. I don't have time to talk about it anymore right now."

Over the next month, Greg bought a '72 Plymouth Cricket, a comfortable little car that got great gas mileage. He had another long stint of 3-11 and 11-7 shifts coming up. Social lives usually die when people work these shifts.

At the end of May, El Guru sent him a letter - actually, a copy of an "Affidavit" dated May 27th.

"The following is a statement from Spec/5 Raimondo D. Guerrero, US Army, stationed in Bremerhaven, BRD, made on 27 May 1975:

"This incident happened on Sunday, 25 May, between 6:00 and 7:00 in the evening. As I was driving down Wursterstrasse on the way from the hospital, I was forced off the road by a black or navy-blue Mercedes that came at me from a side street, right into my path and in order to avoid a collision I swerved to the right. Once I did this, I became angry, stopped, and got out of the car. They were two black men - one had a beard; the other one didn't. They were about six feet tall or so - one was a little bigger - and about 40-45 years old, very muscular and wore well-dressed, expensive looking clothes. They grabbed me and forcibly put me into their car, down on the floor of the backseat. There were no witnesses; no one was around; it was the perfect place to do this kind of job.

"Once I was inside the car, one guy sat on top of me, took my right arm, and twisted it over my back up to my neck, so that if I moved it really hurt. So, all I could do was just lie there. At the same time he was doing this, he took a handkerchief and put that into my mouth. After that, I was blindfolded.

"After some minutes, we changed the car and got into another one. They didn't mention any names to each other but referred to me as 'boy' - 'we have the boy in good hands, etc.' They drove around back roads and secondary roads for about an hour and a half. I do know we arrived in a city other than Bremerhaven. It was a big city, too; I could hear by the type of traffic and the kind of big city atmosphere. I thought it was Hamburg, but I'm not so sure about that anymore. We arrived at a building that I thought might be a consulate. I tried to look out from underneath the blindfold but they kept telling me to keep my head down, look at the ground, don't get any foolish ideas about getting away, and everything would be all right.

"I was pushed down a flight of stairs. We got into a room about 12 by 15 feet. There was a lounge chair in the middle and a small table with a drawer - similar to a small desk. The room itself had been made sound proof, kind of like a music studio. They took off the blindfold.

"The taller of the two appeared to be in charge of the other person. One stood behind the desk in front of me. The smaller one was behind my back, so that I couldn't see him. They both fired questions at me for about a half an hour. I wasn't asked about my political connections, but I was bombarded with how the EAP was using and abusing me because I was a soldier and helping them undermine the US government. They said the EAP was also a subversive revolutionary-type group; that it wasn't really my fault but that I didn't know what I was doing, and what I was involved with, and what the consequences are for being involved with them.

"The only time I was threatened was when one guy waved this paper in front of me, a kind of contract you have to sign when you join the Army, and he told me I could go to jail for what I was doing.

"Then I asked them for identification. They obliged and showed that they were MPI - Military Police Investigators. But I doubt if they were really MPI - they were too good, too professional, too business-like.

"After that, one opened up the table drawer and pulled out a plain manila folder. The file was about an inch and a half thick. I glanced at it for a few seconds and noticed that was once sentence pertaining to me when I was 15, saying that it was the first time I went to Mexico. Then they bombarded how they knew about my political identification when I was a high school student, and what my political views were during the 1973 Middle East War. They had some direct quotes, and read them to me from the file. I wondered if they were not really familiar with me, though. They asked about my security clearance and that I could have been the one carrying out classified information, and that I could be accused of treason. But I already lost my security clearance, which was a normal process when you get out of the Army, which I told them I did at the end of 1972. I felt more in control of their grilling by this time.

"After another half hour, they probably realized I wasn't going to be intimidated anymore, and the shorter one said, 'We figured you might be a tough nut to crack.' He pulled out a syringe, and they grabbed me. I struggled briefly and they injected me with something - I thought it might be sodium pentothal. But after a few seconds, I was out cold. The next thing I remember was being awakened, probably about 5:00 am by slaps in the face. They gagged and blindfolded me again and put me in another car. This time they tied my hands behind my back. They said not to try to remember them because I would never see them again.

"The two people who drove me back to Bremerhaven were not the same ones who abducted me the evening before. They said, 'This is just the beginning and you'd better watch yourself in the future.' I was pushed out of the car about 300 meters from where they picked me up the evening before. It took me a few seconds to get my hands loose and my blindfold off, and by this time, naturally, they were gone.

"After that I went back to my car, where nothing was missing or changed. I drove back to the hospital, went to my room, and tried to fall asleep for a couple of hours before I went to work."

El Guru added a note that he was coming to see Greg around June 10th for a week.

Chapter 21

The Roller Coaster Goes from Down to Up

All Greg could think about was that El Guru had really gone overboard this time, and the EAP must be the European version of the Caucus of Labor Committees. He wondered if his apartment was bugged - he had just finished reading "The Anderson Tapes." Greg's phone rang about 10:30 am on June 9th. It was El Guru on the line.

"Greg, I'm in Plattsburgh at the Air Force Base." Can you come up and get me? I'll get a ride to the bus terminal downtown and you can meet me there."

"Artie! I'll come up now. Here's my schedule: I'm off today and tomorrow, but then I have to work three 7-3 shifts and after that, I'm sure I can switch with someone so I can get Saturday and Sunday off in exchange for nine straight evenings."

"That works out good. You can drive me back up here Sunday. If you're working days, we can't do too much drinking."

"I don't think either one of us drinks as much as we used to. I'm driving a blue Plymouth Cricket. I'll be right up."

"A Cricket! I never heard of it. Sounds like a dinky shitmobile," he laughed.

"It's great on gas but it drinks water. Stop Leak helps a little. A patient on the ward who's a mechanic said, 'Don't drive it over 60, treat it like a baby, and you'll get two years out of it.' But you and me and your stuff will fit in it fine. I'll see you around 1:00 to 1:30."

After he picked up El Guru, Greg asked if he thought the CIA kidnapped him. El Guru said that it was scary for him and that he was paranoid of certain people now - his roommate in the dorm, any of the hospital brass, or someone who may have infiltrated the group discussions about Lyn Marcus' ideas. He even wondered about Ursula at times and the real reason why their relationship ended. Greg wondered if she actually ratted him out to that German bastard who was screwing her. El Guru said that this was probably not the case, but that it just did not work out between them. He felt sad about what happened and he said he was never more in love with any woman more than her, and he would be hurting for quite a while, but he said Ursula didn't like Bremerhaven, and being an only child, she really wanted to live close to her parents. Greg said that long distance relationships are hard to keep going, as he knew from experience.

"Anyway, what happens now? Will you get court martialed for this CIA-like crap? I'm sure the hospital brass knows."

"I'm hoping not, since this thing happened on a weekend and I wasn't AWOL. I wasn't on CQ or anything like that. This is all confidential. At least that's what those shitheads told me after they dumped me out of the car. You know, those guys even knew I was at the Oktoberfest in '71 with you. I want to get out of the Army more than ever now, but I have to keep my nose clean, so to speak."

When they got to Greg's place, El Guru said that he was getting hungry. As he opened the refrigerator, Greg said, "I got enough hash here for the both of us."

"What! What the fuck are you doing with hash and what is it doing in the fridge? I don't do hash anymore and you told me you don't even smoke your pipe that much!"

"No, you ass! It's corned beef hash! Damn! Are you uptight over everything? Relax, man. Do you need a few beers?" They both started laughing.

The next day they walked around Saratoga Springs and later took a ride over to Vermont. Greg worked the next day, while El Guru watched TV and read. When he got home, Greg started talking about his job and the patients on the ward. One patient thought he was under surveillance by the FBI because he was undercover in the Secret Service. El Guru argued that it could be true because he felt that people are probably being spied on everywhere. Greg said that the patient was psychotic - delusional.

"I'd like to meet him. I'll tell you whether he's for real or not. By the way, are you really thinking about going to Canada to live?"

"I have an interview next month with someone from the Canadian consulate about the possibility of living in Montreal or Ottawa. There may be more jobs up there, and I might have a better chance of getting into a doctoral program there. Where I am now is good for a year, but it's a dead-end job. I'll be 30 in two years and I don't want to be in the situation I'm in now."

"Be careful. Big Brother is watching you. Especially because you're friends with me and they know. Remember that guy we met at the Oktoberfest who was supposedly a radical? I'm now wondering if he was CIA."

When Greg got back from work the next day, El Guru asked him about the guy who was "under surveillance." Greg said, "Now he thinks he was really one of the Beatles."

El Guru laughed, "You're right. He definitely is crazy. Any other patients on the ward that you're working with?"

Greg mentioned one guy who was convinced he could play for the Mets, and he was always practicing his batting stance. Also, another big, scary guy was getting angry and threatening people before they found out he was a painter and either the lead in the paint, or paint thinner, or something that infected his brain. He further related there was a real foxy lady in her late 20's - a professional business woman - diagnosed as manic-depressive in the manic phase but coming down from it. She told Greg last week during one of her tirades that he was "the worst bastard of them all." But he said that today, she talked with him for a while and asked, "Greg was I really that fucked up when I came in here? I'm so sorry for anything I said or did to anyone here." He didn't have the heart to tell her she was naked, screaming, and daring any of the guys if they tried to have sex with her, she would rip their balls apart.

"Sounds like she was a raging bitch when she first came in. Did she get raped?"

"No, she said she didn't get raped, but from what I've seen, once manics get that first good night's sleep, they turn the corner toward being normal again.

Then, hopefully, they won't come crashing down toward getting depressed. What I will say is that she is good looking, has a nice body, and is very bright - why can't I meet anybody like that who's stable?"

"You're still in a slump, aren't you?"

"Some one or two daters; not even any possible one-nighters. I really have to get out of this area for more reasons than one."

"Let's go out tomorrow night and see if there are any chicks available who want to play."

"OK, we'll go to Lake George."

At Lake George, there were good bands at a few places but they got shot down everywhere. On Sunday, El Guru thanked Greg for the hospitality and opportunity to talk about what was going on with their lives in person, and he flew back to Germany on an Air Force plane with a layover at Dover (DE) AFB.

That summer, Greg was having conflicts with the Director or Nursing. A very supportive psychiatrist on his team left. The interview at the Canadian consulate did not go very well - he was told he did not speak

French well enough to live where he wanted, but if he had his heart set on living in Canada, he would be better off someplace in Ontario other than Ottawa. Greg drove to job interviews in Steubenville, Ohio and Pittsburgh. The one in Pittsburgh got canceled, but he stayed with his college room-mate, Don, and his wife, and caught up with what was happening in their lives.

After the Ohio interview, he went to Buffalo to look up Dave Wilson, but his girlfriend, Faith, answered when he called.

"Dave and I broke up a few weeks ago. He's living with two other girls somewhere near Rochester, I think."

'Oh, crap. I was hoping to stay with you guys."

"You can stay with me. Let's go out, have a few drinks, and have a good time."

Greg slept with her. Early in the morning, he had to get on the road. He kissed her goodbye and said he'd be in touch. He stopped along the NY State Thruway a couple of times for 15-minute naps, and he had 5 cups of coffee - it was rare for him that he drank any coffee at all, because even one cup would make him feel jittery. Once he got to his place, he took a quick cold shower and got to work just in time for the 3-11 shift. It was a slow evening, with just 13 patients on the ward, fortunately. He sent El Guru a tape, informing him of what had transpired.

El Guru called him just before midnight, on August 10th.

"You didn't! Tell me you didn't! How could you? You violated an unwritten code. You know she and Wilson will get back together. What other woman alive would put up with his crap? And she said they were together for 6 or 7 years? He'll be pissed when he finds out. She'll tell him you stayed with her and more, eventually."

"I am a little ambivalent, the way I feel right now. She's a nice girl and I caught her when she was lonely and we both got horny. What the hell are you doing calling me at this hour, anyway? It's around 6:00 over there right now."

I figured you might be working evenings, and that you wouldn't be in bed yet. I have to go to a USAREUR seminar on race relations. The last one was a joke because no blacks came. I wanted to go to this one to see if anyone cared."

"Do they want you to go before the E-6 Board again?"

"No way. I just got my evaluation for my job. It was great for everything except leadership, so I refused to sign it. I'm a one-person operation in the mailroom. How the hell can they rate leadership? I told them, 'Yeah, you probably think I could be a good leader of a bunch of Communists.' They didn't like my sense of humor."

"There are times when you have to watch your mouth, Artie."

"I say what I feel. Look I have to go. I'll send you a tape when I get a chance."

They didn't hear from each other for months after that. El Guru concentrated on doing his job at the mailroom and staying away from most of the other GIs at the hospital. He now had a single room in the barracks, and when he was off duty, he would put on headphones to listen to a baseball or football on AFN or listen to Radio Luxembourg. A few times, he went to downtown Bremerhaven or Cuxhaven. He wanted to save money for his ETS from the Army. Of the few ladies he met, he immediately compared them to Ursula.

Greg worked a month of evening shifts. He didn't get the job in Ohio. He decided he was going to make an effort to apply to doctoral programs, and go up to Canada in October to sample what living was like in Toronto. A gay cousin and his partner in Toronto welcomed him to stay with them. After a few days of enjoying the sights of Toronto, he decided he didn't want to live in a city of that size. On the way back home, after getting a glimpse of the beauty of Niagara Falls in the early evening from the Canadian side, he decided to call Faith. She told him he could stay there, but she had a female roommate now who was sleeping on the couch. However, her roommate was working a 12 hour shift that night, so she said he could stay with her, but he would have to be out by 7:00. When he got there, they both talked about how they both had mixed feelings about having sex in August. He told her he needed a place to sleep for the night and he slept on the couch.

As soon as he got to his parents' house, he found out that his brother-in-law (who was 37) had died from a massive heart attack a few days earlier and the funeral was the next day. He went to his sister's house to console her; everyone in the family was distraught. During the next week, Greg made up his mind to try to get out of New York State. "Negativity and bad luck here," he thought. He mailed another dozen resumes to various mental health facilities in New England. He sent El Guru a tape about what happened a few days later.

He got a short tape back from El Guru on November 10th. El Guru said, "Wow, you went to Canada—are you on the CIA's shit list too? I know the economy is bad back there with unemployment, gas prices going up again, and inflation, but I will be so glad to get out of the Army. I can't wait to experience some true freedom and dignity again. Hope you get another job someplace - think it'll be in Canada?"

After he finished listening to the tape, Greg got two calls in two hours, both from facilities in northern New England which had received his resume and wanted him to come for an interview right away. As luck would have it, he agreed to interviews at 10:30 am and 1:30 pm that Friday. The second job sounded very attractive to him. He felt like he might not be qualified for the job at the first one - a hospital - but it might be great experience to prepare him for the second interview. He put on his new leisure suit, left his apartment at 7:00 am and arrived at the hospital just in time to meet the interviewers. They asked him all about his experience with mental health patients and working with inter-disciplinary teams, and they liked the references he provided from the psychiatrist and psychologist at his present job. He felt confident, but told them, "If I am hired, I would be here to learn the system and all I can about improving my clinical skills. I sure don't think I have all the answers at this point in my career." They excused themselves for about 15 minutes, and Greg thought, "Damnit, I blew it again. But I know what not to say later today." They came back and gave him a tour of the hospital. When they showed him around one of the buildings with a group of patients obviously psychotic, he thought, "Oh, my God - this is a state hospital! They all look like chronic in-patients." After asking him about behavior modification, contacts with families and other agencies, etc., they started talking about the advantages of living in a smaller state capital city. The starting salary for the job was $4500 more than he was making now and was all day shift work, with no weekends, although they would be amenable to him coming in on evenings and doing some teaching once in a while to the younger mental health workers. Greg was getting blown away - it sounded like they really wanted to hire him. They said they would call him Monday afternoon.

The job a half an hour down the road was also appealing but the female interviewer was slightly seductive and seemed to be curious about him personally. The salary was $2500 less than what was offered at the first interview, and she wanted him to do outreach work, reporting directly to her.

She had others to interview but said she would get back to him in the near future. "Working for an attractive female boss would be interesting, but the bigger career break would be to work at a state hospital," he thought. The state hospital called on Monday afternoon, offering him the job and he agreed to start on Monday, December 8th. He thought, "A new adventure, a new chapter in my life. If it doesn't work out, I can hang in there for a year, my resume will look better and it could possibly help me get into a doctoral program somewhere. He celebrated a few days later by buying his first brand new car - a '76 Pontiac Astre.

El Guru spent Thanksgiving on CQ and sent Greg a tape. "I'm getting short - five weeks to go. My attitude is better because I'm getting out. I'll be back in the US in time to watch the Super Bowl. We are now forbidden to get *Newsweek, Time, the New York Times*, or the *Washington Post* at any military establishment. Do you believe that shit? There is a place downtown that sells the *International Herald Tribune*, and I can get the news from there.

"Hey, I just got the letter from you that you're moving farther north! It'll be even colder there than it is here. Congratulations! Let me know your address so I can come and visit you. It'll be fun to get together for two weeks before I go home to New Mexico. I spent a year in Korea before I went to Vietnam and it can't be colder up there than Korea. This is a big step up for you. Looks like mental health is really your career. Maybe I'll try to go back to school in the fall of '76. Let me know as soon as you get settled and I'll see you when I get up there."

Chapter 22

New Beginnings

Greg's first few days on the new job went smoothly. The man who interviewed him, Dr. Bob Danby, took him under his wing - he introduced Greg to the inter-disciplinary team on Greg's unit, secured a small, comfortable office in back of the unit for him, and went to the first team meeting with him. One entire ward of this unit was behavior modification in nature for patients who had been hospitalized for a few years. The other was half acute patients (there for a few days to a few weeks) and half chronic patients (there for months to many years).

The typical day was similar to the hospital in New York, except that on weekdays, at 8:30, there was a community meeting at which any patient or staff member could bring up issues regarding living on the unit; plans for upcoming hospital-wide events (for example, caroling on grounds a few days before Christmas) were also discussed. The team meeting was an hour later. Treatment plans for patients were discussed in depth, led by the unit psychiatrist, Dr. Paul Delhomme. After lunch, Greg either had therapy sessions with patients who were assigned to him in his office or he met informally with patients on either ward. Also, he co-led group therapy for four to ten patients, with one or two other co-therapists (usually a social worker and/or a nurse), depending on the size of the group. Late in the day, he charted notes or had other administrative matters. For example, he and Dr. Danby met for supervision. They also met to plan converting a token economy system to a point system on the behavior modification ward. Occasionally, someone presented a unit-wide continuing education seminar. There were other monthly meetings for staff members of clinical departments or certain hospital committees.

Greg resided in a room in an old staff dormitory building until he got his first paycheck, four weeks after he started. He was reluctantly given permission to go home for a few days at Christmastime from his Department Head, Dr. Joanna Krech, the other person who interviewed him for the job. Dr. Krech was a German woman who escaped from a Nazi concentration camp in the 1940s. Most of the people around the hospital were friendly and helpful. He liked the hospital and the town, but he thought, "I hope I can survive the winters here. I really should stay here at least two years to build up a decent resume if I want to get into a doctoral program." The year 1975 ended well for Greg. He felt like a professional for the first time since he was the NCOIC of the Psychiatric Clinic in the Army, four years earlier.

El Guru crashed a New Year's Eve party, hosted by one of the German guys who worked at the hospital. Many people were drunk, and he wound up having a one-nighter with a drunken German chick he picked up at the party. He was discharged from the Army on the evening of January 8th. Greg had sent him a Christmas card giving him his temporary address on grounds. El Guru wrote back in his card that he would come up from Ft. Dix to stay in the dorm with him until somebody threw him out. In the meantime, Greg searched for an apartment and found one near the hospital, but the occupant was not moving out until Saturday, the 10th.

El Guru knocked on his door at 7:00 Friday night, dressed in Army fatigues and carrying a packed duffle bag.

"Artie! It ain't much but it's home. This time STAY out of the Army!"

"Getting here by buses was a pain in the ass. I couldn't sleep at Port Authority in New York because of all the shaky characters and beggars hanging around and I got about four hours of sleep on the bus to Boston, and some more on the bus here."

"Did you get something to eat?"

"Yeah, but mostly out of machines. I'm not that hungry, though. I'm just tired."

"As you can see, this room is small, but the radiator keeps it warm. I'm moving into an apartment tomorrow night. We have to see if any place is open to get you something to sleep on tonight. I have an extra blanket and pillow, but no pillow case."

"I have an air mattress folded up in my duffel bag. I'll use a t-shirt for the case. Just show me where the bathroom is, and in the morning when you go to work, I'll stay on top of your bed if you don't mind. I know you have to go to work."

"You lost track of the days - it's Friday night! Your first day of freedom and you want to be a prisoner." They both laughed. "But I do have to go over to the office and on the ward tomorrow to document notes for a couple of hours. I'll get comp time for it."

"I have a book I can read."

"I'll come by around 11:00 and we'll eat lunch. The guy who's living at the apartment now wants to sell me his furniture because he's moving to Colorado. I have to meet him at 3:30 tomorrow and give my landlord the first month's rent and security deposit. I just hope this guy won't want $300 for the furniture because I can't afford that much. It's nice - living room, bathroom, big bedroom, kitchen, and an enclosed porch. Plenty of private parking."

"I'll be careful and I won't go out of the room except to use the bathroom. I don't want to be thrown out on the street, or spend a night in jail for trespassing or get you fired."

"Security comes by every day around 10:00 am. I talked to them the first day I moved in here to find out that information. I told them I didn't want anyone breaking into my room while I was at work. They said they didn't go into rooms because some other guys worked different shifts and they might be sleeping. I got two bottles of Molson Golden on the window ledge outside, just like the old days. Let's celebrate."

The next day they went to a McDonald's for lunch and they stopped at a thrift shop to get El Guru some clothes. At 3:30, they went to Greg's new apartment, in a two-story, 50-year-old brown shingled house several blocks from the hospital. The landlord met them and asked, "It's just you who's moving in here, Greg, right?"

"Just me. My friend Artie will be staying for around two weeks or so."

"I have another place I can rent to you, Artie. It's about two blocks away."

"Thanks, but I'm going home to New Mexico."

Tony, the guy who was moving out said, "Hey, I'm going out west, too. Last week I got a great job offer in Colorado to start on Monday, and none of my friends need any furniture, so I'm hoping to sell it all to Greg at a very reasonable price. Check it out."

Greg and El Guru saw a brown fabric couch in the living room that folded out to a bed, two end tables, a small orange reclining chair, a 13" TV, a small table and two chairs on the porch and a dresser and king size bed. All the furniture seemed to be in good condition. Greg asked, "How much do you want for this stuff?"

"I'll let it all go for $100."

El Guru, who was standing in back of Tony, got wide-eyed and nodded his head at Greg.

"You got a deal," Greg replied, as he handed him five $20 bills. Greg wrote a check to the landlord for the rent and security deposit. The landlord told him to be there at 7:00 that night to move in and he'd give him the keys. Greg and El Guru left smiling.

When they got into Greg's car, El Guru said, "You pulled that one out of your ass. This place is cool and so is the furniture and I can sleep on the couch that folds into a bed. You're on a hot streak!"

"This is wonderful. Actually, my good luck started in November. Historically, every time the year gets off to a great start, I usually wind up having a lousy year."

"Don't be so damn negative. You're going from a flea trap to a palace, so to speak. And you have a great job. Just don't blow it all."

"How long will you be staying?"

"I'll probably be leaving the night after the Super Bowl. I'm gonna take a bus to Boston and fly to Albuquerque on a red eye."

"I didn't tell you this, but I have to go home Super Bowl weekend because my father has cancer - melanoma in his liver and it's spreading. He might not have much time left. I have to say my goodbyes and try to make amends."

"Sorry to hear that You didn't have a good relationship with him, did you?"

"Not really. What I have to do in my spare time this week is get a phone on Monday and go to the Post Office and the bank. I also have to get cable TV so I can get 13 channels instead of rabbit ears Utilities are provided with the rent, which helps. I know you want to go out tonight but let's lay low for a while. We'll go to Woolworth's or Green's and get stuff for this place."

All went well with the move. Greg had an extra key made for El Guru so he could come and go as he wanted. During the next week, they bought food for the apartment, talked a lot about politics, sports, music, various people they knew, great times they had and how great El Guru felt to be out of the Army. El Guru went downtown, talked to various people and spent a lot of time in the library, even getting a library card and taking out *Helter Skelter* by Vincent Bugliosi (prosecutor in the Charles Manson case) and Curt Gentry. They discussed Manson, and then Greg gave him the book, *When Prophecy Fails*, by Leon Festinger and Stanley Schacter. After reading that, El Guru started to become convinced that he probably should not have been involved with the EAP movement, at least while he was in the

Army. However, he declared, "I will be anti-conservative for the rest of my life."

Greg planned to drive home to see his father on Saturday the 17th. However, on the 16th, he and El Guru decided to go to Portland, have dinner, and hit a couple of bars. They ate at the Old Port, and someone told them that the best place for music and dancing was the Merry Manor. They went there and after dragging out a beer, they debated about having one more and hitting the road. Suddenly a couple of ladies sat down right in front of them. Both were attractive and well-built - one was dark haired, about their age, and the other was a blonde about 10 years older. El Guru smiled at the brunette and she smiled back.

"Greg, I think we may be onto something here."

"OK, but remember, I have to be on the road tomorrow by about 7:30. I can only have one more if I'm driving us back tonight."

A few minutes later the band played a new song by The Eagles, "Take It to The Limit." El Guru danced with the brunette, Patty. Greg asked the blonde, Donna, to dance.

"No thanks, but I'd like to talk."

While El Guru and Patty danced to 5 songs in a row, Greg listened to Donna as she lamented that her long-time live-in boyfriend was having an affair with a co-worker. She said to Greg, "I'm not sure if he's gonna end it. The same thing happened about 4 years ago, but if I leave him, I'll have a hard time making it financially. The way I feel tonight, though, two can play that game."

"So, is that why you came here tonight?"

"I don't know. We had a fight after dinner tonight. I told him I was going over to another friend's house, but Patty called and asked me if I wanted to come over. I said, 'Sure.' She lives alone and hasn't had a date in a couple of months. After we had a glass of wine at her place, she suggested we come here. I just want to have a good time out, and Patty is a good friend who likes to party."

After some conversation back and forth, Greg told her about himself. He said, "I'm younger. You sound like you're trapped. I feel sorry for you."

Donna said, "You're a good listener. I like you."

El Guru came back with Patty, introductions were made, and Greg said, "How about if we buy a round of drinks?"

Donna and Patty agreed and went to the Ladies' room, as the band took a break.

Greg said, "Artie, this lady is pissed at her live-in boyfriend who has no idea where she is tonight, except she's supposed to be at another girl-friend's house. She wants to have a good time and she likes me. We're almost 100 miles away from home, I have to leave early tomorrow, and I've never messed with anyone quite like this before."

"See what you can do. It's been a long time since you scored with a woman. Besides, I can sense that my lady is horny and so am I. She giggled at a few of my heavy rap lines. We can't pass this up. Let's see if they want to go back to Patty's place. It's only 10:15. If we're lucky, we can all be fooling around in an hour or less. We can get back to your place and be in bed by 2:00. We both seldom sleep any more than 5 or 6 hours a night."

They had drinks and talked, and after a couple more dances, they decided to continue the conversations at Patty's house. Right after they got there, Patty put on some soft music in her basement, and lit a log in her fireplace. Donna and Greg curled up in front of the fireplace while El Guru and Patty started making out instantly. Donna put her head on Greg's shoulder. A few minutes later, Patty got up, took El Guru by the hand, and giggle, "We'll be back in about an hour," as they went upstairs.

Greg and Donna started hugging and kissing. She took off her sweater and said, "I don't know if I should go through with this. I've never cheated on him before.

"I won't do anything you don't want me to do."

Some more hugging and kissing ensued and they wound up having sex. They kissed and cuddled for a while after it was over.

Donna said, "This was so nice, but it can't happen again. If you weren't from out of town and if I knew I'd ever run into you again, this wouldn't've happened. I know you have a long drive tomorrow morning. I'm sorry about your dad."

In a few minutes, Patty and El Guru came downstairs, smiling. Donna asked Patty to drive her home. "What a night - thank you," Greg whispered to her.

Donna pulled Greg aside and said, "Thanks for making me feel like a woman. I can't see you again, but I won't forget you."

The couples kissed goodnight outside. After Greg and El Guru got in Greg's car, Greg asked him, "How'd it go for you?"

"Man, she was good. She can do it all. As a human being, she's kind of shallow, but she was definitely good in bed. How was your older chick?"

"Best I've had since Celine. I'd love to see her again, but I can't. Her live-in boyfriend must be a prick. She's a nice person"

"Maybe Portland will turn out to be your lucky town. It's been a long time since we both picked up ladies in the same night."

"Welcome back to the USA."

Greg got up at 7:15 and drove home to see his father. His father just retired from work the week before and he looked weak, and had lost a lot of weight. They talked a few times briefly. At this point in his fading life, he couldn't talk for very long and he wanted to take naps most of the time. The whole family was there, including Greg's sister's two young children; everyone seemed a little sad. Greg told them he would be back in about a month.

He left at 9:30 on Sunday, but had to drive slower through the winding mountain roads that were intermittently icy. In fact, he almost skidded into another car head on in Vermont, but luckily didn't go off the road and there was no collision. He started listening to the Super Bowl on the radio.

El Guru was nowhere to be found when Greg got back to his place. At halftime, El Guru called him, saying, "I'm at Hazel Green's. The Cowboys are winning 10-7. Most of the people here are rooting for the Steelers."

"I just got in. I'll be down in a few minutes."

The game was close and the Steelers won 21-17. It was a happy ending to the weekend. Greg drove El Guru to Logan Airport Monday night, again acknowledging that they might not see each other again for a long time. When El Guru arrived in Albuquerque, he vowed to be a civilian forever.

Chapter 23

Greg Has an Affair and
El Guru Goes to College

Greg heard from El Guru by tape in April. "I'm getting settled in Albuquerque. I live with my cousin and I'm driving a '68 VW Bug. Living here is expensive - the price of a quart of milk higher than the price of a quart of beer. I can't find a job. You can't work as a medic in civilian life like you could in the Army unless you go back to school for one of the Physician Assistant programs. My social life is absolutely zero.

"Politics is frustrating, too. Probably 30 people are running for President, and so far, I don't like any of them. I still think we need some kind of revolution in the United States. At least I can get into sports - it was nice to go and see the Albuquerque Dukes, the Dodgers' Triple A team here. I sat in the cheap seats and saw tomorrow's stars today.

"One theater here shows last year's movies cheap. I saw "Monty Python and the Search for the Holy Grail," and I laughed like hell. I read "Jaws," too, which is an excellent book - a lot better than "Moby Dick."

"Your father has probably passed away. If he has, then my condolences. I bet you're freezing you ass of there, but maybe in a couple of years, you can move on to something even better. Portland could be a good place to live."

Greg's department head, Dr. Krech, rode him hard for a few months, but she was much nicer and apologetic toward him when she heard that his father had passed away. Greg and a young social worker, Joan Riendeau, convinced Dr. Delhomme to discharge a manic-depressive patient who was improving, against the advice of many of the staff. This marked a rift between older and younger unit staff, especially when the patient came back psychotic a few weeks later. Greg spent a great deal of time with a patient who frequently argued with staff, and did passive-aggressive things to irritate the nurses. For example, he smoked tea in a pipe (it smells much like marijuana), and he was sent to the maximum-security unit overnight until the hospital lab exonerated him, embarrassing the nursing staff and the MD on call the night before. He assembled food to make 20 hoagies and sold them in the back of the building at a "buy one get one free" rate at lunchtime, to compete with a bake sale the nurses had inside. He bought his own plastic tokens downtown and sold them for a dime a piece to patients in the behavior-mod token economy program. Maybe he got ideas from watching the move "One Flew Over the Cuckoo's Nest," which was playing at a local theater.

El Guru started to let his hair grow longer, in an Afro style and he had a full beard, which didn't help during job interviews. He confronted one prospective employer, at the US Post Office, about his possible prejudicial attitude, stating, "You think someone who doesn't look like you, or dress like you, may be a criminal, or doesn't have a brain. This isn't the Eisenhower era!" However, he got accepted at the University of New Mexico and decided to lay low for the rest of the summer to save enough money to take four courses. He was looking forward to classes at UNM, and even hung out there in August, but after conversing with students, he lamented that they didn't care much about politics.

But in encountering females, he concluded that he finally had a lot of respect for Women's Lib in the US.

Several nursing students of all ages, shapes, sizes, and raw abilities came to do a psych rotation on Greg's unit. Almost all wanted to sit in on group therapy Greg conducted, with Joan as his co-therapist. One of these, Sharon, a tall brunette in her early 30s, who was built much like Celine from a few years before, seemed to be actively flirting with him, even though she was married. Greg liked her right away, and the perfume she wore, Emeraude, had a scent that turned him on. One afternoon, she lamented to him about feeling trapped by her redneck husband (she lived 20 miles away), and after Greg invited her to his place to let her borrow a book about psychotherapy techniques, they almost immediately started having sex. He continued the affair, seeing her once a week at his place, and kept the clandestine meetings going all through July. Sex with her was terrific, he thought - reminiscent of Celine years earlier.

In August, Greg went out to the Midwest to check out some universities that had doctoral programs in his field, but also to look up some long-lost relatives. A new social worker on the unit, Dolph Paxton, gave him advice on areas to explore in Minnesota, where Dolph was originally from. Greg also became interested in doctoral programs at Michigan State after consultants from there came to the hospital, presenting to staff a fairly new independent living program for patients that they hoped the hospital would adopt.

After brief stops at his mother's and Pittsburgh, he went to Chicago. "Driving along Lake Shore Drive with Lake Michigan on the right is really scenic," he thought. He then drove up to Madison, Wisconsin. "Wow, the mayor's only 30, and even the waitresses I talk to are flaming liberals," he thought. Next, he went to Minneapolis. He noted, "It's really clean and I like the campus at the University of Minnesota. This place can't be any colder and snowier than where I'm living." He arrived in Rochester, MN, the next day for an impressive tour of the Mayo Clinic. "I'd love to work here," he thought.

Greg had a New England Patriots bumper sticker on his car as he pulled into Green Bay, and a drunk on a corner yelled at him, "The game's there, asshole!" He realized that the Packers were playing the Patriots that night in an exhibition game in Foxboro, MA. He went into a bar where the game was on TV and two guys next to him were arguing about "Carter."

"They got to get rid of him! He can't stop anyone to the right of him."

"What do you mean? He can beat anyone."

"He's not the same guy he was a few years ago."

"Nobody ever heard of him until last year."

"Who the hell are you talking about—Jimmy Carter—oh, him!"

A few guys at the bar laughed. The Packers had a linebacker named Jimmy Carter; not the man running for President.

Greg went to the Wisconsin State Fair in Milwaukee the next night. Lots of exhibits, rides, and animals—not like the Oktoberfest a few years before. The next day in Michigan he stayed with a cousin he hadn't seen in years, and he visited the Michigan State campus. He liked the campus right away, but unfortunately he didn't get to see the consultants who had come to his hospital. Then he drove to Toronto to see other cousins he hadn't met the previous year. A few days later, after he was back in New England, he decided he would apply to some midwestern doctoral programs for 1977.

The day after he got back, Sharon showed up at his door and said, "I'm pregnant."

They argued back and forth for almost an hour over whether or not he or her husband got her pregnant. Greg learned she had an affair with a college professor right before her involvement with him. Late the next day, he met a physician's assistant, Will, who was known to flirt with Sharon quite a bit. Greg asked him if he was having an affair with her. Will seemed surprised, and looking nervous, denied the implication saying, "I never did anything with her, but I know her brother-in-law did." Will left his position at the hospital a month later; he avoided Greg and never talked to him again. Sharon had an abortion. She asked Greg if he wanted to continue seeing each other if she divorced her husband, but Greg declined the offer. They never saw each other again. Greg vowed, "No more married women, ever again."

El Guru called Greg after receiving a tape from him in late September. "Greg, I'm a New Mexico Lobo now. I'm living with a Junior from Syracuse."

"How's school going so far?"

"I'm taking Anthropology, Psychology with a lab, Spanish, and American History - 13 credits, and that's all I can handle after being out of school for 10 years. I wanted to take History of Communism, but I had to take Political Science first and I couldn't get into the Intro course. I have about a C+ average so far - I have to learn to write papers and essay questions better. I go to the library to study instead of my apartment."

"Living with a Junior should help."

"We don't agree politically. He's a New York Giants, New York Yankees, and Notre Dame fan, so what's that tell you about how conservative he is? We argue some, but he's OK."

"I'm going to New England Patriots' games. They're off to a good start. I hope they beat the Oakland Raiders next weekend in Foxboro."

"You had a good trip to the Midwest. It was funny about 'Carter' in Green Bay. Did you drive off your hangovers?"

"No, that night was the only one that I had more than one beer. By the way, there's a bar on every corner in Green Bay. About Carter—I decided I'm going with McCarthy '76 for President. We need a third political party."

"I may write someone in. I don't trust Ford or Carter."

"This call is costing you a lot of money. I'll send you a tape in a few weeks."

El Guru's grades improved somewhat, but he felt a generation gap between him and most of the students. He had his highest mid-term grade in Anthropology. On the American History mid-term exam, there was a 20-point essay question in which he gave his own opinions about the Whigs and slavery instead of facts, and it cost him - he got a D on the exam.

Greg wrote and designed a program, sticking closely to the Michigan State model, and a Michigan State psychologist regularly consulted with him, a social worker, and a ward aide about it, along with some other staff. Nine patients were to live in a separate part of the hospital, making all decisions for themselves as a group, with guidance from the aide, who reported to Greg and the social worker. The goal for the group was to move out into a small house at a town 50 miles away, about eight to nine months later, for them either to have part time jobs or doing volunteer work. Greg was also making friends with Dolph Paxton and Jack Orvanis, a graduate student doing an internship.

Greg's social life was poor, but he met another older lady - a 34-year-old buxom redhead he met in southern Vermont while driving around to see the last of the fall foliage. They dated the next weekend. She had five cats in her apartment, so he thought it would be a "kiss her goodnight and drive home," but after they saw a movie, she insisted that he come in and have a glass of wine with her. As they were drinking, she cuddled next to him and implied that she wanted to get amorous. Greg didn't pass up the opportunity, and they were naked in her bed in 15 minutes. Right as they started having sex, one of the cats jumped on his head, and wouldn't get off. She started laughing uncontrollably, but after two minutes of wrangling with the cat, Greg jumped out of bed, quickly put on his clothes and scurried out the door while she was screaming about "leaving me hanging." He had hoped to get a girlfriend closer to where he lived to help him make it through the bitter, snowy winter that was being forecast, but to no avail. He sent El Guru a letter telling him about the incident.

El Guru sent him a tape laughing about the cat, at first. About his own social life, El Guru was seeing a German lady who was in his Anthropology class, but they were not sexually compatible and her political opinions were too conservative for him. He thought he had a solid final week - Psychology, particularly, was more enjoyable after the prof stopped talking about stimulus-response topics and more about personality, attitude change, and mental health disorders. He did not get an A in Spanish because the transition from conversational to writing (proper tenses, spelling, etc.) was more difficult than he thought it would be.

Greg, who had not had a roommate since he lived with Buck, moved in with Jack in a house on a lake right after Christmas. Jack's black lab, Bo, liked Greg right away and Greg and Jack seemed to enjoy the living arrangement in the cozy two-bedroom house with a tiny kitchen, a fireplace in the living room, two snow covered cords of wood outside, and a dock on the small lake out in back. Greg enjoyed mentoring Jack professionally, even though Dolph was Jack's supervisor. Greg's program at the hospital was going very well, so far. He called El Guru at the end of February.

"Artie, que pasa?"

"I'm glad you called. You're having a bitch of a winter up there."

"Yeah, 28 below zero one day last week. An 18-inch snowstorm a few days ago. There's no break in this crap, either. It's all over the east coast, especially here."

"Your job is going OK, at least?"

"Yeah. I moved in with that guy Jack I told you about last year. He's only 24, but he's done lots of traveling, likes '70s music, is a Redskins fan, has a nice dog, and plays chess. He also says what he feels and he's politically aware. We live in a nice little house on a lake outside of town. He's dating two chicks both named Lori - one's white and one's black. They aren't aware of each other."

"Like the song out now, 'Tryin' to Love Two.' He sounds like a cool dude."

"How'd your GPA turn out? What courses are you taking now?"

"You won't like this, but I decided not to go back. I got about a 2.8, but I can't deal with this generation of students and some of the professors. Too many people there don't give a shit about this county, the state, and even where they are going with their lives."

"Damn. I'm disappointed that you didn't give it more of a chance. You were doing great for not having been in school for years, and you didn't even take Political Science."

"At this time in my life, it's not for me. It was an adventure, and maybe I'll go back and try it again, someday."

"You proved to yourself you can do it, and if you want to get a decent job, a college education sure helps. I know you're turning 29, but you don't want to be 35 and floundering. Are you looking for a job?"

"Yeah. I'm moving out of here at the end of the month. I did pick up a chick at a party named Shari, and got to spend the night with her. She is in Colorado right now, but I hope I can live with her temporarily when she gets back next week, or until I get a job. She's a little unstable, though. She said her 2-year-old boy is the only thing that keeps her from suicide."

"Be careful. Sounds like you're Mr. Marginal Man' again."

I have some leads on jobs. I'm confident everything will work out OK. I'll get back to you when I'm settled."

Chapter 24

Europe Part II - for Greg

Greg applied to seven doctoral programs and was rejected by all of them. He applied to the wrong program at Michigan State; the consultant for his project told him, "If it was our program, given the progress of your project, we probably would have accepted you." The hospital project that he was involved with, along with guidance from the Michigan State consultant and mental health personnel where the group planned to move, was a success. Jack started seeing Joan Riendeau exclusively after that, even though she went to graduate school in Virginia. Jack moved out early in June to do another internship at a town 60 miles away, which meant that Greg needed to find a place very soon.

In mid-June, El Guru called him. "Greg - sorry I haven't been in touch. I bought a cheap cassette player and I left it on the dash in the car and it melted two weeks after I got it."

"What happened to you? You never sent me an address so I wrote you a letter and it came back 'Unable to Forward.' I have to move out of here at the end of the month, and I don't know where I'll be living. Decent apartments are hard to find in this town."

"I got a job in the mailroom of a big hospital here, the job is OK, the pay is OK, but I joined a union, which was a big mistake. The leaders are sleazy. There are over 500 people in this union, but only five or six regularly show up for the meetings. I asked the president of the union about the finances and to explain how what is taken out of paychecks is used and associated benefits, and they gave me bullshit excuses. I told them that, according to the Articles of the Union, any member can see the books at any time. Then he said, 'Any member in GOOD standing!' Then the son of a bitch called me a Communist and said, 'We know all about you and your past.' I was shocked!"

"That's bullshit. Were you rabble rousing at the meetings?"

"You know, I did bring up some things that Karl Marx would have appreciated. These people are supposed to be pro-worker."

"Here we go again."

"Let me tell you before you pass judgement - I went to Phoenix to see my cousin last weekend, and when I got back my apartment had been ransacked. Fortunately, nothing was taken. It took me five hours to put things back together. I can't prove it, but I wonder if it was one of those people."

"I hope my own phone isn't being bugged. Let's talk about something else in case it is. How's your love life going?"

"It didn't work out with Shari. Some women I've met are dummies, but a few others are really friends, but nothing beyond that. Either I've cooked for them or they invite me over to have dinner. We usually have wine, and in one case, we actually shared a joint. But I've reached the point where I don't fantasize about every lady I meet being a potential lover."

"I think I got to that point last fall. My roommate, Jack, even slept with somebody at the house, who just wanted to sleep with nothing sexual going on. He said he's done that a few times and it's OK with him."

"That's hard to do."

"Yeah, hard literally (they laughed). Jack had to move out, but he will always be a friend. As housemates, we've had our arguments. Sometimes it was about stupid stuff, like last month, I took off to Portland for the weekend and I had a good time. Before I left, I bought a package of those new Double Stuf Oreos, and we each had one just before I left - delicious, man. But when I got back Sunday night, the bastard had eaten all but two of them! Man, I was pissed, but he couldn't stop laughing when I confronted him. He promised to buy me more, but he never did."

El Guru laughed loudly and said, "You love chocolate anything, don't you? Would you rather have a delicious chocolate cake or get laid?"

"Shit, man, that's not a fair question (laughing)—depends on the cake and the woman. Would you rather smoke great dope and get high or pick up a chick and get laid?"

"Same as you—it depends," he said, laughing, "but I don't get high much anymore."

"Seriously, Artie, I was hoping to hear from you and get your phone number because I've decided to go to Europe on vacation for two weeks in August. Are you in?"

"Wow, Greg, I'd love to go. I'd have to quit this job, and the union has put a real sour taste in my mouth. I'd probably have just enough money to pull it off. Do you want to go back to Cologne, Dusseldorf, and those other places again?"

"Yeah, but I was thinking of also going up to the Scandinavian countries and you could show me around the Bremerhaven and Cuxhaven areas for a day, and maybe we could go all the way back down to Luxembourg, or take a Rhine cruise for a day."

"That sounds cool. Let me get back to you soon."

"I have to start making reservations soon. I met a travel agent who could get us a great deal on flights, and even get a whole European train schedule ahead of time."

"Can you call me back in about two weeks?"

"OK, I should have a better idea of where I stand with things by then. But let me know if you can go. I'll call you Sunday night, the 19th."

He called El Guru on June 19th and told him that he would fly into Brussels on Aug 6th. El Guru told him he could meet him in Dusseldorf at 1:30 that Saturday afternoon on the 6th. He said he was planning on quitting his job on July 29th, and that he'd live at home for a while when he got back, and look for another job. Greg told him that he would get back to him in a few weeks for some more planning about other places that they might want to go to and what they might want to do. He asked Greg if he had found a place to live yet and Greg said, "No, and it's getting down to crunch time. I'm always either looking for a place to live, or a car, or some kind of a girlfriend, or a job. I rarely have them all at the same time." El Guru said that it was exactly the same for him and replied, "That's what life should be all about for us at our age."

Greg found a place to live on the 29th and soon after he moved in, he spent all of his spare time either listening to Red Sox games on the radio, recording music, or planning the trip. He called El Guru on July 16th.

"Artie, here's where we should go and what we should see."

El Guru cut him off. "Wait, Greg, I hate to tell you this and I hope you don't get pissed, but I'm not going. I've decided to go back to school at UNM and give it another chance. I'm almost 30 and it's now or never. This time, I might go into nursing or another medical area. I didn't quit the job, but I had a long talk with Dr. Vargas, a surgeon, last week when he came by the mail room and he told me there was an opening for someone with my experience as an OR tech. He also convinced me that it would be better for me to go back to school to have more options open for me later on. I'm keeping my apartment. You're not pissed at me, are you?"

"Not really, I guess. I am disappointed, but I agree, you really need to do this. Maybe we can do another trip after you get your degree, if we're both still single. But I won't back out now because there's a chance I may never get to see parts of Europe I always wanted to. Are you already working in the OR now?"

"I started on Monday. I can work full time until school starts, and then 20 hours a week. Buck Williams did something like this when he lived with you a few years ago, didn't he?"

"He did, but he worked his ass off and lost a lot of weight. Did I tell you I heard from him several months ago? Instead of medical school, he's finishing a program in North Carolina as a physician's assistant."

"I thought he'd sure make it and be a good doctor but a PA is the next best thing."

"Don't you want to do that? There are more and more programs for PAs starting up."

"I don't know. Maybe, or maybe something else. But I am probably better off in the medical field. I don't have to be involved with a union on this job. Hey, have a great time in Europe. Get in touch with me when you get back."

El Guru liked his job at the OR. He ran into the same in house political issues as in the mail room, however—management vs employees regarding issues of overtime, retroactive pay, and people filing grievances and losing. He was meeting more women, but when he did get dates, he started talking politics and got upset because their views were the opposite of his.

Greg went back to his mother's one weekend, and he met a very attractive younger girl, Sandy, at a disco in Lake George. They agreed to go out the next Thursday night to see Star Wars. Star Wars was sold out when they went to see it, but they saw another movie and went to a nearby bar for drinks afterwards. Sandy was a tall, Lynda-Carter-like brunette who was turning 22 the next month. She was a secretary for a state government agency in Albany, and her father was retired career military. She had never been out with anyone as old as Greg before, and he had never been out with anyone 8 years younger, but Greg thought she was a very nice person. Within 10 minutes of going back to her place later, they started making out hot and heavy, and wound up going to bed. They both thoroughly enjoyed the encounter, and they kissed and cuddled for a while afterwards. At midnight, she said she had to go to work the next morning and he said he had to pack to fly to New York and Europe the next day.

"I can't wait to see you when I get back," he said.

"Send me a post card," Sandy said, with a glassy-eyed smile.

"What a great start to the vacation," Greg thought. "I like this girl a lot – maybe she could be the one, after all these years."

Greg thought about Sandy all through the trip. He flew into Brussels, went to Dusseldorf, checked into the Hotel Continental and tried to look up Peter Herkt at the New Orleans Club in Konigsallee. The bartender said he hadn't worked there for a few years. Later he was at Lord Nelson's and the place was packed. He didn't even flirt with any women because he kept thinking about Sandy.

The next day he took a train up to Bremen. It was raining, so he only saw part of the city and took off for Copenhagen the next day. He woke up to a big, delicious Danish pastry outside his door and later went to explore the city - Tivoli Gardens, the Little Mermaid statue, Stroget, etc. On a walking tour, he met a young guy named Henny, from Amsterdam, who wanted to know all about America because he was going there the next year to upstate New York, northern New England and Montreal. They had dinner at a sidewalk café, talking and drinking for over two hours. Greg told him to stay in touch.

Greg took an early morning, very long train ride to Oslo. After dinner, he was shocked to see that it was still daylight - the sun did not set until after 10:00 pm. The next day the weather was gorgeous, about 70 degrees and sunny. He walked around Frogner Park, admired the statues, and later took a boat ride around the fjord. He relaxed but was surprised there were no high cliffs. At the end of the day, he went to the site where the Nobel Peace Prize is awarded, and then to a museum with Viking ships and the Kon Tiki raft. He bought Thor Heyerdahl's book. At dinner, his waiter encouraged him to see Gothenburg, Sweden, instead of Stockholm because Stockholm was the most expensive city in Europe.

At Gothenburg, the desk clerk at his hotel seemed angry when she saw that he was an American, and went through the check-in as quickly as she could, almost throwing a map of the city at him. He wondered if some people still thought of Americans as Nixon-types. Later he went to a disco where every fourth song played was by ABBA, some of which he had never heard before. He soon left and went back to the hotel because it was difficult to stretch money in Sweden. He decided to go to Aalborg, Denmark, the next day. That night he went to a bar where a rock band was playing. The guy next to him at the bar was a very friendly Norwegian who told him that the bar closed at 7:00 am! The beer was cheap and the band was really good, but he kept comparing the women he met to Sandy.

The next day, he took a brief tour of the city of Aarhus where there was a magnificent area of Lego structures. But he had to go to Hamburg, Germany, because he promised to meet a woman named Kirsten, who had been an intern at the hospital last year. He had written to her a month before he left, asking if she would like to meet him for dinner that Sunday. He met her for an early dinner and they caught up on what had happened in their lives during the past year; she asked about many of the staff and patients. She was going to finish her doctorate in Psychology that year and she told him what to expect about doing a dissertation someday. Afterwards, they took a stroll along the harbor for an hour, ending at the Hauptbahnhof during the clear, cool evening, and he took pictures along the way. She caught a train to Kiel to meet a friend that night. Greg checked into a hotel, and walked to the St. Pauli district where there was a carnival. From there he walked to the Reeperbahn, observing many tourists gawking through the doors of the clubs of this famous red-light district where he saw, from a short distance, someone getting the hell beaten out of him by two men outside of a club. A couple of prostitutes tried to pick him up as he scrambled to get out of this area. He took a brisk walk back to his hotel.

On the 15th, he hopped on a train to Cologne. He stayed at the Hotel Kommerz, as it rained on and off. He hoped that the night life would still be as good as it had been five years ago, but first he went to Alt Koln, his favorite restaurant, for dinner. Then to Hohenzollern Strasse - he smiled as he walked, feeling "at home again in Europe." He went to the St. Marlena

Café, and played chess, but was checkmated in 20 minutes. It disappointed him to discover that most of the places he knew from the early '70s were gone or had changed radically. Some were now casinos; some turned into clip joints; one even turned into a McDonald's. Old Mac had evolved into Chico's Mexican Jazz Club, but it was dead. The Santa Cruz was still good though; Margo, a bartender El Guru liked, was still there. She laughed loudly when Greg told her the story about Mr. Bangladesh and the Viking back in '72. He went to the Scandinavia Bar, a place he frequently went to wrap up the night. People there were very friendly but he was getting drunk, and he wobbled back to his hotel. Greg was hung over the next morning, but he went into the Dom to take a few pictures and he had to spend money at Kaufhof (department store) because he was out of shirts and had no time to wash his clothes.

Later, he took a train ride to Koblenz to board a Rhine cruise to Bingen. An attractive, 35ish woman, Ruth, from California shared the cab he was going to take to the dock. As they pulled away, a girl yelled, "Wait for me!" in Spanish. Her name was Gail, from Peru, and she spoke fluent English as well as Spanish. She was cute, emotionally expressive, and had a great sense of humor. Ruth had a bottle of wine and drank a good bit of it before they boarded the boat. After a while on the cruise, Ruth withdrew from the group on the deck and got drunk alone, while Gail, Greg, and several others were talking, laughing, and taking pictures of castles along the way.

Gail was partially American-educated in Florida, had a father who was influential in Peruvian government, and he did not like Americans. Gail seemed to be turning on to Greg, however. When the boat docked in Bingen, Gail wanted to stay with Greg to save money, and he agreed. When they got back to the hotel after dinner, she said she just wanted to sleep, and take a shower in the morning, which was OK with Greg. "If Jack can do this, I can, "he thought. However, in the morning, they wound up having sex and it was enjoyable. Afterwards, at the train station, they exchanged addresses and kissed goodbye, even though they realistically knew they would never see each other again. Greg hoped that this would be his "last fling' before possibly starting a long-term relationship with Sandy when he got back to the U.S.

Gail took a train to meet a relative in Frankfurt, while Greg went back to the old hospital in Bad Kreuznach just to see it, before he went to Luxembourg. When he got there, it started raining while he walked to the hospital. However, he suddenly realized the place was deserted and had apparently shut down, although he did walk around allowing memories to soak in before he got soaked himself. He hopped on a train and headed to Luxembourg. Once he arrived, he went to the Hotel Italia, and later went to Black Bess's, but the place was all teeny boppers now. He dropped into the Royal Bugatti Pub, which was lively, and they played all Elvis Presley songs - someone broke the news to him that Elvis had just died. He asked a lady to dance, who was dressed in a chic Army fatigue-like outfit but he started laughing when he saw a "Philadelphia Eagles" label on her chest. He tried to explain to her what it was, but she didn't believe him and was turned off to him. He talked with several other friendly men and women who wanted to discuss Elvis - one guy even bought him a Henri Funk beer By 11:00, he was feeling no pain and someone suggested that he go back to his hotel and sleep "alone."

In the morning, Greg travelled to Aachen. Nothing had changed from five years before except the Hotel Hospitz ("Mr. Tailer and Mr. Horning!") was gone. He returned to the cathedral and museum there, but he suddenly decided to make Brussels the last stop on his trip because he had to catch a plane from there the next day to fly back to the US. The Hotel Galaxy there was a rip off but it was not far from the airport. Nobody had ever been friendly to him in Brussels, but he hung out briefly at La Grande Place before going back to the hotel in the evening.

In New York, he missed his connecting flight, but he found a clerk who told him he could take a limousine to Newark Airport and he was the last person to get a seat. At Newark, he rushed to the Allegheny Airlines desk and asked the clerk there to get him on the flight to Albany that was leaving in 10 minutes. The clerk said, "That flight left 10 minutes ago."

"What? They lied to me at JFK about the time of the flight! I at least want a refund for the limo that brought me here."

"OK, we'll credit your American Express card, but that's all we can do."

"You're going to put me up at a hotel out here, so I can take the first flight out in the morning, aren't you?"

"We can't do that."

"Christ! Air India did that for me the last time this happened six years ago!"

"We're not Air India and it's not six years ago."

"What am I supposed to do now? Do I have to wait in this dump all night?"

"I can't help you. This counter is closed. Take a bus to Port Authority in New York and take a bus to Albany. We can't get you out on a flight."

He shut off the lights, locked up his desk and left. Greg was forced to do what he'd been told, plus take a taxi to his mother's house. It cost his almost every cent he had left. He arrived at his mother's at 4:15 am. To top things off, he went back to the Albany airport just before noon and when he went to the Allegheny Airlines desk, he noticed his bags were strewn in a nearby corner along with a few others—not even at the baggage claim area! He went over and picked them up, and in an angry voice, pointed to the Allegheny desk and yelled, "I'm filing a complaint with the Civil Aeronautics Board and Ralph Nader against you bastards!"

When he got back to his mother's she said, "By the way, you got some mail about two weeks ago." The letter was from Buck Williams who was getting married in Boston that afternoon. Greg got his parents' phone number and called. Buck's father answered and said the wedding was at 4:00. Greg explained that he had been out of the country and just got back into the US and that he was sorry he didn't know sooner but he couldn't make it there in time. Buck wasn't there, but Greg gave his father his phone number and asked if Buck could please call him when he got back from his honeymoon. Unfortunately, he never heard from Buck again.

Chapter 25

Good Times and Bad Times in the Late '70s

$\mathbf{E}$l Guru went back to the University of New Mexico, and he liked a girl who was financing her education by prostitution. He wanted to go to bed with her but she asked him for $40. He then told her he wanted to be friends, but she declared she didn't want to be close to anyone. He met another guy who was an Air Force veteran but they argued about politics. He joined what he thought was a fairly liberal discussion group, but he told the group in the second meeting that they were all actually more conservative than he was. He felt that his classes, even Political Science, were boring. They only other person on campus he met that he liked was Michael Cooper, a star basketball player. He quit school after about four weeks.

El Guru continued working in the OR, but after his second month there, he was irritated by the apathy of many of the staff because they did not care about making any changes in the system at work. He became more outspoken with his opinions, and he began making as many enemies as friends. One guy told him to cool his "quick, ornery attitude, and shave his beard," but El Guru replied, "I've worked in hospitals for years now and I know that the worst thing for improving a workplace is to just do your job and shut your mouth. The situation never gets better that way. And my beard is staying until one of the docs or head honchos here talks to me about it." The surgeon who helped get him the OR job, Dr. Vargas, had taken an interest in him, and was supportive of his opinions. But when Dr.

Vargas took a leave of absence, El Guru started working permanent nights on a surgical ward. He bought a new boom box and sent Greg a tape in November in response to the one Greg had sent him.

Greg was upset that El Guru had quit school again, and in a tape to him declared that El Guru never gave UNM a chance. "College is not like pledging a fraternity for four years. I hope your decision doesn't bite you in the ass later, but at least you have a job in a hospital environment, some interesting patients, and you're not just stocking supplies on the ward all night."

Then he told him about Sandy. "I really liked her. I went out with her again in September, but she told me, 'We have to talk.' She had been going with a guy for over two years and he was there when she got my postcard from Europe. She said he wants to get married now, but she thinks that she's too young for that. Her family likes the guy. I told her that this year I have felt the pull to settle down. She said that she wants to see the both of us for a while. We agreed to leave things open for now. I told her I would send her a Christmas card, and to send me one back if she was still interested. The other guy has been with her since '75. He just landed a good job in Massachusetts, he can see her almost every weekend and maybe even during the week, and he's a lot closer in age to her. It would be like fighting with my right arm tied behind my back. Maybe I'll hear from her, but I don't want to get into a 'Let's you and him fight' game. Anyway, I just had a date with a young psychologist and it went really well."

Work went much better for El Guru during the winter. He spent time with several friends, and a roommate named Pedro, who worked days and helped with expenses. In January, they had a lady named Elena move in - like a "Three's Company" in reverse. El Guru dated a couple of women off and on. With things going so well for him, it made the colder and even snowier than normal winter there enjoyable. "Nothing better than having several friends, having some wine, and just talking around a fireplace," he said to Greg in a Christmas card. El Guru performed CPR on a patient one night and saved her life. His 30th birthday party in March was a memorable one with about 10 people at his place to help him celebrate, complete with a decorated cake and a bottle of Jägermeister. A lady he had just dated was at the party and spent the night with him. El Guru was on a hot streak.

Greg's life was the opposite of El Guru's. He was having a difficult time at work and he was convinced some nurses sabotaged treatment plans for patients. Any possible relationship with the young psychologist fizzled out; she got rid of him after the third date. He never heard from Sandy. His car was giving him lots of trouble. His apartment was intermittently cold. It was a rough winter in New England and it seemed like there was either a snow storm or an ice storm every weekend. Aside from work, Greg was doing nothing but watching sports on TV or recording music. Instead of taking his usual vacation in the summer, in April he decided to take off for 10 days and go to Canada. The second night he was in Ottawa, talking and dancing at a downtown disco when they played the Village People's song, 'Key West.' Suddenly he thought, "This is stupid. What am I doing here? I should be in Key West." He left the disco, went back to his motel, got up early the next morning, drove to his mother's house, and went to a travel agency that got him a fly/drive package to leave from Albany to Miami the next day.

The trip was well worth it - 85 degrees and sunny every day, palm trees and blue-green ocean water. In Miami, he wandered into the Orange Bowl where Dolphins coach Don Shula was trying out a punter. After a few minutes, security guards chased him out, but gave him a "hot off the press" 1978 schedule of Dolphins' games. The next day, he drove to Key West via the narrow Seven Mile bridge, checked into a motel, and stayed there for several days. He spent one relaxing day at a beach. Then he went sightseeing for the next two days—he was impressed with the tour of Hemingway's house. He spent one of the evenings going to a couple of bars on Duval Street. At Sloppy Joe's, he had a long talk with a lady about his age whom he wanted to date the next night - she told him she liked him, but she didn't want to date him because she was a local and he was a tourist. She said, at one point, "How can anybody live in northern New England? For me, that would be positively weird." He spent his last day of the trip in Miami, and while basking in the sun on Coconut Grove beach, the lady in Key West's words resonated in his mind. He thought, "You know, I could probably live or go to school in Florida. Too bad I'm not rich and I could spend summer and fall in New England and winter and spring here."

El Guru called Greg the night of May 15th. "I'm surprised you're home, but I thought I'd try, anyway. I thought you might have bought yourself one of those new answering machines for your birthday."

"Too expensive. Today was probably my worst birthday ever. Nobody in my family called me, and you are the only friend I've heard from. At least my mother sent me a nice card."

"That sucks, but is that's all that's bumming you out?"

"No. Just as I got in the parking lot at work this morning, it started raining like hell, and I got soaked. Then I got into a loud argument with the head nurse in the team meeting bitching about what kinds of things we should be doing in the state mental health regional planning - I was fortunate to get on a huge committee for that."

"Wow, you're moving up in that system."

"It's a combination of luck and taking advantage of breaks. Anyway, in the afternoon, I'm in group therapy with eight patients and two co-therapists, and hardly anyone wanted to talk for the first 15 minutes. So, I said, 'OK, let's just sit here in silence and to reflect on what you're experiencing nonverbally.' Right after that, a patient comes in late with a half-gallon of ice cream saying, 'Hey, you guys, you gotta try this Deering's Mint Chocolate Chip,' as he went to pass it around, and that disrupted the whole group. I got pissed and threw him out, but three other patients went with him. Later on, I saw a new patient in my office and after a little while, he started screaming that everyone who worked in mental health was nothing but a bullshit artist, me included. To top off the day, I was supposed to get a new car after work, but they told me it wouldn't be ready until tomorrow. Then a few ladies who work on another unit were supposed to meet me at Hazel Green's at happy hour, but they didn't show up. I watched the Red Sox lose to the Royals on TV and I'm on my 4th Heineken, alone."

El Guru started laughing, "For you when it rains, it pours—even literally. "

"I'm fucked the wrong way. Not even any cake or ice cream."

"You should have ripped off the ice cream from that patient and told everybody it was your birthday, and you deserved all of it. The second side of your tape was fuzzy, but apparently you had a good time in Florida. Did you almost score with that chick from Key West?"

"No, and the way I feel at this moment, I don't even want to. I'll probably try one more time to apply for doctoral programs, but if I don't get accepted anywhere, I'll try to get into a Masters program for Health Care Administration. Looks like there's a good one at the University of Missouri at Kansas City."

"Why not try New Mexico? Or Florida?"

"Too early to tell now, but Florida may well be an option. I keep thinking about what that chick at the bar on Duval Street said about it being weird where I live. What's up with you?"

"I'm having a real good year so far. The job is going great, but it's frustrating that I can't do a lot of the same things on the ward that I did as a medic in the Army. You have to be an RN or LPN, but I get a lot of respect from people who work here. I've had dates with a few women, but nobody serious. In fact, as friends, I have more female friends than male friends right now, and that's OK. I go to Albuquerque Dukes games when I can. I haven't smoked a bowl or a joint in a long, long time."

"I'm starting to make more female friends, as friends. I only have you and one other male friend who aren't married."

"Like you, I have to get a new car pretty soon. My old VW is starting to leak oil a little bit, and I'd rather get a more recent used car. What car are you getting?"

"A '78 Plymouth Volare."

"A Volare? Good luck. Hope it's better than that aluminum block engine Astre and you don't have all the trouble with the transmission and engine you had when the weather was cold."

"You know, we're both in our 30s now. I don't know about you, but I've been thinking lately about where I am in my life and where I expected to be by now. Things are different from six years ago when I got out of the Army, but not really what I thought they would be for me."

"Yeah. Back in '72, I never thought seriously about going into the Army again, and it was a big mistake when I did. I thought I'd either be living in Europe or be working at a decent job at a hospital, even as a lab tech or something, while I'd be going back to school and getting a degree. I thought I'd be married with a family by now."

"By this time, I thought I'd be married with a family, too, or at least married and owning a house. I thought I'd either have a doctorate in Psychology, Counseling, or Social Work, or in some kind of work in mental health management. And I've have a bad-ass car, and making real good money."

"In those days, I thought we'd unfortunately be doomed with Nixon until '77 and America would go further downhill from there. That's why radical or revolutionary stuff is attractive to me at times. The Carter administration comes off as amateurish, to me. I always knew I'd stay as interested in sports and music as I was then."

"The job I have is good, but it's a dead end in the long run because I don't have a doctorate. I could become a young dinosaur by the mid '80s if nothing were to change in my life. At least our health is OK, and we're both staying active physically. I bought some weights, and I'd really like to get on a softball team. Like you, I'm as interested in sports and music as I always was."

"I still love travelling but I can't do it right now. You're lucky you can. Another thing - six years ago, I just wanted to pick up any chick I could if any opportunity presented itself. Now, I can appreciate women as human beings first, and the Women's Lib thing really needed to happen. My relationship with Ursula started changing my attitude."

"We were more free-wheeling, hedonistic, and thinking we'd be zooming on the Trans European Express Train to success in life in our 20's. Now, we're taking the local train."

"That's a good analogy, but it isn't all bad or disappointing. We're still young, and we're not ready to die by a longshot."

"Send me a tape sometime, Artie."

"Hope your birthday isn't an omen for the rest of the year."

El Guru and Pedro moved into a new place, but soon things took a turn for the worse in El Guru's job. A new Director of Nursing came to the hospital, and he was assigned to a new supervisor. He clashed with both of them regarding almost every ward procedure. Once again, he started to preach his political ideas to people in the hospital, and except for a few friends, became more of an outcast at work. He was even arguing more often with Pedro, and one night in August he decided to quit his job and soon ended up in Huntington Beach, CA.

In October, he wrote to Greg that it was not as expensive as he thought it would be and he even went to a couple of Dodgers' games. The only females he met were 'WASPs' - no Chicano ladies yet, and he got a job in a hospital OR.

He said that he was the only minority in the department, but he did not feel disadvantaged at all. He was able to speak some Spanish with the patients, though. A month later he had to go back to New Mexico to help out his parents who were both having health problems. He told his supervisors that he would like to try to come back next year if there were any openings; one MD said that he would write him a letter of recommendation despite only having worked two months there. El Guru later sent Greg a Christmas card telling him why he was temporarily back in New Mexico and he would get in touch with Greg in the spring.

Later that summer, Greg met a lady from Quebec City, Octavia, at Lake George one weekend. He and Henny, from Holland (who he met last year in Copenhagen), were at the same disco in Lake George where Greg had met Sandy the year before, and they each met French-Canadian woman about their ages. Henny's chick was from Montreal, and he got to spend the night with his lady. Greg got an address and phone number from Octavia, who told him to call her so that they might go to the Quebec Provincial Fair in Quebec City in August.

The drive to Quebec was interesting for Greg. The temperature dropped about 10 degrees as he drove up US 201 on a two-lane road with only a few passing cars. He had the windows down and there was a pleasant odor of balsam and other evergreen trees as he sped along. "It really smells like Christmas," he thought. In about a 25 mile stretch of 'nothingness,' he saw a couple of moose grazing near the road, and at one point, he saw a porcupine with its quills up on the other side of the road, but surprisingly, no deer. He passed through Customs into Canada and drove to St. George where he called Octavia, who was pleased to hear from him. They spoke half French and half English to each other. She laughed, "Call me at 1:00 tomorrow. Je vous donne le grand tour of Quebec." Greg stayed at Le Chateau Frontenac, overlooking the vast St. Lawrence River, a hotel which was upscale for him. He hung around there for a while after he checked out, ate lunch at a café and called Octavia.

Octavia, a 5'7" blonde with short hair, average build and a 'baby' smile, was two years younger than Greg, and single. Directions to her place were very easy, and after he got there, she drove them all over the area, walked through quaint parts of downtown, and the dinner at the Chinese restaurant there was the best Chinese food he ever had. They went to the fair and saw the Patsy Gallant show (a bi-lingual French-Canadian pop-rock star). It was a very enjoyable evening for them. When they got to her place, he asked Octavia if he could stay with her. She agreed but said, "Nous sommes fatigue," as she giggled. They started kissing and caressing, and after some conversation, they wound up having sex but Octavia lit up a cigarette in bed, which slightly irritated Greg.

"Many times, I do smoke avant sommeil (before sleeping)," she said.

"Ce n'est pas dangerous?"

"I am eveille (awake) when I smoke in bed. C'est aide for sleeping. Seule une (only one). Jamais (never) two"

They agreed to meet in Montreal in September for a weekend, but Greg began to see some drawbacks to Octavia. On the positive side, she liked to laugh and she had a good sense of humor; but they weren't very compatible sexually, she blew things out of proportion getting too emotional, and she also smoked a pack of cigarettes a day, even though she recently had a collapsed lung. "I don't know where this is going," Greg thought on the drive home from Montreal. A few weeks later, Octavia invited him back up to Quebec to meet her brother, her sisters, and friends at a party at her brother's house. He liked her brother and they talked about American football and hockey (Greg was impressed that a few friends she had growing up were well known NHL players). Everyone spoke French. Greg had a good time but he felt out of place, even though they were a fairly friendly bunch. He invited her to come to see him for a weekend in late October to see Manchester, NH, which had a French-Canadian section of town.

When she came to see Greg, he showed her around the area, and they spent part of an afternoon with Dolph Paxton and his family. Octavia did not seem thrilled with Greg's apartment and although she seemed to have a good time, some arguments started over her smoking. Also, she started dropping hints about Greg moving to Canada to live with her. The last day of her visit, while they were lying in bed, she admitted she wanted to get pregnant and get married, but for Greg, he decided this was not the future he wanted with her. And winter was coming soon.

A few days after this, Dolph's 15-month-old son had a terrible fall, resulting in a head injury that left him fighting for his life. The little boy wound up at Children's' Hospital in Boston and Greg drove down there one night to be with Dolph and his wife Jane when it looked like the child was not going to make it. For the next month, Greg spent a great deal of time with Dolph and his family, decreasing communication with Octavia. He called her on her birthday a few weeks later, but their talk was fairly brief - there were silences and elements of a "dangling conversation." Winter was coming fast, and he had no other dating prospect in sight. He sent her a Christmas card - he didn't get one from her - and soon after that he wrote her a break up letter, telling her she was very nice and they'd had some good times, but he listed many reasons why their relationship would not work in the long run.

To close out the year, Greg was excited about a phone interviews he had for jobs as a branch director of a mental health clinic in Indiana, and at the Mayo Clinic in Minnesota doing only group therapy for substance abusing clients. He was assured he was the leading candidate for both positions. However, after the first of the year, both places notified him that they had decided to hire someone internally. Aside from the help and support he was trying to give Dolph and Jane, he felt he was not getting much satisfaction from his life - the job was really just a 'job' now; the state regional planning was scrapped because of a political upset for Governor in November; more patients coming into his hospital unit were actually sociopaths claiming they were suicidal, trying to spend the winter there. On weekends, he spent his time either recording music, watching hockey or old movies on TV, and drinking beer alone.

Greg decided to apply to several doctoral programs in Ontario, Wisconsin, Maine, Florida, West Virginia, and for Masters in Health Care

Administration in Missouri. The last two accepted him to start in the fall of 1980, but for different programs than what he wanted. The first three rejected him. However, on St. Patrick's Day, he was accepted into the Florida program and he excitedly wrote to them saying, "Yes, I will come down there to start in September." Of course, there would be no assistantship, and he would be on probation for a year, but that didn't bother Greg - he was on probation when he started every job and every academic endeavor for the past 15 years. All he had to do was save money, which he had been doing anyway, all winter. Things were looking up for him in 1979.

El Guru sent him a tape in mid-May, in response to a tape Greg had sent to him in April. "Wow, man, it's been a long time since we've been in touch with each other. A lot has been happening with me. I finally fixed this old tape player and bought a used truck. I don't know why I didn't get in touch with you about this soon, but I got a girl named Lorraine pregnant as a result of my 30th birthday party last year, and I have a five-month-old daughter. Her name is Kris, and she is a delightful little girl. I'm living with them now. Lorraine works part time but mostly stays at home. I pay for whatever child support she needs.

"I quit my job at the hospital and became a correctional officer a few months ago. I work evenings. The money is good and it's a raise in salary for me. I don't give the prisoners any breaks - they always ask me for coffee, cigarettes, and other stuff but I say 'No.' This is a hard place to escape from but inmates keep trying. I got a great probationary evaluation. They have psychiatric and medical services and I'd like to work at either one but there are no openings right now. Some guards bang prisoners around, but I won't. One of them moved up to be a new supervisor and everybody hates him except the warden. I try to avoid working with him - he's a flaming asshole.

"I haven't smoked anything at all in over a year now. If somebody offered me a joint at a party, I might not turn it down, but I don't go out partying any more.

"You're gonna move to Florida in September? Good luck. I hope it works out for you. Send me a tape or call me when you can."

Greg called him in July. "Hey, amigo. Greetings from a hot summer up north!"

"I was hoping I'd hear from you, Greg. Let me tell you what's happened with me and Lorraine. A few nights ago, I asked her to marry me. She said, 'No,' and that we wouldn't be happy with each other in the long run. She said that things were OK for now, but she would prefer that soon we should go our separate ways. She probably wouldn't want me involved in Kris's life, and she wouldn't even want me to pay child support. This whole thing is on the order of what Ursula told me without any outside sex being involved. It hit me like a ton of bricks. She was almost objective and impersonal about it. Wow!"

"Sounds like it was pretty cold. What are you gonna do now?"

"I can't cry over spilled milk but I can't quite afford to leave now, either. I told her I was hurt by this and I didn't see it coming at all. She said she had been thinking about sitting down with me to discuss this for about a month. She said sex had nothing to do with it. She was sorry and hoped we could remain friends and she was willing to let me live here until I found another place. At least, I appreciate her honesty."

"Which was worse - this or what happened with Ursula?"

"I don't know. With Ursula, I was in love and it would have been a new start for both of us. With Lorraine, it would be a real chance to settle down with my own family, and I like her but I thought I might grow to love her. It's disappointing, but I have to move on."

They talked about other things going on in their lives. Gas was up to 88 cents a gallon, but there were no long lines at the pump like there were a few months ago. El Guru was in a power struggle at work with a black female correctional officer over treatment of the prisoners. He was put on duty with two black females to see if he can work with blacks, and the ladies agreed with him that it was ridiculous. He was making $11,500 a year, and he said he could see where people would get burned out working in a prison, which is why he said he would rather work in a medical or psychiatric unit here.

Greg told him that he was enjoying the summer and hanging out a lot with his friend Dolph and his family. Unfortunately, Dolph's youngest son could not yet walk or talk, but the toddler seemed happy for now. Greg related that he was on a state agency softball team playing shortstop, and hitting well. He also said he was going over to the beach whenever he could and had a great tan built up. He planned on going down to New York to see his friend from college, Mort, in a month. He also called Kent Stone and told him he'd be in Charlotte on his way to Florida. Stone said he was looking forward to having a few beers together and cooking a southern breakfast for them.

"Man, you're having some good times. What's Stone doing now?"

"Nothing. He's independently wealthy. Never worked or went back to school."

"Isn't that nice! Will you try to look up Buck Williams?"

"No. He's somewhere out in western North Carolina, way out of my way."

"Send me your address and phone number by cassette tape after you get to Florida."

On August 10th, Greg told everyone at the hospital he was leaving. There were some shocked looks, but people were happy for him and most hoped he would return someday. That night he went to the Red Blazer, a local restaurant and bar. After he had one beer, he noticed a lady sitting at a table with her friends who were nurses in another building of the hospital. A year ago, he had seen her in a parking lot and asked the Chief of Social Work who this gorgeous lady was. He told him that her name was Janie and she worked days on one of the units but he didn't know which one and he thought she had kids but didn't know anything else about her.

"She looks like the quintessential foxy older chick for me," Greg replied.

The band started playing the Peaches and Herb song, "Reunited." Greg thought, "What have I got to lose? Here goes…"

"Hi, would you like to dance?"

She stared at him briefly and started to smile.

"Well, I didn't ask you to marry me, did I?"

She gave a big smile, grabbed his hand and led him to the dance floor.

"I know your name is Janie and you work on one of the units at the hospital."

She drew back her head and asked, "And you are?"

"My name is Greg James."

"Oh, I've heard your name before. You worked on the regional planning team."

"That's right, but I resigned today and I'm moving to Florida in a month."

"Hopefully, you'll live on the beach. I know I'd love to have a place on the beach if I ever wind up there."

They then danced to a couple of fast songs. Greg asked if he could buy her a drink and meet her friends. She said, "Sure. I'm drinking White Russians tonight."

He went over to her table and she introduced him to her friends. They all talked for a while about the hospital, what people they knew, some patients, and what happened with the regional planning. Janie was 5-8"; four years older than Greg. She married right out of high school in Vermont, but divorced after 10 years. She had been an RN for several years and started working at the hospital in 1976. Her friends seemed surprised that Greg was still single. After a few more dances, Janie told him that he couldn't take her home, so he asked her if she wanted to go the next night to see a movie someplace. She said, "There's a Burt Reynolds double feature at the drive-in. I love Burt Reynolds, and I can't remember the last time I went to a drive-in."

"Me, either. It'll be fun."

She went back to the table and wrote down her name, address, and phone number, and told him to come to her house at 7:00 the next evening. She said her kids and her mother (who lived next door) would be there, and they would go to the drive-in from there. He wrote down his name, address, and phone number and gave it to her. Then he left and went home, even though it was only around 10:30. He could not believe his good luck. "I've got to make the most of this; no mental errors," he thought.

The date was interesting. Janie had a beautiful 17-year-old daughter, a 14-year-old son, and a 10 year old daughter. Her mother was a woman in about her mid-70s who was a big Red Sox fan. In fact, all the kids liked sports and pop/rock music which was a big plus for Greg. The movies (Hooper and Gator) were just fair but they had their laughable moments. After they went back to her house, they talked, kissed and cuddled for hours and Greg left about 3:30 am. He didn't 'score' but he really liked this lady and her family, and they had many things in common. He was going to his mother's home for several days, but he definitely wanted to see her again.

"Maybe you can come over for dinner next Thursday, but you're half Italian so don't come back here unless you bring some prosciutto ham," Janie smiled and said.

"You got it. I'll bring some ice cream, too."

She gave him a nice long kiss goodnight. A couple of new songs, 'Heaven Must Have Sent You' and 'Hot Summer Nights,' were playing on the radio the way home. "How appropriate," he thought.

Greg began seeing Janie every few evenings, and some days, taking long walks; long rides to the beach in Ogunquit; going out to dinner; staying home with her kids and watching Red Sox games. One night he made them delicious home-made pizzas. At the end of the month, sex at his place was definitely good. He even told her he was in love with her, which startled her, He said, "That freaked you out didn't it?" This was more than the 'Je t'aime' he jokingly said to Celine years ago.

But a month went by quickly, and he had to move out of his place by September 8th. He spent his last night at Janie's place, but he slept on the couch. They said a sad goodbye the next day as he left for the long drive to Florida. He promised Janie he would send her his address and phone number as soon as possible and he thought about her almost all the way there.

El Guru left his job in late September. He wanted to transfer to a medical, or at least a minimum-security unit, but this wasn't possible. Somehow, he got unemployment, and he went to San Diego, but he could only get temporary work for a month as an aide in a state hospital on a geriatric unit, with no chance of being employed permanently. He then went to Los Angeles, but he couldn't find work there. He wound up going back home to Albuquerque because he was running low on cash. It was a frustrating year for El Guru, the opposite of Greg's.

Chapter 26

Good Year - Bad Ending

Greg had a smooth three-day trip to Florida. He checked out some civil war historic spots near Fredericksburg, VA, and made it to Charlotte, NC, to see Kent Stone. They stayed up late into the night drinking beer and talking about old times and what had happened to them over the past seven years. Kent made Greg a delicious southern breakfast including bacon, grits, cornbread, and some kind of gravy in "liver mush." After Greg drove into Florida, he drank from the Fountain of Youth in St. Augustine. "I'm good for another 30 years at least," he thought. He drove his car on the beach for a mile at Daytona and, later on, he stayed at a motel near I-95.

He spent the whole next day, into the evening, looking for a place to live. As the sun was setting, he noticed a small bungalow development on the beach on Highway A1A that had a vacancy, and he decided, "What the hell, I'll check it out. If they don't require a lease, I'll see if I can stay here for a while until something comes up that I can afford." Greg stopped in and shook hands with Ronnie, the manager (not the owner) inquiring about the vacancy.

"It's only a one-room place and you'd have to clean it up, but it's furnished. The washer and dryer in that shed over there are free."

"How much do you want?"

"Let me show it to you first."

Ronnie was about Greg's age and lived there with his wife and two kids, managing eight bungalows. The owners were in New York City, only came down once a year, and didn't stay there. Most of the bungalows were really one room L-shaped apartments, but two families lived in larger units. The one he showed Greg had a couch that unfolded into a bed with one tiny gas heater, a window air conditioning unit, a small bathroom with a shower, one closet across from the couch, a small table with two chairs, and a small kitchen where several cockroaches (called Palmetto bugs) were crawling around. In the back of the bungalow, there was a large hibiscus bush and a fairly small kidney shaped in-ground swimming pool.

"The pool ain't been right since Hurricane Frederick hit here around Labor Day," he said, as they walked on a path across a lawn that led to the ocean.

"I'll be going to school here full time," Greg said.

"You like to have a beer or two, watching sports - boxing, football?"

"Yeah."

"I could use a buddy. How's $250 a month sound?"

Greg was stunned - he thought any place on the ocean was worth at least twice that amount. He said, "Sure! Can I move in tomorrow?"

"Yes, you can, but the price comes with a few favors."

"What favors?"

"We have cable TV here but it's mostly illegal. The company comes out every few weeks and tears it down – you have to help me hook it back up. Sometimes I go to wrestling, and I want you to go with me - I'll pay for the tickets. There's a new topless bar that's gonna be opening up - I do land-scaping for the owner. If I'm in there sometimes drinking and I need a ride home, I call you and you come get me. If there's a good fight on TV Saturday afternoon, you'll watch it with me at your place. Same thing for Sunday afternoons if there's a good football game - you buy a six-pack for us. Clean the pool once every two weeks. I'll show you how to do it; it's easy."

Greg agreed and he moved in the next day, after giving the place a thorough cleaning and spraying to get rid of the bugs. He went out to buy groceries and a few things for the kitchen, but the next day, he bought a five-gallon container of spring water because (as he quickly found out) the tap water was so hard that you could not drink, cook, or clean effectively with it.

He completed registration for school on Friday and began course work the next week. After being out of school for six years, and in his 30s he was unsure of how difficult it would be, so he took the least possible full-time credit load, consisting of one class in the afternoon and two others in the evening. Two out of the three seemed tough, but they all held his interest. A couple of younger guys quickly became friends of his - Gordy was from a small-town south of Pittsburgh; Pete was from a city south of Boston; and there also was Gus, a guy about 40 who was local. Living on the beach was quite pleasant because the weather was a continuation of summer as he knew it, so he spent a few hours a day lounging on the beach or body surfing or taking long jogs or walks at low tide. He felt it was almost like living in exile, or being retired 35 years early, but he really missed Janie. Greg called her a couple of times, but they kept the conversations fairly short because of the long-distance charges. They also wrote to each other a few times and he sent her a couple of tapes, too.

In late October, El Guru recorded a tape for Greg that took two weeks to make because of various interruptions. He said he was living on $77 a week from unemployment, and depositing some money into a bank account created for his daughter, even though Lorraine didn't want any of it, and he was able to move into a new, big apartment in Albuquerque with a lady named Linda, her three year old daughter, and a cat. "Nothing sexual," he said. "I've known her for a little while but we seem to trust each other as friends. She needed a roommate because she was burglarized one night while they were asleep. The cat is a pain in the ass but I can tolerate it."

He said that Carter was in Albuquerque. "I saw him speak, and he comes off as being out of his league as President. He even called New Mexico, 'Mexico.' I know he did a good job with Sadat and Israel but I think he's in the dark dealing with the Russians. I can see him possibly being a one term president. Reagan will probably run for the Republicans next year, so I may vote third party."

He related that he had cancelled one job interview because he had been invited to a bachelor party the night before and was hung over. A women's state correctional facility wanted him to work there as a CO, but no way would he pursue that. Then he had to cancel another job interview because he blew a tire on the way there. "It pissed me off but nothing like the next day when I had a job interview with the VA hospital, and first thing in the morning I blew out another tire! I didn't get a chance to shower or shave, although I did have decent clothes on. I couldn't cancel that one because I had already told them I wanted to work as a nursing assistant on a ward instead of housekeeping or in food service." In the interview, he played up his experience as a veteran who had worked mainly in hospitals, and he thought the interview went very well even though he asked them to excuse his appearance. "You never know on interviews, though, as you found out. But federal government salaries are OK for me, and I'd rather work here than anyplace else."

A few hours later, El Guru continued the tape by saying, "You got to hear this new super song by Supertramp - 'Take the Long Way Home' - I just love the lyrics. After another brief pause, he said, "Hey, I just got a call from the VA and I got the job! So ends my streak of bad luck, hopefully. I start next week. My probation is for one year."

He continued the tape a week later, saying that he had a friend who used to work there until earlier this year, and she said, "Knowing you, you probably won't last six months there, the way you're intolerant of stuff that goes on in hospitals and systems." For the first few days he worked, he thought everyone seemed very polite. "The job seems very much like it was in the Army on the ward - things you really have to get done, things you can skim over if you don't have time, and even a little bit of ghosting time if you need to get away. The supervising nurse I'll be working with reminds me of the 11-7 nurse on my ward when we were in Germany. I'll be working nights with her. Right after I started here, I got an offer from the US Government Energy Commission but they wanted me to relocate to Amarillo - no way. I like the environment of a hospital. I hope this works out. Things are finally going good."

Things went well for Greg, too. He was getting A's and B's for papers he wrote and exams he took. He felt bad that he couldn't make it over to Tampa for Jack and Joan's wedding because he was swamped with academic work and he actually had a test that day.

After mid-October, he went to the beach only for walks at low tide. Greg fulfilled his agreement with Ronnie, including pulling him out of the topless bar once and going to wrestling one night - Greg mostly laughed there. Ronnie's wife had a car accident and their '79 Chevy Chevette was just about totaled, so Ronnie either borrowed Greg's car for errands or occasionally Greg drove him.

Greg had some trouble with static on his phone intermittently, so his talks with Janie continued to be brief.

However, he thought it was strange he couldn't get in touch with her for most of November. They did talk briefly on Thanksgiving, but again the conversation did not last long because Greg was leaving for Thanksgiving dinner at a friend's house and Janie had her whole family plus some other company there. Greg was going to fly to upstate New York a few days after final week in December and he planned to drive over to see Janie the following weekend. Janie told him he couldn't stay there because there would be relatives at her house right through Christmas and New Year's. Undaunted, he replied that he really wanted to see her the weekend after he got back up north and she agreed. Greg called Dolph, who said that Greg could stay with him and his family that weekend, which helped because Janie's house was about a mile away.

Final week went well for Greg. He thought he aced his exams, and since he would be low on cash, he hoped he might find a part-time job for January.

He mailed some resumes right after Thanksgiving and cold-called a few places, but got only one interview. A mental health clinic, 20 miles away, wanted to hire him to start as soon as he could to be a one-man Family Violence program coordinator. His duties would be supervising two mental health technicians, speaking in the community to organizations once a week, writing weekly three-page narrative and statistical reports, and using his own car to be on with the two techs to go out and break up family fights - 25 hours a week for only $7,000 a year! Greg felt insulted and turned the job down.

El Guru sent Greg a Christmas card just before he went up north. He said his job at the hospital was still going well, although the night shift head nurse was getting demanding. He hoped to switch to the 3-11 shift soon after he got his preliminary evaluation, but probably someone on that unit would have to quit. On the back of the card, El Guru wrote that his cheap tape player bit the dust. "Maybe I'll get a new one for Christmas. I may have to move out because Linda doesn't like the idea of me not being home nights, but I am losing patience with the cat, anyway." Finally, he told Greg that he was glad things were still going well with Janie, despite it turning into another hard to sustain long-distance romance.

Greg did some Christmas shopping with most of the last of his money (his GI bill check never came) - it was weird shopping and seeing Santa Claus, lit palm trees and ceramic snowflakes when it was 75 degrees out. He flew up north in mid-December. People were in angst because no snow had arrived yet and the Olympics in Lake Placid was only two months away. However, it was much colder than he was used to in Florida, and he thought, "Your blood really does seem to thin out, just like when I got home from Vietnam." Greg called Janie that night and they agreed to meet Saturday at 1:00 at a mall about 20 miles away from where Dolph lived.

Greg arrived at the mall at 1:00 and waited for Janie. After a half hour he called her house, and her daughter, June, answered and said Janie would be "a little late because she had some things to do first." He tried calling her twice in the next two hours before she finally arrived, smiling and saying, "Hey, you look nice and tan."

Greg replied (obviously irritated), "You kept me waiting for 2 ½ hours. I have presents for you and your family that I brought up from Florida."

She retorted, in a hostile tone, "I had things to do - you know my family is important."

"Why the hell didn't you tell me ahead of time? Am I supposed to go to a bar here and get drunk waiting?"

"You have balls to talk to me like that. What a bastard you are to insult me like this!"

"Insult you? I haven't seen you in over three months, and now you're turning into an instant bitch! What's wrong?"

"I don't need you goddamn gifts! I'm going home."

She left. Greg went to a bar, had a beer and calmed down. He thought, "I don't believe this - I've never seen this side of her before. She might be having a bad day, but if this is the end for us, I don't want it to end like this. I want to be with her for New Year's Eve."

He finished his beer and got in his car and drove to her house. He thought, "Tonight I'm gonna ask her to marry me. No, that's absolutely crazy. I'll apologize and see if she'll talk to me about what's going on. I'll leave the presents at her place, even if she throws me out."

When he got there, her kids and her mother were there. She motioned him in, took him aside out in the hall, and whispered, "I'm sorry." She took his presents and put them in a closet. The family, who had just finished eating dinner, seemed happy to see him. Her mother asked him to stay for dessert, but Janie quickly said they were going out for drinks and be home later.

They drove to Osgood's, a bar downtown. After a few minutes of silence in the car, Janie said, "Greg, I shouldn't have acted like a bitch today."

"I accept your apology, but what the hell was that for?"

As they were parking, she said, "Let's order some drinks and we'll talk."

He got a Bass Ale and ordered her a Southern Comfort Manhattan, straight up. There was an uncomfortable, almost somber aura.

Greg broke another silence saying, "I hope we can get together New Year's Eve."

"I'm afraid I already have plans," she said as she looked down.

He had a sad look on his face as he instantly thought, "Oh, shit, she really is dumping me. How can I handle this assertively? I don't want to come off like an asshole." Then he said, "We had a lot of good times last summer, didn't we?"

"We did," as she nodded, half smiling.

"Sounds like things aren't the same anymore, are they?"

"No. While you were away, I met somebody here I really like, and I've been seeing him for about a month or so."

"I guess I never should have left."

"No, that's not it. At that point in your life the doctoral program was a 'now or never' thing for you. You were great, but I knew, even if you went back and forth between here and Florida, I just couldn't deal with it. I'm grateful for the good times - it was really fun. Being with you was almost like being on vacation."

"Tell me about this guy."

"He's older than me. He's an air traffic controller. He wants to get married, and at this point in my life, that's what I want. The kids like him. I like the stability. I can't pass this up."

"I couldn't give you that for at least several years. Hell, all of you are going to be disappointed with your Christmas presents."

"I know you're broke. I feel bad for you. Whatever, the thought was there, and that's nice. I do appreciate it."

They talked and had a couple more drinks. They laughed at some of the good times they had last summer. He drove her home and they had one last, nice kiss goodbye at her door. She promised that she would keep in touch with him, as friends.

"Rotten ending to an otherwise real good year, and to the decade," Greg thought.

Chapter 27

The New Decade Begins

El Guru started working on the evening shift, but he was becoming disillusioned. He felt that many staff members were lazy and unprofessional but, on the other hand, a few of the nurses were rigid. He tried to suggest what he felt were ways that certain procedures could be done more efficiently in Army hospitals and clinics where he had worked in the past. His ideas were either ignored or sometimes ignited shouting matches. He had burned bridges with the head nurse on nights, and he refused to work on that shift again. However, the day shift would be worse because he would either be a combination glorified errand boy and janitor, and he would not be able to help with any medical procedures or spend much time with patients, even though the day shift staff were more pleasant people. He was unable to transfer to another unit in the hospital. El Guru shared his opinions with doctors and patients about various medical treatments, which also angered some of the nurses. In every medical facility where he had worked, he said what he felt - usually he had one of the physicians or treatment specialists as an advocate for his opinions, but not at this hospital. True to his personality, he rebelled against a "my way or the highway" approach. Like Rodney Dangerfield, he thought, "I don't get no respect."

El Guru's social life was going downhill, too. He started smoking pot occasionally again and he spent New Year's Eve getting high with a bunch of acquaintances. He was ready to leave after the first bowl went around a few times, but someone brought up the hostage situation in Iran and what possible solutions there could be to free the Americans. Arguments broke out regarding whether or not "we should bomb the hell out of them," or "blockade them economically," or (his approach) "make a deal with the Russians, because they're a stronger country than we are and the Ayatollah would listen to Brezhnev." Almost everyone in the group rejected his ideas on the subject, so he left right after midnight. When he woke up the next day, he had a big argument with Linda over his smoking pot, not being around for her protection, the cat, and dropping big hints about wanting to get sexually involved with her. They kept bitching at each other, on and off for the next week, when he finally said, "Get yourself a house boy - when I get my paycheck next week, I'm gone." He moved out the weekend of January 12th and got a tiny one-room apartment where he paid rent week to week, not far from the hospital.

Greg returned to Florida and took a bigger credit load for the next quarter. He immersed himself in school work, despite still doing various favors for Ronnie. Gordy was spending a lot of time with a new girlfriend who was a student and Pete's wife was pregnant. Gus, who was recently divorced, moved in with his girlfriend and her two beautiful Old English Sheepdogs. It was too cold to go to the beach, other than to take his daily strolls at low tide. A couple of weeks later, he was feeling lonely and he spent a weekend with Jack and Joan in St. Petersburg. When he returned, he had a couple of dates with a young widowed lady but he thought, "She's nice but she's a little shallow. I hope the next female who comes along is as good as Janie or better."

There were no single females in his classes who turned him on, except one cute, fairly young chick - a 5'5" blonde with a beautiful smile. On Valentine's Day, during a break between classes, she happened to be walking near him so he introduced himself and tried to make small talk with her. He thought, "This is out of character for me. I'm curious about her, and I'm not in a bar situation at all." She gave him a weak smile and said her name was Jean, but he was getting vibrations that she was the most unavailable woman that he could ever meet. After about 30 seconds, she gave him a quick nod, and a sideways smile, as she quickly ducked into the ladies' room. "Maybe I came off like a jerk," he thought.

His bad luck continued. Later that day, his car was rear-ended near a busy intersection on a four-lane road as he was going home by a guy who was driving without his glasses. Greg wasn't hurt (although he would experience a bad whiplash the next morning), and neither was the other guy, but Greg worried that maybe his car was totaled. The cop investigating the accident told him about a nearby autobody shop where his car could be towed. Greg had his car towed and called Ronnie to give him a ride home. Right away, Greg notified his insurance company but could not get a rental car until Tuesday. After recovering all weekend, Ronnie drove him to school on Monday, but said he couldn't pick him up until about 8:00 that evening. Greg told him he would hang out at the library on campus and call him then.

After his last class, as he walked out of the room, Jean, the chick he met the other day came up to him with a concerned look on her face and said, "How are you? I saw you standing there last week with your car smashed in and I felt so bad for you."

Greg thought, "Wow. This is the same girl who blew me off the other day, right?"

He replied, "I'm OK now. I have to pick up a rental car tomorrow. Right now, I have to hang around the library because I don't have a ride home until 8:00."

"I can give you a ride home."

"I live over at the beach. Is that out of your way?"

"That's OK, I can bring you there."

They talked as they walked to her van and told each other about themselves during the half hour ride. Jean was going to turn 25 next month. She was single and lived in a small trailer with a little dog. She had just broken up with a guy recently. Jean was an only child - her father was a retired

Army officer and her parents lived a few miles away. Like Greg, she liked to sing, listen to the radio, and she also liked to laugh and had a good sense of humor. She had gone to a Catholic college in Connecticut, and like Greg, was now a full-time grad student. Greg thought, "I like this girl. I can't believe I'm hitting it off so well with her." They got to his place and he invited her in and gave her the 'grand tour' of his little L-shaped bungalow. They sat on the couch and talked for a few minutes. At the door, he took her hand.

"Jean, you've been a lifesaver for me today. Thank you, thank you so much."

"My pleasure," she said with a big smile.

Suddenly he thought, "You only go around once in life, I'll take a chance here." As he moved closer to her, he said with a smile, "I've never done this with someone I met in a class, but…" He kissed her. She didn't resist, and it was a long kiss that got him instantly turned on. Then he said, "I'd really like to see you again soon."

She grabbed his hand and replied, "Come on, let's go to my place."

Just as soon as they entered her little trailer, they started hugging and kissing, and tumbled into bed. He thought, "She is so pretty! She is so responsive! Wow! What good thing did I do to deserve this? It was well worth the car crash."

They cuddled and talked for over an hour afterwards, and she brought him home. He thought, "The way I feel now, it probably doesn't get any better than this!"

For the rest of the month they saw each other every few days, after his insurance company got him a cheap rental car. They went to Jai Alai and he won some money, so they went out to dinner afterwards. One day when she was at his place, as they got a little bit of studying done, the Good-year blimp flew right over his back yard and Greg took a few pictures. They saw Ordinary People at the movies. Near the end of the month, it got below freezing one morning (Greg's tiny gas heater in his non-insulated bungalow didn't provide much heat.) and he called her at 5:30 am saying he was in desperate need of warmth and she invited him over. They were at his place one evening and watched the US Hockey Olympic team beat the Russians in a monumental upset. And the great sex just kept on coming. Just as important, this was the first woman that he ever spent the night with, whom he felt comfortable with in the act of sleeping. Better than Gretchen, who would wake up off and on all-night; better than Celine, who fought like hell with him over the covers all night; better than Octavia, who had to have a cigarette in bed before she went to sleep and smelled like one the next morning.

El Guru called him on the 29th. "Greg, I have to tell you about what's happening with me. It'll freak you out."

"I got news for you, Artie, and it'll freak you out more!"

"You first," El Guru said.

"Janie got rid of me just before Christmas and I was bummed out to the max for six or seven weeks. But I met a younger girl here named Jean, who might be as good, if not better. She's a grad student like me. She's pretty, smart, vivacious, we like a lot of the same things and sex is very compatible. Believe it or not, I met her because some bastard smashed the shit out of my car as I was pulling up to a red light. She saw the aftermath and felt sorry for me."

"Wow, Greg, I'm happy for you again. She sounds really good and I hope it lasts. But our lives are going in different directions again."

"What happened?"

"I had a blowout argument with Linda last month and I started living in a little apartment alone, and the job got to be a pain in the ass because I didn't like the way they did things, so to make a long story short, I quit. My last day was today. I think I'll go back to California or Arizona to see what I can find at a good hospital."

"Artie, you're going to turn 32 next month. Isn't it time you got more stable instead of jumping from job to job? If you have a resume, this doesn't look good. You've only had one job for at least one year since you got out of the Army and you need more than one recommendation from someone in authority over you. If you keep pulling this crap, nobody will hire you. What are you going to do if you're still 35 and still drifting?"

"Don't you give me this shit, too. I don't compromise my values, my opinions, my feelings, or the way I look for anyone. Dammit, I am going to do things my way, especially with hospital patients - it's the right way. I've always had the support of at least one doctor everywhere I've worked. Maybe I have to go to Russia or South America or somewhere. In fact, I'm seriously looking at moving to Costa Rica - they have a better government than we have. But I am more determined than ever to fight systems and to try to change things to the way they should be done - with work or anything. I don't need any goddamn lecture from you."

"A lot of new jobs are opening up as paramedics on ambulances. You have experience as a lab tech and an OR tech. Or try to get into a PA program somewhere. Buck did it, so you can do it. You have talent and you're bright, but you can't keep going on this way in the working world. At least get somebody to show you how to do a resume. Your life is oozing away, professionally."

"Hey, don't try to get in touch with me. I'll get in touch with you."

El Guru hung up. Greg didn't hear from him for several months.

In March, Greg and Jean went to the beach at his place a few times, taking walks together at low tide, holding hands. They took a trip to Cape Canaveral, exploring all the NASA exhibits. They sang to songs on the car radio. One day on campus, a fellow classmate named Stu congratulated him - "I hear you're going out with Jean. She is nice! Lucky you."

Ronnie had four strip-teasers from Maine move into another bungalow on the property for the month of March, but right after he saw Jean, he said, "I was gonna introduce you to them for some good times, but holy shit, your chick is better than all of them." Greg thought, "This is last summer all over again."

Jean brought Greg to her parents' house. Her father was a graying man with a moustache and glasses and a big, wide smile. They talked about aspects of military life. Her mother, a blondish-gray haired woman with glasses, didn't say very much. She just sat in her chair and smiled a lot. After they left, Greg remarked that her father seemed like a good guy but he didn't know what to make of her mother yet.

Jean said, "I've always had problems getting along with my mother. We argue all the time. You can say I'm a 'daddy's girl.' We talk to each other about a lot of things. He's one big reason why I'm enlisting as an Army officer after I get my doctorate. It's actually part of the deal I have for school here."

Greg thought, "This is the opposite of me growing up. Maybe Jean turns onto me because I'm an older guy with glasses and a moustache and I was in the Army. Maybe that's why when my mother was at Disney World last week, she didn't want to go with me to meet her for dinner. Too bad - I think they'd probably like each other."

On Jean's birthday, St. Patrick's Day, they went to a major league spring training game with Greg's friend Pete and his wife Katy. It was a fun time, and Greg and Jean had more fun at his place afterward. Later that week, final exams for the quarter began, and Greg was rapidly running out of money. After his last exam, he tried looking for a job in Florida but had no success. He had no real choice but to go back to New York, or see if he could live with Jean. He thought, "Living with Jean would be moving too fast in this relationship. What if I get her pregnant? I'd have to do the honorable thing, but neither of us has any money. Dolph told me there are no openings at the hospital. She would never go up there with me, anyway. The only alternative would be for me to go back home for a few months, and hope that she can tolerate the long-distance relationship for a while. Janie couldn't, but Jack and Joan did, and they got married." He told Jean about his plans and although she seemed a little sad, she understood his predicament. They discussed his need to come back for classes during the summer, and the possibility of one or two summer sessions in Switzerland through an overseas program the school had, although neither one could afford both sessions there.

They had one last relaxing time together on March 31st. She gave him the book "Love" by Leo Buscaglia and wrote on the inside, "To Greg - In friendship and in love." Did she tell him she loved him? No, not explicitly. Did he tell her he loved her? No - Greg said that to Janie last year and got burned. He and Jean had a tearful goodbye. He surrendered his key to Ronnie and drove up north.

Greg lived with his mother for three weeks before he started working at another facility in New England for the developmentally disabled - he had a connection there through a man he met during state regional mental health planning two years earlier. Jean wrote to him about four times a week, and he answered all her letters but not quite as often as she wrote to him. He was living cheaply, and saving every cent he could to go back to Florida for one six-week summer session and to Europe for the other six-week session; the GI bill would also help. He made a deal with Personnel that even though he would be away for no longer than 10 weeks without pay, he guaranteed that he would return and work there at least until the end of the year.

During the first week of May, another letter came from Jean. As he read it, he threw it down and yelled to nobody in particular, "What the fuck?" She said she met a grad student there and had a sexual encounter with him that was a 'peak experience,' and went on about what a great time it was. Greg paced for a while and had a beer to calm down. He thought this was probably reminiscent of El Guru and Ursula in 1975 but he didn't know where El Guru was. He called Van (now divorced) Dolph, and Mort in New York, but their phones rang and rang. Jack answered but said he couldn't talk and said he'd get back to him tomorrow. In the background in the living room, a new song by the J. Geils Band, "Love Stinks," was playing on the radio.

A few hours later he wrote a short, angry letter to Jean, effectively breaking up with her, telling her he could not compete with someone well over 1000 miles away. He asked why she even told him this, and what was she thinking? In any event, he said that he had made up his mind that he was going to Europe, not Florida, for school in the summer. He drove over to the post office to mail the letter thinking, "Another female who can't handle a temporary long-distance relationship."

He received a reply from her in a week. She said she was shocked and cried when she got his letter. She said she thought they had no secrets between them, the guy was only a one-time thing and, "What am I supposed to be, the woman who waits? Why didn't you ever call me from up there?" (He had just got a phone installed two days before.) He didn't answer her letter - he was still hurt. "I don't want to ever get serious with a young chick again," he thought.

On June 1st, El Guru called. "Hey, Greg, I'm at my mother's. Belated Happy Birthday. I can't talk for too long because this is costing a lot, even if it is Sunday."

"Artie, what happened to you? Are you still pissed at me?"

"No. I made it as far as Guatemala for a few weeks and those people either don't know what's going on or they are violent in terms of any political revolution. I felt uncomfortable there, but it was nice to speak only Spanish for a while. I'm back with my tail between my legs, but I'm trying to regroup."

"Did you get a job?"

"No, but I have some leads in Santa Fe. It isn't that far away from here and it's a nice area generally. I know a guy who lives there."

Greg told him all about what had happened with him and Jean. El Guru said, "This girl may be an immature bitch, but at least she was an honest bitch."

"All I could think of besides, 'How could she?' was 'Could I ever be good enough for her?' I wonder how I would react if I ever met that guy."

"You know, you broke some hearts over the past 10 years or so. This might be payback. Did you ever tell her you loved her?"

"No, I said that to Janie before I went to Florida and it was the kiss of death for me."

"This girl was probably waiting for you to say that to her. Hell, she gave you that Leo Whatshisname's book on love. That may have been a big hint."

"Speaking of countries, my school has two six-week summer sessions in Switzerland. Could you get enough cash to make it over there for a while?"

"I couldn't get enough money to go even for one week. I wish you'd told me about that a few months ago. I would have stayed at the VA job and bailed on them in June. But stay in touch by letter or tape and have a great time in Europe."

Chapter 28

Two Lives Like a See-Saw

El Guru began work at the medical unit at the state prison in Santa Fe. He also, in his spare time, did some volunteering for Andrew Pulley, a Socialist Worker party candidate for President (who was essentially a Communist). El Guru could not support Carter—he felt Carter had botched the rescue of the hostages in Iran; supporting Reagan was out of the question for him, and John Anderson was too conservative. He felt the regular Communist candidate, Gus Hall, was a "whack job"; Pulley was a minority, a Vietnam veteran, and young. El Guru knew Pulley had no chance of winning, but he felt that this was a start to at least get people opening up about the possibility of radical views like they did back in the '60s.

That fall, El Guru started seeing a 21-year-old girl who had just graduated from college, although she was more interested in arguing with him good naturedly about his political views than having them become romantically involved. He got a cozy little apartment and bought another '75 VW "Bug" that gave him no trouble. Things went well for him for the rest of the year, although he was only in touch with Greg a couple of times.

Greg did go to Europe that summer, but he wasn't totally sure of a place to stay. He got in touch with Gordy who told him he could sleep on the couch at his apartment. Gordy had written to the landlord who said it was OK if Greg would pay his part of the rent in cash. On the flight to Frankfurt, Greg's luggage was lost. Getting off the plane, he met an attractive lady in her late 20s from Ohio, who had also lost her luggage and she spoke fluent German. Two hours later, the airlines found their bags, and after a long train ride to Freiburg, she agreed to let him stay with her at a pension (small hotel) they found which had only one bed on the condition he would not touch her. She said, "Look, I'm engaged. You don't even kiss me goodnight or hug me. We just sleep, period, or you're out of here." Greg didn't get much sleep, but he kept his end of the deal. When they left the next day, they did hug each other and wished each other luck. She told him, "I know you know my name, and you know where I'm from in Ohio, but please don't ever try to look me up."

When he got to Lugano, Switzerland, he met Gordy at the train station. He was very grateful for Gordy's hospitality. The couch proved to be large and comfortable. Unfortunately, it seemed that almost every morning, it rained when they walked to the classes and Greg hadn't brought a jacket or hat with him, but at least he enjoyed the academic venture there.

Gordy, who was 27, met an older, attractive woman, Giselle, and spent a lot of time with her on weekends, while Greg got a SwissRail pass and made a few overnight trips on weekends, staying at one city for a day and night to stretch his money. He went to Geneva, which was the most expensive city in Europe at that time and he could only afford to eat at a McDonalds. At Lucerne, he had fun at an open-air festival, including watching a great Dixieland jazz band. He saw the bear pits in Bern. In Basel, there was a friendly American bartender and they conversed at length. He didn't meet any women, but at least he found cheap places to stay. "It feels good to practice speaking German and French again," he thought. He had plenty of time to concentrate on getting good grades for his courses, anyway. Switzerland was worth the expense for him, and he experienced no anti-Americanism.

Near the end of July, he flew home, unpacked, repacked and drove to Florida for the second summer session. When he got there, Ronnie said he couldn't move in until mid-August, but to "drop in periodically in case someone leaves, and I hope we get to watch some pre-season football and boxing together."

The next day on campus, Greg immediately asked around if anyone needed a roommate for the next five weeks. A guy introduced him to a grad student, Kathy, from New York City who was looking for a roommate. She was five years older (she claimed she was 28 though) and she happened to have a nice apartment about two miles up the beach from where Ronnie was. Greg paid cheap rent to live with her, but this time it was a disaster. They argued over everything. Fortunately, after the first five days he was there, Kathy got a boyfriend and spent most of her time at his place.

Stu, a grad student Greg knew, met him on campus and said, "You're living with Kathy? She's a flaming hysteric. What happened with you and Jean?"

"I'll just say it didn't work out. Tell her I said 'Hi' if you see her."

"She's in Europe. She was hoping you'd be there."

"I just came from there. She must have gone over for the second summer session."

"Anyway, she's a lot better than Kathy for you."

"Almost any woman is."

Ronnie had an opening August 10th and Greg jumped at it. When he wasn't studying or going to classes, he occasionally hung out with Ronnie or he would go to a happy hour at a dive that was probably the last quarter draft bar in America. Greg couldn't wait to get out of Florida. The best part of his time there was when he spent a long weekend with Jack and Joan in St. Petersburg to avoid Hurricane Allen, which luckily didn't hit Florida.

After his summer session was over, he went back to his job in September. His academic program in Florida offered several non-required courses lasting five full days each quarter that could be taken for credit, and he convinced his employer to give him time off for one of these in early November. Greg flew to Florida, rented a car and stayed at a Best Western. The next morning, he was about to walk into the class when Jean came up to him, hugged him and tried to kiss him, saying, "I'm so glad you're here."

"Whoa! Are you in this class?"

"Yes. I knew you'd be here. I have to talk to you."

She started to say she was "sorry" but Greg cut her off and asked, "Is Mr. Peak Experience here?"

She had a sad look on her face and said, "That's him over there." Mr. Peak Experience looked over at them with a smile on his face. Greg said, "I can't sit next to you."

"Can we please talk?"

"Let's go out to lunch and we'll talk. Definitely not here."

Greg sat about five seats to the right of Jean; the class was in a circle, and he either looked down at his notebook or right at the prof and stayed silent. He stayed in his chair during the morning break. Greg and Jean went to lunch at a fast food place, and they talked for 45 minutes straight, barely eating. Greg admitted that he did miss her, but now that he has a face to connect in his brain to Mr. Peak Experience, it might take a long time for him to get over that image.

At one point, Jean said, "I saw Gus last month and he said, 'Both you and Greg were coming off relationships, and maybe this was a rebound thing for both of you.' "

Greg replied, "Maybe Gus was right, but what happened was something you should have kept to yourself instead of giving me the details. Look, I realize that neither one of us had the right to control the other, especially from such a distance and long time away. But this guy is right here in the class, almost laughing when he looked at me this morning - that's hard to get over. I think you're basically a good human being, and I would like to stay friends. But beyond that, it's doubtful -at least at this time, right now."

For the rest of the week-long class, Greg went to class, avoided taking breaks, and did not participate much. The last day of class, the prof briefly mentioned Maslow's "Peak Experience" and what it meant. Greg and Jean looked at each other, somberly, for an instant. And when Greg looked across the room at Mr. Peak Experience, the guy had a big wide smile on his face. The final exam was a "take-home paper." As they left the room, Jean mentioned to Greg a book she needed for a class in the spring. Greg said he had it up north and he would call her next month when he found it.

When Greg returned to work the next week, he found that some regulations had changed. He didn't mind working with the developmentally disabled population, but he was really more interested in dealing with mental health in-patients, and also administering programs. He called Dolph, who was now a Unit Director at the state hospital. Dolph said he had an opening on his unit and would love to have Greg start work there at the end of December as program director of a ward. Greg replied that he would report for duty on December 30th.

In the meantime, Greg sank some money into car repairs and he had to temporarily move to a tiny apartment because of electrical problems where he was living. If he had to spend another winter freezing in northern New England, he would try to get a girlfriend to help him through it. When he went to see Dolph in early December, he was lucky enough that evening to meet Annie, a divorcee a few years older than him, who spent the night with him after a date on Saturday. They made plans to spend New Year's Eve together, and he signed a six-month lease on another apartment, not far from the hospital, a week later. It looked like his streak of mostly bad months was over.

He called Jean because he found the book she wanted, and he promised to give it to her when came to Florida for another week-long course in late February. It was a very friendly conversation, and after he hung up, he started thinking that maybe he should try to reunite with her after he got back to Florida. Both he and Annie seemed to agree that their relationship would be temporary. Annie dropped hints that she was uncomfortable with a guy who was several years younger, and Greg felt that Annie was no match for Jean, but she fulfilled what he considered to be his basic needs.

For the first time in six months, El Guru contacted Greg by letter. His job was going well, but many inmates were hostile and violent. Word spread around the prison that he was a "Communist," which did not endear him to many people, even though he declared he was a Socialist. He said, "People here don't understand what Socialists are. The Scandinavian countries have the right ideas about Socialism. I want to live and work in a country where people can speak their minds, help each other, and maybe positive changes will result. But it won't happen with Reagan as president."

Greg sent El Guru a Christmas card and updated him about the changes in his life, including working at the hospital again, and his new address. The year 1981 was looking better for Greg, but not for El Guru. Again, it seemed if things were going well for Greg, they were not going well for El Guru, and vice versa.

Greg knew some of the staff on the hospital unit fairly well, including a nurse, Penny, who was Janie's best friend. In fact, Janie knew most of the people Greg would work with, so he decided to call her and they had a nice talk about the different staff members and her opinion about what the program needed. About 15 minutes later, she said, "I got married in June."

"I heard. You got what you wanted," he said, somewhat sadly.

He's working at the new Hartsfield Airport in Atlanta, and we're moving there pretty soon. I'm going to be a southern lady."

"Wow, that's a big change for you after being in New England all your life. Hey, drive down to St. Augustine for a weekend, if you can. It's a really nice area."

"I'll suggest that to him. You had a good time there, I remember."

"I'm glad we're still good friends."

After Greg hung up, he pondered, "I'm living in the here and now, or for the short term. Annie is just for the winter - she's a good cook, sex is good, and she's attractive, but she's so superficial. Janie is gone, but I'm starting to miss Jean. I'll be back and forth between here and Florida for the rest of the year. Thank God for Dolph and some people I know in Administration who will let me take a leave of absence in pursuit of a doctorate, provided I work at the hospital for a few years afterward. I've got to get on some hospital committees to re-establish my reputation at the hospital. I need to go back to Florida for the whole summer, even if its unpaid leave, but I can use annual leave and comp time to fly down there for two week long courses in the next few months. My car is acting up periodically, but I won't have any money to buy one for a long time. My apartment is all right, but I doubt if my landlord will let me sub-let it for the summer, so I'll have to move out. My future is uncertain, but at least I have my friends and family and a good job."

Just before he flew down to Florida in late February, Greg got a tape from El Guru. "I borrowed a tape recorder. My job is OK but the violence at the prison is unbelievable at times. The other day, on the maximum-security unit, one prisoner was murdered, and one of the correction officers was hurt so badly he had to resign. No more than one prisoner at a time should be out of their cells, but four were out when this happened. More often than not, it seems like a group of inmates control this place and the correction officers are just pawns. And the warden doesn't seem to give a shit, or if he does, he gets no back-up from the state. I try to get along as well as I can with most of the prisoners, but you just can't trust any of them.

"I hate Santa Fe. Environmentally it's nice, but I've been treated like shit by most of the people in the town I've tried to get friendly with. This is worse than what you felt about living in Massachusetts years ago—cold, cliquish, phony, and unfriendly people. Maybe the Russians should drop a bomb on this place.

"I was seeing a married lady briefly a few months ago. She got cold feet about going through with her divorce and it got too dangerous for us, so we agreed to break if off cleanly. I remembered what happened to you a few years ago. I'm seeing that other young chick I told you about. I like her intellectually but that's all. She's about to start a job in Arizona soon anyway.

"I can't wait for baseball to start again. Your Boston Celtics are looking good. Best song I like is "Celebration" by Kool and the Gang. Send me a tape and keep me updated on your address in case you move about seven times like you did last year."

Greg sent back a tape later in March. "Things are going well for me at the hospital. I like the people I work with and the program I'm developing is off to a good start. Right now, I'm home—sick with a cold and sore throat that I can't seem to shake ever since I came back from Florida several weeks ago. While I was there, I saw Jean, and as I got to her place, I thought 'maybe we can have a long talk about getting back together.' She greeted me with a big smile, and right after she invited me in, she flashed a rock on her finger and said, 'Look—I'm getting married.' The guy is apparently an engineer or has some professional job with one of the companies in the area. I told her I was happy for her—I don't know if I let my disappointment show—but it's probably all for the best. She has an agreement where she has to go into the Army for a number of years after she gets her degree. I really wonder what she's going to be like 10 years from now.

"Anyway, I got rid of Annie after I went to her house one night and was about to talk about plans for her birthday when she pulled out a loaded gun to show me. She said she would seriously think about using it on her ex-husband if he bothered her about her kids again. Anyone who keeps a loaded gun in their house is a deal-breaker for me. Did I tell you her ex-husband is a transvestite! At least she got me through a fairly rough winter.

"I would get rid of my car, but I can't afford another one right now. At least my place is warm enough. My address and phone number should be the same until June. Then I have to go back to Florida through August to finish up my course work.

El Guru replied quickly with a short tape. "As I speak, Reagan just got shot! This asshole sounds just like the guy who shot John Lennon a few months ago. But it's coming out now that he did this to impress Jodie Foster! You work with people like this - is he crazy, a rip-roaring asshole, or both? Maybe this will change some attitudes about guns - this country is getting more conservative redneck every day. Looks like Reagan will survive OK. I wondered for a little while what it would be like with Bush as president. Reagan's men, Deaver and Baker almost sound like Haldeman and Ehrlichman from 10 years ago. I'm getting beaten down about any revolutionary ideas I express, but if it gets worse, maybe I'll see if I can go back to Europe to live. Mexico is too corrupt and Canada is too cold.

"The governor here may be a Democrat, but he is a shithead. He and the legislature are squabbling over money for the Department of Corrections and what their goals should be. About one inmate a week either gets stabbed or severely beaten up. The pricks in administration are worse than the inmates. At least I started working nights on the medical unit with an on-call MD, and I get every weekend off, so that helps.

Greg called El Guru on April 8th. "Artie, we are both getting screwed the wrong way right now. I'm still sick and just can't shake this cold and sore throat. I feel much like I did in '74 when I was unemployed, living at home, and sick for months, but the only differences are that things are going really well at work and I have a neat little apartment."

El Guru replied, "This may be the last time we can call each other for a while. They want me to come in on my time off from work when they can't get a hold of the doc on all, but what the hell am I supposed to do? I don't want to come in on my time off and I'm not an MD. Plus the phone bill is expensive and the service is lousy."

"How do you like working nights there?"

"It keeps my contact with these 'animals' at a minimum. The only time I see inmates regularly is from 6:00 to 7:00 am, and I chart notes and leave. I'm doing some reading, but I'm literally in jail for eight hours a shift. I'm getting tired of it. I don't like living in this town, either. I haven't had a woman in many months and I have no desire to smoke a joint. I only drink a few beers a week. I'm losing weight."

"That's the night shift for you, especially with not much decent human contact. I'm losing weight, too. I haven't had a beer in weeks, I've felt so miserable. In fact, since I slept through a thunderstorm in Florida at the end of '79, I don't drink as much as I used to anyway. I've had a couple of dates, but then I got sick again, and both of the women got sick and they're probably pissed off at me. At work there are a few days when I try to keep distance from everybody else and I end up going home early or just stay in my office. People are starting to scream at me to go see a doctor, but then I feel OK for a few days in a row."

"No ladies on the horizon for me either, lately. You really should see a doctor. I know I would if I were going through the same crap you are."

Greg said, "On the positive side, baseball starts tomorrow. People here are hopeful about the Red Sox, and I'm hopeful about the Pirates. Watch out for the Montreal Expos - I like them to win it all."

"I bet the Dodgers will take it all. Some of the guys they had in Albuquerque in AAA are coming into their own now. Hey - get your body straight. I'll get my head straight. Or I'll move on to the next job. I'm frustrated right now."

"Don't quit until you've been there for one year and get one or two letters of recommendation."

"My six-month evaluation was finally done last week but they won't discuss it until tomorrow. I'll see if they give me comp time or overtime to stay until 8:30."

"Good luck, stay in touch or send a tape when you can."

Chapter 29

The Future is Uncertain

Greg finally started feeling better physically in early May. He decided he would quit smoking anything forever. Although he never smoked cigarettes, and quit cigars in the early '70s, he always smoked at least one bowl of pipe tobacco most days for many years. He did quit for six months in '74 when he had a similar long-lasting sore throat and eventually felt better. He called Ronnie because he needed a place to stay in Florida for the summer to finish his course work, and Ronnie said his old place would be ready in mid-June - same deal, same conditions.

Greg's birthday fell on a Friday so he decided to take the day off and go to Montreal for the weekend. On the way, his car gave him trouble again, and he wound up bringing it to a Sears in Burlington, VT. Since it took a few hours for the repairs, he checked into a motel there. Later, he dropped into an upscale bar and noticed a beautiful, slightly older tall brunette four or five stools down from where he sat. After checking her out for about half hour, he determined she was alone and he wondered why. He decided to move to the stool next to her, introduced himself to her, and after brief small talk he said that he was stranded in Burlington on his birthday.

"I'm Amanda - Mandy. I've never heard that line before."

"No, it's true. Here's my driver's license."

She looked at it, smiled and asked, "Am I too old for you?"

"Come on - you can't be any older than me. And you look younger than that."

"I like you already. Why are you stranded here?"

They talked for about an hour over a couple of drinks, moving to a quieter table after the first one. Mandy was 39. She was divorced with three kids -her ex had custody of two teenage daughters while she had custody of her 10-year-old son. She was a buyer for a furniture company. Like Janie and Octavia, she smoked. Even though she was dressed casually, there was something elegant about her, like Janie, and she was interested in Greg's work at the hospital. She liked contemporary music and the Red Sox. She was out tonight because she "just needed a break from home."

At 11:00, after their third drink together, she said, "I'd like to get to know you. Not just sexually."

"You have someone watching your son but my motel room is open."

"It's your birthday but I can't spend the night," she said.

They went back to his motel room; Mandy had the body of a woman 10 years younger. They hit if off romantically, and it was great for them. She did light up a cigarette lying in bed, but Greg did not care. He thought, "What a birthday present. She could be like an American Celine all over again." She wanted to see him the next day.

"Come over and meet my son, Freddie. You can stay until Sunday morning if you want."

He went over to her house the next morning, but Freddie was whiny and didn't warm up to Greg very much. They went to a carnival later, which was fun for Freddie, who went on a lot of rides. But he still didn't seem to trust Greg who walked around like a drunk after he got off the Tilt-a-Whirl and the Pirate Ship. Mandy invited Greg to stay for dinner and spend the night while Freddie stayed overnight at a friend's house; Greg did not refuse. He left early the next morning, promising Mandy that he would return to Burlington to see her next month before he took off to Florida. Greg thought, "What an interesting birthday weekend. Good thing this is long distance because this kid and I aren't going to get along, I'm afraid."

Greg went to Florida for a week in May for another elective course. Soon after he returned, he received a tape from El Guru on June 1st. "I hope you're not in Florida yet. I got an outstanding evaluation on the job, and I'm proud of it but I don't know how much longer I can stand this place. I'm still working nights, and essentially 'on call' for any medical problems I can handle, but the prisoners are getting to me. I get off work and I'm angry because of how they insult me. A lot of them act like wild beasts, yet they say they want to be treated like men. Because I'm working nights, I don't have as much contact with them as I used to. My car is all right, my place is all right, but I'm getting so that I'm just living for the weekend. Still no women on the horizon either—the only ones I've met are dummies real shallow people. There are so many freaking snobs in Santa Fe, too.

"About baseball. Those bastards might actually go on strike in the Major Leagues. I can't believe they would do this in the middle of the season. If for some reason it does happen, they won't keep it going so that there's no World Series because that would absolutely kill baseball. And football and basketball are probably more popular than baseball is. I love this rookie pitcher the Dodgers got - Fernando Valenzuela. I bet the Dodgers make it into the World Series. I don't think the Expos will make it - did you get up there to see a game this year? I always liked that one Expos pitcher, Bill Lee, 'the Spaceman.' Probably because he's a head, he's a liberal, and he says what he feels. Send me a tape before you leave if you're not in Florida yet."

Greg went to Vermont to see Mandy - Freddie went to his father's, and he stayed with her for the weekend. But on the way back, he thought, "Good thing I'm leaving. I don't know how I can keep this going. Since Jean, I don't feel the pull to settle down now like I did in the past few years. Besides, even though Mandy is sexy and I like her in many ways, she smokes too much, the kid would be a pain in the ass, she's almost six years older, and I don't get any 'falling in love' feelings from this thing we have. I may not see her for long, or not regularly."

Greg moved out of his apartment and left for Florida on June 13th.

He breathed a sigh of relief when he was assured that his job at the hospital would be held through the summer, even though many positions around the hospital were being cut as a "trickle-down" from Reagan's budget axe; it helped that Greg's unpaid leave would save the hospital two and half month's salary. Besides, Dolph advocated for him with the new hospital superintendent, and the unit program Greg built was very successful; also, unlike some other programs in the hospital, it met every JCAH requirement. He dictated a tape to El Guru telling him all about what had happened during the six weeks before he left.

Greg arrived in Florida on the 16th and went to meet his friend Pete and his wife Katy for dinner. Greg's car wasn't air conditioned and he was sweaty when he got to the Chinese restaurant. After greetings and hugs, he looked at the drink menu and said, "Yeah, this is what I want—a Suffering Bastard—because that is what I feel like." He stayed at Pete's for the night and called Ronnie, who said, "The last tenants trashed the place a little, but as part of our deal, you have to clean it up." Greg agreed (he had no choice) and moved in the next day. The place had about 100 cockroaches, and Greg bought two cans of Raid and a few Roach Motels. He didn't buy any groceries until the bugs were all dead two days later. He fixed the toilet and the closet door, and one of the kitchen cabinets, with Ronnie's help. A week later, his wall air conditioning unit conked out. He bought a fan, and had to leave the windows open. It took 10 days for the A/C to be fixed - Ronnie had no other bungalow vacancies.

He started classes that Monday. Gus was in one, but except for him, there were only a few people on campus that he knew because a lot of people he knew had finished their course work and were taking their comprehensive exams, working on their dissertations, doing internships, or already had their Masters' or Doctorate degrees. Greg worried whether his program at the hospital would fall apart while he was gone. Even worse, he left his book with all the addresses in his office at work, or maybe at Kent

Stone's where he stayed one night on the way down. The courses were more difficult than he expected - it was one long summer session now instead of two six-week sessions. By the end of July, he was truly a "suffering bastard."

He immersed himself in his coursework. It was too hot to go to the beach except for walks in the evening. Greg helped Ronnie get his wife's Chevy Chevette on the road again. The frame had been bent from the accident, making it almost rhombus shaped, and Florida had just done away with inspection laws. Ronnie had stolen a speed limit sign and welded it onto the passenger side of the car. The engine ran, however, and Ronnie used it for around town only.

After Greg's final exam, he went to the nearby Holiday Inn bar to have a celebratory beer at happy hour. An acquaintance from one of his classes came in and sat next to him.

"Hey, it wasn't a bad final," the guy said.

"Not that bad at all. I don't care if I get an A or a B. This was my last class. On to the comprehensive exam in October, the internship, and the dissertation," Greg replied.

"It may be tough getting an internship with Reagan's budget cuts."

"I'm lucky I still have a job to go back to for a while, at least. Maybe I can get an internship over in Europe. I liked Switzerland."

"I was there last year - you weren't there," the guy said.

"Yes, I was, for the first six-week summer session. I didn't see you."

"I was there for the second summer session."

"I lived with a friend of mine, Gordy. Do you know him?"

"Gordy had Jean living with him. Do you know her? They didn't get along at all. They were bitching and fighting about a guy named Greg half the time. I don't know if she was Greg's girlfriend, and Gordy was Greg's friend, but Gordy had an older lady he got rid of right after Jean moved in with him. She had no place else to live and because he was Greg's friend, I think she trusted him at first. Gordy wanted to get into her pants, I think.

307

The conflict between the two of them was really funny, I thought. They fought like hell."

As Greg listened to him, he thought, "I'll be dammed. Why didn't Gordy or Jean tell me anything about this?" He had just seen Gordy a week before in St. Pete Beach when he went over to visit Jack and Joan. Gordy was pissed at Jack because Jack couldn't help him get a job.

"Ask me my name - I know you're Rick."

"You're Fred."

"No, I'm Greg!"

"Holy shit! You're Greg!" Rick started laughing loudly and said, "Let me buy you a cold one. You knew all this was going on, didn't you?"

"Hell, no! I'm stunned."

"What happened to Gordy and Jean? I haven't seen them around all summer?"

"Gordy flunked out a few months ago. Jean was engaged to some guy, an engineer or businessman. Knowing her, I'm pretty sure she's married by now."

"Why didn't you stay around for the other session in Switzerland last summer?"

"I was running out of money. I had just enough so I could go back to Florida but not enough to stay over there."

"Why did you and Jean break up?"

"I don't want to go into it. Let's just say that she couldn't tolerate a temporary, long-distance relationship after I went back up north." After he finished his beer and went back to his place, Greg couldn't stop wondering what would have happened and how he would have handled it if he had committed to stay in Europe and Jean showed up at the apartment with him and Gordy there.

Greg left Florida early the next morning. He was running low on cash again so he stayed with Kent Stone in North Carolina. All they did was drink and talk about old times. At least he found his address book. Greg stayed at his mother's house for a week; he was supposed to start working at the hospital right after Labor Day weekend. He had enough money to get a room in a private home, but not an apartment. So, he did the unthinkable - he went to the Saratoga Race Track that Friday, bringing only $15 with him. "You never know," he thought.

He hit the daily double. Then a 35 to 1 longshot in the third race came through for him. He scored with an Exacta in the fourth race. After he lost a few races, he put $10 on a 14 to 1 underdog in the feature (8th) race, and his horse won. He left with $228 and a huge sigh of relief; he never had good luck like this at the track before. He went back to New England the next day, stayed at a cheap motel for a night, and got a cheap apartment with a six-month lease in a lower-middle class neighborhood that was a mile away from the hospital.

El Guru had a rough summer. He was essentially living for the week-end, but he hated living like that. He was upset at the baseball strike and he vowed to only follow football for the rest of the year. Aside from a few acquaintances in Santa Fe, he had no friends there. In August, some inmates took three officers at the prison hostage and killed one of them. That was the last straw for El Guru, and he quit, saying in his exit interview that he felt nobody was safe working at the prison in any job on any shift. He went back to Albuquerque and got a tiny apartment that he rented by the week and he had to use food stamps. He took off for California and Arizona again, to try to find work but nobody would hire him - many people all over the country seemed to be getting laid off. In fact, Reagan had fired 11,000 air traffic controllers for going on strike and banned them from working at any government jobs.

Because of their moving around, El Guru and Greg were unable to get in touch with each other, except El Guru had Greg's mother's address in

New York. He wrote to Greg in late September. Greg couldn't respond right away because he was studying for the comprehensive exam - 10 days away.

El Guru told him that he couldn't afford a phone until he got a job, and he didn't have a cassette recorder, but would try to get one within the next month.

Greg wrote back, in mid-October, saying that he thought the comprehensive exam went well, and that he planned to look around for an internship right after the first of the year, but he had to accumulate money because an internship would mean a big drop in salary. Socially, Greg told El Guru he couldn't afford to get emotionally involved with anybody because huge budget cuts in the state might eliminate his job, even though his program at the hospital was working really well again. And he thought that even if any females were interested in pursuing something serious with him, he was convinced any younger woman would eventually dump him. Greg left Mandy "hanging" over the summer. However, he wrote that he would try to see her again but he wasn't sure when. He told El Guru he didn't want to get married now or be monogamous because his future was so uncertain. At least his car was running well, after a series of repairs.

El Guru wrote back at the end of October, saying, "Why don't you see if you can get an internship for a year in New Mexico.

I'm living with a young chick named Jennifer—she's only 22, but we're very physically compatible. She has a two-year-old son who is, ironically, named Greg. I know she's young, and you have said that younger girls will probably get rid of you eventually - sooner, rather than later - but I like this girl. I think this might work out OK for me. I like her little boy a lot. He's a smart kid.

"Hey, my Minnesota Vikings are hot - they're on a winning streak. As usually, the UNM football team is going nowhere. Maybe they'll be better in basketball."

They weren't in touch with each other all through November. In early December, Greg sent El Guru a tape. It was designed to be a humorous interview with El Guru, using comments he had actually made. He wished him a Merry Christmas and Happy New Year at the end, and told him that he would consider New Mexico as a possibility for an internship next year.

Chapter 30

Not a Merry Christmas or Happy New Year

El Guru's relationship with Jennifer became more tense with frequent arguments in the last two weeks of November. On the 27th, after coming back from looking for work at a few hospitals, El Guru yelled at her, "We both need to get jobs. Not just me!"

Jennifer screamed back, "I can't afford to work with a two-year-old child. I need to be here with him until he's old enough to go to school!"

"I can watch him if you get a job. I can take care of the kid. If you get a job and come home from work, I can work someplace during the evenings and nights. Or I can work days, if you work evenings."

"Yeah, you need to get a job. You made pretty good money in the past, or you said you did. I don't think you've seriously looked for any work in about a month. I don't get child support and my family won't help me. Right now, all we have is your unemployment."

"I haven't seen any openings at any hospitals. I'll be damned if I'm going back to work in any kind of jail or prison. I pissed off some people at the last place in Santa Fe and who knows - maybe some of those inmates will try to find me and get revenge. I don't want to get shot or stabbed to death."

"There are a lot of other jobs you can do. I'm living with you because I thought you would be able to help me and the baby. So far, it's been big talk and no action. All I'm getting lately is bullshit from a bullshitter."

"Why you bitch - you were nothing when I met you! I could get you out of my life instantly. But I care about you and I want to make this work for us, but you're not helping!"

"You probably have some whore on the side instead of going out looking for work."

"I do like hell! It's you and me and the baby. Right now, financially we're in a hole, but we both need to pull us out of it, not just me. There's got to be a way where we can both work at different times. Even if it's only for six months or so until we build up some cash. I can't look any farther than Albuquerque - gas prices jumped up again last week."

"You're 11 years older than me and you don't have a job. You're always bitching about how people look at you and give you no respect. For Christ's sake, do something about it! How many people would hire you the way you look now?"

"You respect me for what I am as a human being and I will respect you. Let us both get off our asses and look for work right away. I'll try to get anything I can for a while, until something better comes along, and you should do that too. Deal?"

"Another thing, Artie, you got to cut down bitching about stupid things like sports and all this political crap. I'm getting dammed sick and tired of it. That's all you want to talk about. That's all you watch on TV."

"I'm sorry, but those are things that won't change. You knew that when I met you. I'm ME! This is who I am and those things just won't change."

There were many times over the past month when she thought she was trapped in this relationship. He wondered if he'd made a mistake by living with her. He loved her son and her son really liked him. El Guru played with him, comforted him when he cried, and sometimes, even fed him, changed his diaper and took him for short walks in the neighborhood. El Guru enjoyed being a "daddy." He rarely got to see his daughter any more.

On the morning of November 30th, El Guru went to a barber and got his hair cut short for the first time in almost six years, and he shaved his moustache for the first time in 15 years. When he came home, Jennifer told him that he really did this just to shut her up. He admitted that he finally looked around and saw how society had changed from the '70s, and maybe a new appearance might help him get a decent paying, satisfying work. He wondered if he should try for an EMT position, work in an OR again, or get re-trained as a lab tech. He had the medical experience and a couple of recommendation letters from his last few jobs. He also was conflicted about whether or not to leave Jennifer, because of the increasing tension between them, even though she was absolutely right about his needing to work. They went to see his mother later that day in Albuquerque.

Mrs. Guererro said, "Raimondo - is that you? You look so young and handsome now. Jennifer, doesn't he look so nice? And what a nice little boy you have."

"Yes, Raimondo looks different. He looks good enough to die. I could kill him," Jennifer said, with a wide smile.

They all laughed. El Guru talked about some hospitals, clinics, and laboratories where he could try to look for work. He said that even though the economy was not good, there were a few new health care facilities opening, and maybe he would finally find a job and workplace that would last. He was hopeful that next year would be a better year for him. Jennifer stayed mostly silent and her little boy fell asleep in her arms. But while smiling again, she said at one point, "It will be interesting to see what happens for Raimondo."

That day, he got an unemployment check and cashed it. Later, they ate dinner at a small, inexpensive restaurant near where they lived. El Guru was looking forward to watching the Monday Night Football game on TV, Philadelphia Eagles vs. Miami Dolphins. Jennifer was upset because she wanted to watch MASH and Lou Grant. El Guru said that she could watch them next week - this was one of the most crucial games of the NFL season.

He asked her if she would feel better if he watched the game at a local bar. She said in a resentful tone, "Go ahead and watch it here. I'll be in the bedroom."

Greg was very busy at work all month, and he was looking forward to taking some time off. He also had an interview for an internship in Maine in early January, to begin July 1st. Jack and Joan, who were spending Christmas with Joan's family, called him at work on December 23rd. Greg said that he would be taking some time off that afternoon to buy one more Christmas present before he went to his mother's the next day, but he invited them to come to his place later on. Jack said that they would get there at 3:30, and Greg gave them directions.

The doorbell rang at 3:30, and there was a cold blast of air as Jack and Joan entered. They smiled and hugged Greg as he greeted them.

Greg said, "This is a lot different than what you're used to in Florida. Here it's about 50 degrees colder with snow on the ground."

"Don't I know?" Joan said. "I grew up not far from here."

"It's cold but you and I lived in this weather before," Jack said.

They drank the bottle of wine they brought with them and Greg had a beer. They laughed about not having any Double Stuf Oreos and that Greg always had a corkscrew for whenever he went on a first date. They drank a toast to 1982. After Greg put on some music, he told them about his program at the hospital that was going very well, and that a lot of staff they knew from several years ago were gone. He told them his car was "hanging in there," and he had no date for New Year's Eve, "as usual."

They asked how Dolph and Jane were doing. Greg replied, "They're doing good. The older boy is 10 now, he's bright and he'll be an athlete. The younger kid is four and unfortunately, he's about the same. He's not talking, but he seems happy—always smiling or giggling. Hey, there's the mail. I'll be right back."

A few seconds later, Greg came in and said, "What the hell?"

Jack asked, "What happened? Bad news?"

"A tape I sent to my buddy Artie in New Mexico came back to me and it says, 'Deceased.'"

"That's weird," Joan said.

Jack asked, "When was the last time you were in touch with him?"

"Last month. Maybe this is somebody's way of playing a joke on me. But I didn't get a Christmas card from him and he always sends me one. I did send him this kind of joking tape for Christmas, but 'Deceased?' That bothers me."

They talked for another half hour or so and Jack and Joan said they would try to get up with Dolph and Jane before going to Joan's family for dinner. Greg said he was going to wrap presents and take off early the next day for his mother's.

Christmas weekend was pleasant for Greg with his family and relatives, but he was obsessing about El Guru most of the time. He went back to work on the 28th and called El Guru's mother when he went home on his lunch break. They talked for only a few minutes because the phone connection was very bad and she had a thick Hispanic accent that was very hard for Greg to understand, and she also was crying. Apparently, El Guru somehow died tragically. He asked her to write him a letter and gave her his address.

El Guru was watching the Eagles–Dolphins game on TV at home on the night of November 30th and it was exciting. He was having a couple of beers and yelling at the TV. Miami won the game 13-10 on a fourth quarter field goal, but just before that happened, Jennifer came out of the bedroom angry.

"You sit here and scream at the TV with your fucking football game, and the baby and I are trying to sleep, and I can't watch any of the shows I want. You control me and I'm sick of it!'

"Shut up, goddamnit! The game's almost over."

"Why didn't you go out to some bar then?"

"You told me to stay here. I can't afford that, anyway."

"Why don't you get serious about looking for a job? All you ever want to do is watch sports lately. That doesn't bring in a damn cent to help me."

"I'm tired of your goddamn bitching and nagging. I've been as good to you and your son as I could possibly be. I just got a haircut for you. I shaved my moustache for the first time since I was in basic training in the Army. I told you I would go out looking for a job tomorrow. Nobody's going to hire me until the first of the year for something decent anyway. You should get some shitty Christmas job somewhere so you can help."

"I have a two-year-old kid and you promised me you'd support me."

"I'm trying. Right now, I have unemployment money and a little bit from my mother. All the other girlfriends I've had worked. They weren't parasites."

"You're just a fucking loser. All you want from me is just to get a regular piece of ass."

"I've had enough of your shit. I'm going to bed." He thought, "That's it. After the holidays I have to get rid of this bitch, even if I have to move back with my parents."

Jennifer went into the living room. She waited until about midnight. El Guru was asleep. Her son was asleep on the living room couch. The day after Thanksgiving, while El Guru was out looking for a job, she had gone to a nearby pawnshop and bought a secondhand .22 caliber pistol with some ammunition, and she hid it in a closet. She pulled the pistol out of the closet, went into the bedroom, and fired five shots into El Guru's head. Immediately afterwards, she shoved the gun into El Guru's right hand and started screaming loudly. She ran to the apartment next door and hysterically yelled, "Artie killed himself!" The neighbor ran to where El Guru was lying in blood on the bed, and he took the gun, saying, "I don't want anybody else to get hurt."

"Don't call an ambulance. I think he's dead," and she started to sob.

"Hell, I'm calling the cops," the guy replied.

The police and an ambulance came and El Guru was pronounced dead at the scene. Police investigated, and the next day Jennifer was arrested for the killing. It was determined that there was no way El Guru could have fired that many shots, in those locations, considering the angles of the gunshots. They didn't totally believe Jennifer's story that he was depressed over not being able to find work, although she admitted that they argued over a TV program. After interviewing the neighbor and other people who lived in the building, they also dismissed any idea that the neighbor had anything to do with El Guru's death. Bond was set at $10,000, and a hearing was scheduled for December 21st. The trial was to be on January 13th.

Greg was distraught over learning of El Guru's death, but he couldn't find out any details. He tried calling the Albuquerque police department, but they stonewalled him. He wrote to their Chief and got no response. The newspaper, the Albuquerque Journal, told him he would have to order a year's subscription to the paper which wouldn't get to him until the end of January. He considered flying out there to ask his own questions about what had happened, but he wouldn't be able to afford that for many months. Mrs. Guererro told Greg what had happened in a half Spanish, half English letter on January 18th.

Jennifer got two public defenders to represent her, while the state had an assistant to the District Attorney. The charge was reduced to Voluntary Manslaughter. Greg felt sure this was a case of 1st degree murder because Jennifer planned it, and Mrs. Guererro even testified to what Jennifer had said when they visited her that day, "He looks so good enough to die." Greg thought, "At least the charge should have been second degree murder." Greg knew El Guru could not have known that Jennifer had bought a gun - El Guru was always an anti-gun person.

Epilogue

In the ensuing months, Greg went into psychotherapy to deal with El Guru's death. Dave Wilson wrote him a letter saying he hoped to see El Guru later in the year and asked if Greg could give him El Guru's current address. Greg sent him a post card informing him that El Guru had been murdered - he never heard from Dave Wilson again. Kent Stone was drunk when he called Greg one night and when Greg told him what had happened to El Guru, Stone laughingly said, "Serves him right for that asshole to get involved with a bitch like that." Greg angrily hung up on him. At times, Greg was angry at El Guru for the poor judgement he used in the last year of his life. He thought, "He didn't go back to school; he didn't stay with any good job at the VA; he could have gone to Spain and worked if he wanted to. I told him, 'Young chicks will probably get rid of you,' but I never dreamed it would be like that. He kind of threw his life away, and things could have been better for him if he hadn't been so damn stubborn."

Greg made no attempt to get an internship until 1983. Instead, he worked on his dissertation and earned his Doctorate a few years later. Three years after he left New England, he met a lady in Pittsburgh who seemed to be kind of a combination of Celine, Janie, and Jean, and he married her. He also started giving an annual contribution to Handgun Control, Inc. and he had a good house, a good car, a good job, and a good wife - all at the same time, for years to come. This long-term combination was something El Guru, unfortunately, never got to have.